The 100 Greatest Moments in St. Louis Sports

Bob Broeg

The 100 Greatest Moments in St. Louis Sports

 MISSOURI HISTORICAL SOCIETY PRESS • SAINT LOUIS

© 2000 by the Missouri Historical Society Press
All rights reserved
Published in the United States of America by the Missouri Historical Society Press
P.O. Box 11940, St. Louis, Missouri 63112-0040
04 03 02 01 00 5 4 3 2 1

Library of Congress Cataloging-in-Publication Data

Broeg, Bob, 1918–
       The one hundred greatest moments in St. Louis sports
                   p.   cm.
       ISBN 1-883982-31-6 (cloth : alk. paper)
       1. Sports—Missouri—St. Louis—History—20th century—Chronology.
       2. Athletes—Missouri—St. Louis—History—20th century.
       I. Title:100 greatest moments in St. Louis sports. II. Title.

       GV584.5.S2 B76 2000
       796'.09778'66—dc21

                                                                                            00-029199
                                                                                            CIP

Distributed by University of Missouri Press

Design by Robyn Morgan
Photo edited by Josh Stevens
Regent Publishing Services Limited/St. Louis, printed in China

∞ The paper used in this publication meets the minimum requirements of the ANSI/NISO Z39.48-1992 (R 1997) (Permanence of Paper).

Contents

Foreword

Throughout 1999, St. Louis's all-sports radio station, KFNS, ran a series of daily vignettes covering "A Century of St. Louis Sports."

Greg Marecek, the station's president, asked Bob Broeg to write them, and me to voice them. Broeg, I was assured, would pen them "in your style." On this point I was, shall we say, skeptical. Bob Broeg cannot and should not write in any voice or style but his own. Those who heard the programs can judge for themselves how well I did interpreting Bob's compositions. I know I learned a few things from those scripts, and I had a great time doing them.

Bob Broeg is an amazing man; slightly eccentric, totally endearing. He probably has seen firsthand more of this past century of St. Louis sports than anyone now living, and it goes without saying that he recalls all of it in great detail. But those who see this Hall of Fame sportswriter as simply a font of recollections of days gone by miss a large part of the point.

Nearly always, Broeg's reflections go beyond nostalgia to illuminate some connection between past and present events—some precedent, coincidence, or irony, some perhaps forgotten person or circumstance that foreshadowed or set the stage for what was to come.

And even if that were not the case, where else would we turn for anecdotes and insights into the lives and times of such worthy characters as Doc Counsilman, Ed "Strangler" Lewis, or Flint Rhem?

Now here's one last thing you should know. In his own way, Bob Broeg is as memorable an individual as many of those he has chronicled; a happy warrior now well into his eighties, who retains his vigor and a keen interest in the world around him. This seems odd to say of someone Bob's age, but there is something eternally boyish about him. His enthusiasms are genuine and undiminished. Whether it's baseball, old Westerns (Bob notes that the films of Tom Mix were so squeaky clean, he kissed the horse instead of the girl), or Civil War history (still to come, an article on the comparative merits of Ulysses S. Grant and Jim "Mudcat" Grant?), he still revels in it all like a schoolboy. But only with the passing of many years does a man accumulate this many memories.

Here then, a century of St. Louis sports, as only Bob Broeg can remember and tell it.

BOB COSTAS

Acknowledgments . . . and Alibis

If you've lost count and swear you passed 100 chapters, don't fret because you're right. A hundred isn't necessarily 100 just as 14 really was 10 back there in boxing's famed "long-count fight," 1927.

This geezer was a kid of nine then, wrapped up in the excitement of a year that brought St. Louis's second-worst tornado ever, a killer, and the utter excitement of young Charles A. Lindbergh's historic first-ever transatlantic flight. Uh-huh, and a flash named Frankie Frisch won a permanent spot in the boy's heart as the Cardinals' new second baseman.

Yes, it really isn't important to count even if it's only to five. Colorado won a national college football championship in 1990 only because the Buffs needed a fifth down to beat underdog Missouri 33–31—and this rankles even more than the mistake: they still didn't score. The officials muffed the goal-line fifth-down call about as bad as Don Denkinger did that critical first-base play in the 1985 World Series.

About the long-count fight in '27—see, I know I do tell you how to make a watch when you only want to know what time it is!—heavyweight champion Gene Tunney got off the floor with a referee's extra five seconds and back-pedaled to a repeat victory over Jack Dempsey.

If you'd like more trivia, Tunney's share of the gate from a 100,000-plus crowd at Chicago's Soldier Field was so big that, dramatically, Gene gave the promoter a check for $10,000 and said, "Now give me one for a million!" With different king-sized dollars and only $11,000 income tax, that check, duly framed after Tunney cashed it, would be worth probably 100 more millions now.

If you are weary of my gee-whiz approach, as noted in Bob Costas's tender foreword I deeply treasure, there's a point to my shilly and shally. Reluctantly, I've got to get around to explain why the editors and me—or vice-versa—left out your favorite sports memory of the twentieth century.

Heck, learning early not to take myself too seriously, I can second-guess me, too. With 14 sports described in these pages, it could have been 15 if I had insisted on the bowling Budweisers' record 3,858 score in 1958. I hope former Buds will forgive me, i.e. Dick Weber, Ray Bluth, Don Carter, Pat Patterson, and Tom Hennessey.

Others were unhappily omitted, including many about my favorite traveling partner, baseball's Stan (St. Louis's Man of the Century) Musial. Also, Bill White after a record-tying 14 hits in back-to-back doubleheaders in 1961, memories of famed John McGraw's one year in St. Louis uniform in 1900—even if he did ditch it off the Eads Bridge when his train left town—and many who saw Joe Medwick's dramatic return to the Cardinal in 1947. Muscles hit a pinch double that turned back the sentimental clock to when he had been a hero, not an enemy heel.

Many more of those who wore the heavy woolen flannel, including Babe Ruth and Lou Gehrig dismantling the Cardinals in the 1928 World Series, Jesse (Pop) Haines pitching the frosting-on-the-cake no-hitter on TD Day in 1924, retiring Casey Stengel for the last out. And the Cardinals' scoring the record 28 runs in 1929, aptly described by a personal favorite, Sam Muchnick, the sportswriter smart enough to become a wealthy wrestling promoter.

So many in football: among them Knute Rockne's bringing his Four Horsemen to St. Louis in 1923 to beat Bob Hannegan's Billikens in a rainstorm at Sportsman's Park 13–0. Dear "Rock" invited a kid sideline usher named Muchnick to share protection of the Irish's canvas bench cover.

KFNS's top 50, an interesting addendum prepared by Greg Marecek and his staff, included Mel Gray's hotly disputed end zone pass that helped the long-gone Big Red to a critical victory over George Allen's Washington Redskins in 1975. A good choice I omitted. And Jim Bakken's record seven field goals in a 1967 game.

Golf had some good ones that fell under the editor's pencil, particularly when St. Louis–based pros won national honors, twice Ralph Guldahl of Sunset Hills Country Club with the U.S. Open in 1937 and '38. Also Westwood's physically handicapped Ed Furgol at Baltusrol in '54.

Heart warming was St. Louis's rooting from afar as gifted all-around hometown athlete Bob Cochran reached the finals of the British Amateur in 1960.

And Jimmy Jackson was a constant local and state amateur contender and champion before an early death.

St. Louis's career "Mr. Basketball," Ed Macauley, appears alone rather than with alma mater's Cinderella NIT champions of 1948. Another All American, Dick Boushka, was a left out, too. And also the Bills' brief brilliant hockey success when Bill Selman turned the Blue and White briefly into a national college hockey power before red ink turned off the Jesuit fathers.

The big-league Blues' Mike Crombeen's dramatic overtime goal in a 1981 championship playoff was not an oversight. Neither was Virgil Akins's brief welterweight boxing championship nor sleek young Joe Louis's winning the national amateur light heavyweight title here in 1934 at the Arena. Three years later, a group of sports-minded St. Louis guys took a roundtrip private-car train ride to watch the Brown Bomber win the big one at Chicago. They had such a good time they came back and became a still-prominent group named Knights of the Cauliflower Bar.

So many memories of so many moments, many enjoyed first hand, and happily many more to come for many of you, hopefully more than for a guy running out of fifth downs. Just think, as the new century began and the third millennium, too late to classify was Washington University girls setting a national record and the basketball Bills bumping off the national No. 1, en route to a dream-team conference conquest.

Thanks to KFNS's energetic Greg Marecek for thinking of the series for his all-sports radio station and for luring a busy old friend, Bob Costas, a giant of the entertainment field, to narrate a guy's copy.

Thanks again to Marecek for approving the series' use as a book and to the Missouri Historical Society for wanting it. And to many others, too most certainly Pulitzer's Prize and my first literary love, the *Post-Dispatch*—for pictures and permission.

Gratitude to others who lent time, attention, and worthy photos, including my colleague on the St. Louis Cardinals' Encyclopedia, Jerry Vickery, Missouri Sports Hall of Fame curator.

Others: Bill Mathis, Steve Pona and Ellie Jones of Mathis-Jones Communications; Flo Ryan, Frank Borghi, Eileen Waters, Mike Kalist of CYC, Steve Prange, Val Palizzaro, Bill Eppy, Belleville Archdiocese, Bob Carson, Tim Boggan, University of Illinois, University of Missouri, University of Indiana, Doug McIlhagga and Saint Louis University, Washington University, Arizona Cardinals' Bill Burdick and the National Baseball Hall of Fame, St. Louis Olympic Committee Archives, Bob Goalby, Karen Sue and Allied Photocolor, U.S. Tennis Hall of Fame, Ellen Thomasson, Friedel Geisert, and Rick Salamon.

And also thanks to the Historical Society's peach of a pair, Matt Heidenry and Josh Stevens.

BOB BROEG

The 100 Greatest Moments in St. Louis Sports

1899

The Day They Came to Town

Behind Famed Cy Young, the Cards Came from Cleveland a Winner

The metaphor for the end of the "old" century, the nineteenth, was captured, in effect, in the rousing song "76 Trombones" from Meredith Wilson's *Music Man*. You know the line about the day when John Philip Sousa, W. C. Handy, and all the great bands came to town? That day would be the arrival of the 1899 St. Louis Cardinals.

From poor Ol' Chris Von der Ahe, Cleveland streetcar men Frank and Stanley Robison had bought the bankrupt Browns and, miffed by poor Cleveland attendance, moved their National League franchise and team, the Spiders, to St. Louis.

At the time, the former Cleveland Spiders were a good ball club. They had .400-hitting outfielder Jesse Burkett, slick shortstop Bobby Wallace, and the granddaddy of all pitchers, Denton True (Cy) Young.

Cy Young was so good that when he was at the twilight age of 88 in 1955, a young reporter asked him how many games he had won. Cy smiled around watery blue eyes, "Sonny, I won more games than you'll ever see!"

That well could be because he had 511 victories, of which St. Louis saw many, usually on the wrong side in Cy's 22-year career, which began in 1890. The city did see 45 in the red raiment of the Redbirds or, as an enterprising reporter called them, "the Cardinals."

Young pitched the first game for the new ball club on Saturday, April 15, 1899, at rechristened League Park on Natural Bridge and Vandeventer. The park later was renamed Robison Field, in honor of the brothers whose efforts to better the old St. Louis ball club were rewarded that opening day with a handsome capacity crowd of 18,000.

The fans were all there following a morning parade downtown, led by the mayor, John Zeigenhein. Ziggy was best known for his reaction to criticism about skimpy public use of precious new electric lighting. Huffed his Honor, "Vell, we got a moon yet, ain't it?"

By happy coincidence for hometown fans, even then pretty sporting, the first-day foe was the old NL Browns the Robisons had swapped to Cleveland. Here in '88, managed by Tin Hurst, later a National League umpire, the Browns had a 39–111 record. As the Spiders at Cleveland, they did even worse—so bad that

many games were played elsewhere. Hence, caustically called the "Exiles," they finished 12th again in the 12-team league with a 20–134 record.

Bless St. Louis; folks even cheered the poor blokes before the game as they did eagerly future Hall of Famers Burkett, Wallace, and of course, Young. Cy needed just an hour and 50 minutes to polish off Cleveland, 10–1.

Of the red-clad locals, two of the 16 hits came from manager first baseman Oliver (Patsy) Tebeau and three by catcher Jack O'Connor. Both were hometown guys from north St. Louis's Goose Hill district, which lay near the ballpark Von der Ahe had slapped together a few years earlier, confusing everyone by giving it the same name as the one at Grand and Dodier—Sportsman's Park.

As pilot, Patsy Tebeau soon would become a patsy, but not at first. That '99 team won its first seven games, still the most of any Cardinal ball club, but with strong early support and an attendance more than double Von der Ahe's last, 150,000, the team finished fifth with a good record, 84–67.

Big blocky Cy Young, age 33 and about halfway through his career, didn't like St. Louis's summer heat, even though he went 26–16 that year. Chances are, Old Tuscarawas, the Ohio sodbuster, might have done more here, but when the American League came along a year later and founder Ban Johnson dangled $600 more, Young jumped to the Boston Red Sox. The legal NL limit was only $2,400.

At Boston, he pitched with success for several years; but in his second go-around there, the incredible guy who did win more games than many saw got so bulky at the belly—his 6'2" frame well above his normal 220 pounds—that the club bunted him into retirement. For baseball, Young was old at 44.

★

CY FOR CYCLONE: That's what the shortened nickname of big Denton True Young, baseball's winningest pitcher ever, meant. Young, transplanted from Cleveland with the original Cardinals in 1899, won their first game here and got two hits. Old Tuscarawas pitched until he was 44, then too heavy to field bunts—and complained he had one more career victory coming, 512.

1900

The Davis Cup

Dwight Davis's Most Famous Tennis Trophy

A big rich kid from St. Louis, playing tennis left-handed and with enthusiasm at Harvard, came up with a capital idea at the turn of the century—an international tennis prize. It was named after him. Everyone knows the Davis Cup.

Dwight F. Davis, most certainly a shining jewel of the twentieth century to St. Louis and the world, lives on with a game that ranks internationally just behind soccer.

By modern standards, Davis didn't live long. After years on Portland Place in the Central West End, he moved to New York's exclusive Southampton area of Long Island, and he died in 1945 at age 66 in Washington, D.C. Dwight Davis did far more than bequeath the Holy Grail to the game he loved.

First, as a young man he was public parks commissioner in St. Louis and won huzzahs from kids and others when he ordered the "Keep Off the Grass" signs removed from Forest Park and other potential play areas.

With a political as well as civic interest, Davis eventually became Secretary of War under President Calvin Coolidge in the Roaring Twenties, and from 1929 to 1932 he was governor-general of the Philippines. The biggie, of course, was the notion for lawn-tennis play that was named the Davis Cup in 1900.

With Dwight himself playing, the United States won the first tournament in 1900. Great Britain won the third through the seventh. Australasia, as Down Under was spelled then, scored for the first time in 1907.

Uncle Sam surged forward in the Big Bill Tilden era immediately after World War I. The French had a five-year run into the depression led by a man, long-lived, who would become better known—and wealthy—as creator of the famed Alligator sports shorts—René LaCoste.

After Britain's last run, from 1933 to 1936—the Fred Perry era—America's red-haired Don Budge brought the United States into a 30-year dogfight with Australia. The Aussies' nonplaying coach,

Harry Hopman, was as famed as his stars.

Fact is, the box score at the close of the millennium is 31 victories for America and 20 for Australia, but in 1974, a delightful thing happened that would have pleased Davis, an ecumenical man.

In 1974, neither the United States nor Australia reached the finals. South Africa topped India. Since then, other than the occasional 1–2 powerhouses, national pride has soared for Sweden, Italy, Czechoslovakia, West Germany, and France, with an overall total of nine countries winning the prize.

Led by energetic S. E. Freund, St. Louis built the handsome Dwight F. Davis Center in Forest Park. In 1963, Davis became the first person elected posthumously to the Missouri Sports Hall of Fame.

For the ceremonies at Columbia, Dwight Davis, Jr.—Pete Davis—came from New York. Pete told about a time his father was invited by the president of France to listen to a debate in the Deputy of Chambers.

The doorman was adamant in his refusal to admit Davis, unmoved by the fact that he was governor-general of the Philippines. Former Secretary of War? A polite shrug. Ah . . . "Why, I'm the man who gave the Davis Cup to tennis!" exclaimed Davis.

The Frenchman was apologetic. "Why didn't you say so, monsieur. Entrez-vous, s'il vous plaît!"

★

FAMED FELLOW: Dwight Davis, creator and donor of tennis's greatest international prize, played his left-handed game in 1913 when serving as superintendent of recreation for St. Louis. (inset) The Holy Grail itself.

Olympic Laugh

The Comic-Opera Marathon at the Famous Fair

The 1904 Olympics, held in St. Louis as part of the famed 1904 World's Fair, featured a comic-opera finish to the most storied of all athletic accomplishments, the marathon.

Unfortunately, the Russo-Japanese War that steamy summer nearly a century back took some glamour away from the Louisiana Purchase Exposition. The fair itself overshadowed the Olympics, which weren't steamed up enough by ancient automobiles and dust-choked dirt roads.

The infancy of the horseless carriage itself left byways far from highways and, in fact, roads dusty enough without the heat of a good ol' St. Louis summer. Also, sadly, not enough countries came to contest the United States on its home turf for the first time.

The limited entries represented Germany, Ireland, Canada, Australia, Greece, Hungary, South Africa, and Cuba. Britain and France were conspicuously absent.

Because rich, eastern U.S. colleges passed on the event, athletic clubs dominated, and the United States won all 22 of the track events because the one competitor not from the United States was a French-Canadian cop from Montreal. He won the 56-pound weight event. Milwaukee's little Archie Hahn won three sprints: the 60, 100, and 200 meters.

If you'd like a contrast from the present, in different days and equipment, pole vaulters could reach only 11'6", while now they reach 20 feet.

The marathon featured the most colorful character of the 1904 Olympics, Cuba's one and only entry, a little Havana postman named Felix Carbajal. Felix begged, borrowed, and stole Cuban hearts for enough pennies to get to the States, then immediately blew it all in gambling joints in New Orleans. He was an odd duck in raggedy clothes when he got to St. Louis, where he received favorable hospitality, including food, shelter, and what he already had enough of— encouragement.

That day at the starting line at Washington University's ornate Francis Field, the pint-sized Cuban stood there in heavy street shoes, a long-sleeved shirt, and long trousers. A sympathetic bystander snipped off the shirtsleeves and reduced the long pants to knee-length shorts.

The 26.2-mile race started in the stadium and moved quickly into the countryside, where a mounted squad marked the course in red flags. Of the 40 entrants, 17 were from the United States and 10 from Greece. Cuba's one and only, Carbajal, jogged tirelessly, cracking jokes in broken English, picking roadside apples, and snatching a couple of peaches from an accompanying car.

When Felix finished fourth, the consensus was that properly equipped and handled by a trainer he would have won the race.

The winner? Well, that's another story altogether. Among the many who fell by the wayside in heat, dust, and heart and lung exhaustion was Fred Lorz, who cramped up nine miles out, hopped in a car, and rode to within five miles of the finish.

When the auto broke down, as so many did back then, Lorz finished on foot. After all, his clothes were back at the stadium.

At the finish, representing her father, President Theodore Roosevelt, was daughter Alice—celebrated in the song "Alice Blue Gown"—and just when she prepared to hand Lorz the trophy, actual winner Thomas J. Hicks of Cambridge, Massachusetts, appeared and was declared the winner.

Hicks, given small doses of strychnine, brandy, and egg whites throughout the race, finished in a fog, unable to stand up long enough to get his prize. He fell asleep on a streetcar ride downtown to the Missouri Athletic Club. His winning time was 3 hours, 28 minutes and 53 seconds—nowadays an embarrassing time!

★

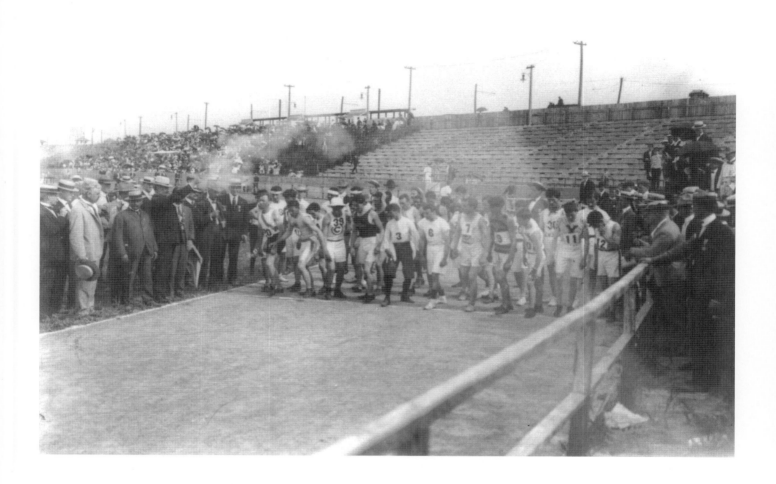

GET SET—TO LAUGH: *Unfortunately, funny was the big marathon at St. Louis's 1904 version of the Olympic Games at Washington University's Francis Field. The winner at far left, near the starter, was Thomas J. Hicks of Cambridge (20). The biggest good-humor man was in the middle, Cuban Felix Carbajal (3), his black long pants scissored off at the knees to beat the blistering August heat.*

When St. Louie Was First at the Fair

The $50,000 Handicap Won by a Hometown Man at Fairgrounds Park

If St. Louis had a crowning moment as a major metropolis, a swinging site early in the century and maybe a sin-and-fun city, it was at the World's Fair in 1904 when the old hometown hosted a $50,000 horse race won proudly by a local entrant.

The impact of the $50,000 World's Fair Handicap, as the event was called, can best be captured by a comparison to the Kentucky Derby, already a venerable quarter-century race that paid off only $4,500. So half a hundred thousand dollars just coming out of the nineteenth century must have seemed like . . . well, the moon filled with green cheese.

But the victor, St. Louis brewer Otto Stifel, a bristly mustached millionaire, summed up the situation grandly. Announcing that he would give half the winner's $41,000 purse to trainer C. E. Rowe and pay off jockey A. W. Booker handsomely, Stifel said, "I would have raced for the stake even if there hadn't been a cent in it. The pleasure of winning in my hometown is all I wanted."

Nobody spoke for Colonial Girl, the mare who won the prestigious, pricey event by out-gaming the favored Hermes in the stretch, herself aided by a decided weight factor, 97 pounds to 130. Her time of 2:09 1/2 was considered great for the track that was cuppy after rain.

That track has to be, of course, the centerpiece of limited turf recollections in St. Louis. The Fairgrounds Jockey Club was located along Natural Bridge in Fairgrounds Park, just west of Grand and across the spacious street from the National League baseball park.

St. Louis was the nation's fourth-largest city, behind New York, Philadelphia, and Chicago, and the community already had been strait-jacketed by the divorce from St. Louis County in 1876. Still, the city had just about the most of everything, including thoroughbred interest, which was quickly lost in the stroke of a conservative governor's pen.

So the famed Fair, still the sentimental favorite of a French fur-trading post begun in 1764, became a hazy glow of memories, along with many other reminders of the aggressive growth of the Gateway to the West.

About the directions of entries, attracted by the glittering circumstances and the high cash price, Mayor Rolla Wells's "guests" came from all over. That late June date, the customers, too, were cosmopolitan and from high society. Many women dressed simply because of a threat of rain. Still, the prevalent full-length white was tempered with an occasional pink or red hat. Predominating the style of dress were the long lines and flying white veil of Alice Roosevelt, the president's daughter and a constant attraction at fair events.

So, in fact, it was a great day for ladies, especially Colonial Girl. She opened at 4 to 1, second to Hermes's 8 to 5. Mr. Stifel's four-legged beauty, however, lost ground with odds and went off at 5 to 1.

The race was delayed. A celebrated turf judge from Baltimore was tardy in his arrival. Streetcars, tallyhos, and the latest horseless carriages had brought a crowd that shoehorned in at 35,000 (ultimately nearly 50,000), enough to keep club-wielding cops busy.

Another delay was caused when Colonial Girl's regular jockey couldn't make the weight, giving Booker the chance, and he was off on Colonial Girl, a close second to Hermes in the most significant mile-and-a-quarter ever run in St. Louis.

Not until the stretch did Stifel's four-legged lady stick her snout in front. Hermes gamely passed her until Colonial Girl surged again, winning by two lengths. She carried the white-jacketed, pink-sashed, and pink-capped colors of Stifel's stable.

Afterward, Colonial Girl pranced around with a blanket of red roses, best associated with the Kentucky Derby, but that June day in 1904 would have been just another "routine" race run at Churchill Downs in Louisville.

★

ONCE UPON A TIME: Briefly, St. Louis, a city of fun and sin, had most of everything, including a giant racetrack on what now is Fairgrounds Park, Natural Bridge at Grand. The St. Louis Handicap, a sporting feature of the 1904 World's Fair, paid $50,000 to St. Louis brewer Otto Stifel for his winning filly, Colonial Girl. The illustrations show the vast stands and the close-up of the grandstand.

CLUB HOUSE,
Grand Stand & Race Track
=St. Louis Fair Grounds=

Father of the Forward Pass

St. Louis's Eddie Cochems First Used a New Rule in an Unbeaten Season

In 1906, Saint Louis University's football team had a perfect season, largely because those early Billikens were the best at using a newfangled offensive weapon—the forward pass. They were also first to use it, thanks to their coach, Eddie Cochems (coke-ems).

On September 5, 1906, in a practice game against Carroll College, a big ham-handed man named Bradbury Robinson completed a pass to a teammate who became his favorite receiver, Jack Schneider. History was not only made, but also refined, because through that first season, in which throwing the ball forward was legal, the Billikens were the best.

Fact is, when they ended a perfect season with a 39–0 rout over Iowa before a large crowd of 18,000, referee Horatio Hackett of West Point paid them a great tribute.

The week before, in a 34–2 victory over a strong Kansas team, Robinson had completed seven of nine passes, including one for 48 yards to Schneider. Against Iowa the team hit 8 of 10 and was, as Hackett put it, "nearly perfect."

The official noted that he had seen Yale and Harvard throw high passes that were easy to cover, but St. Louis's were strong, hard, fast, and thanks to Eddie Cochems, first!

Because President Theodore Roosevelt, himself a roughneck like his famed cavalry Rough Riders, was appalled at football's roughness, he had called for liberalized rule changes, or else. One new rule made it legal to throw the ball, but penalties discouraged it. On an incomplete pass, the ball went automatically to the foe.

Cochems, 30 years old, a former Wisconsin player and head coach at three schools, charged ahead with his plans, encouraged because Brad Robinson showed that his sizable hands enabled him to spiral the larger ball then used.

With players lured from the Wisconsin area to St. Louis to attend medical school—virtually all became doctors—Cochems received permission to train at Lake Beulah, Wisconsin, and to meet small Carroll College in a practice game. He didn't plan to use the new plays they had practiced, but Carroll put up just enough of a fight.

So Robinson threw the first pass—short, incomplete, loss of down and the ball! But the next time, Robinson called, "Hike!" a signal to St. Louis teammates to block downfield, he hit Schneider 20 yards downfield for the first aerial touchdown!

THE PASS MASTER: Saint Louis University's football coach, Eddie Cochems, threw the first legal forward pass in 1906, the year the pass was legalized. His battery (right to left) was Brad Robinson throwing to favorite receiver Jack Schneider. The unbeaten Billikens included a 34–2 rout of Kansas at cozy Sportsman's Park, rebuilt in 1909 and enlarged in 1926.

Despite the sensation of Notre Dame's upset of West Point in 1913, a result of forward passes from Gus Dorais to Knute Rockne, even Dorais and The Rock hailed Cochems as first in 1906.

The Bills won four practices games and all seven official games, scoring 407 points to only 11. Robinson insisted he had once thrown a scoring pass 67 yards.

As the former good quarterback of Captain Clarence (Pike) Kenney's team, Dr. Robinson was quite full of himself on occasional visits back to the old brick-and-concrete campus of St. Louis U. They even convinced him finally that his longest pass was "only" 48 yards, mighty good with the big-bladdered ball.

After all, when most coaches figured on underhanded tosses or little end-over-end flips, Robinson made a memorable name for himself with the deep pass, as did Cochems. By the time Eddie checked out in 1953 at age 76, cynics called football "basketball on cleats," but like baseball's home run, the forward pass had become the game's glamorous play.

★

1911
Heroic Rail-Wreck Redbirds
Roger Bresnahan Saved His Team and Helped Them Save Others

Roger Bresnahan, early day Hall of Fame baseball catcher, went from hero to heel in a romantic moment in which he saved the Cardinals from a train disaster and then lost his job because he didn't know how to treat a lady.

Back in 1909, fleet enough to lead off, Bresnahan, nearly 30 years old, was offered as trade bait by New York when the Robison brothers were eager to turn the Redbirds into a contender. If the Cards would name Bresnahan player manager, manager John McGraw would give them the Duke of Tralee in exchange for a couple of pretty good players.

So ordered, a magnificent salary of $10,000, but the Duke—that Tralee—was phoney for a guy who never got closer to Ireland than his hometown, Toledo. Trouble is, Rog caught only half the games and just about half as well in three playing seasons with the Cardinals, but he did become a hero.

Train wrecks were seldom, though back in '03 when the Browns and Cleveland were on a special, a wreck had caused a hand injury and apparently psychological shock to hometown right-hander Willie Sudhoff. A 20–15 pitcher that season, Wee Willie soon faded.

In the Cardinals' case in July 1911, Duke Bresnahan's third year with a sub-par team, the Redbirds were making first-division noise as loud as their eastbound train. The manager grumped angrily about the noise. At a time when baseball made good use of trains, the railroad made an obliging switch. The New York, New Haven, and Hartford's Federal Express—called President Taft's train—placed the Cards' two sleepers back at the caboose.

Near Bridgeport, Connecticut, the train derailed at a viaduct, pitching all cars onto a street except for the last two. The coaches that had replaced the players' Pullmans upfront jackknifed and crashed. The Cardinals, upright and shaken but unhurt, spent the night pulling out the 14 dead and many injured others.

The 15-hour effort of the players was hailed. They were led by the big Bohemian Candy Dropper, as they called slugging first baseman Ed Konetchy, and, of course, the man who had saved his players, manager Bresnahan.

Even though the ball club understandably fell off, the Cards finished over .500 for the first time since 1901. The new owner was grateful. She was the daughter and niece of the deceased Robison brothers, Helene Hathaway Robison Britton. Called "Lady Bee" by the press, happy with $165,000 in profits that overcame old debts, Mrs. Britton extended the manager's contract—oops.

Miffed because the boss wouldn't sell the ball club to him for $500,000, Bresnahan fell back from fifth, 75–74, to a familiar sixth, 63–90. Called in on the royal carpet for an accounting, the Duke wondered vulgarly what the living what the blankety-blank woman knew about the game or his job?

The dear lady ruled him out of bounds and out of her house, but the ball club owed him $40,000 for four more years. Attorney James C. Jones talked fast and hard to get the Duke to accept half the money and a managerial job with the Cubs.

P.S. He lasted one year with Chicago.

Put off about his departure, Bresnahan hinted at a romance between his replacement, little second baseman Miller Huggins, a bachelor, and the divorced club president, but, you know, that would have made a real heel out of the train wreck hero.

★

HANDSOME HERO: Player-manager Roger Bresnahan (left) saved the 1911 Cardinals in a train wreck, helping his players move out of harm's way by requesting a new compartment. The move rescued many in a mishap that killed 14. Another stalwart was the big right-handed-hitting first baseman, Ed Konetchy.

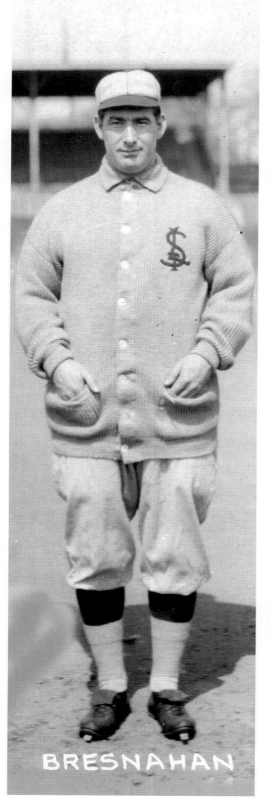

BRESNAHAN

KONETCHY

1917

A No-No Novelty

Two Days, Two No-Hitters, Ernie Koob and Bob Groom

Ernie Koob and Bob Groom had three things in common other than the ability to reach major league baseball. They were losing pitchers, they lived most of their lives here, and they shared a rare honor— no-hit games on successive days.

That fluke on an early May weekend in 1917 would have been even more remarkable, of course, if Koob and Groom had pitched hitless baseball in successive games, but Groom's no-hitter came the second game of a doubleheader with the Chicago White Sox at Sportsman's Park.

The double-dip victim, swept three straight, was no humpty-dumpty ball club like the local Browns, who sagged from a sorry start into a seventh-place finish. The opposition was the Chicago White Sox, en route to the American League pennant and a World Series win over the New York Giants.

Pitching was paramount for manager Pants Rowland's so-called Pale Hose. Eddie Cicotte, who had a scandalous Black Sox date with misfortune two years later, won more games—28—than Koob and Groom combined.

Koob, a St. Louis resident by way of Keeler, Michigan, was 6–14 in '17, his third of four seasons, but he was unhittable in that Saturday game and won 1–0 on an error by Chicago shortstop Swede Risberg and a base hit by the Browns' brilliant young first baseman, George Sisler.

Koob's no-hit game of five walks was marred when Browns manager Fielder Jones sweet-talked the official scorer into changing a questionable hit into an error. After his pitching career, Ernie stayed in St. Louis and died in 1941, only 49 years old.

Groom died in '48 at age 64 in hometown Belleville, Illinois. Belleville Bob, bigger at 6'2" if not

stronger, had a career of more ups than downs with a
122–150 overall record that began in 1909 with a 7–26
season at Washington and sagged to 8–19 in '27, his
second-to-last year. But he'd had his years and moments,
including his record of 24–12 for the Senators in 1912.
But no game matched that early May Sunday shortly
after America entered the World War.

Groom needed no help from anyone against a
batting order that included Hall of Famers Eddie
Collins and Ray Schalk and sidetracked Cooperstown
honorees Cicotte, Shoeless Joe Jackson, Happy Felsch,
and Buck Weaver. The best break in his performance of
three walks came from shortstop Johnny (Doc) Lavan.
Doc moved in quickly for a slow-hit ball by third
baseman Weaver. Buck stumbled as he left the batter's
box and was retired on a bang-bang play.

Groom's win over the Sox followed a wild game by
Allen Sothoron in the first game. That one was saved in
relief by future Hall of Famer Eddie Plank in the 42-
year-old left-hander's 17th and final big-league season.

Actually, a wild throw by Sisler at first base, trying
for a 3-6-3 double play, had hit the sliding Eddie Collins
in the head, forcing Sothoron to the showers.

By then, the Brownies had learned not to chastise
Sisler, a good pitcher converted into a great first
baseman. He was headed for a .353 season, but he also
went 3 for 3 for Bob Groom that day. Uh-huh, after
once chastised crudely, he dumped the big pitcher on
his flanneled backside.

★

NO-NO NOVELTY: Ernie Koob (right), pitching for the St. Louis
Browns, threw a no-hitter in 1917 against the Chicago White Sox. Next
day in the second game of a doubleheader, big Bob Groom also no-hit the
championship-bound Sox. Groom was 9–18 that year, lefty Koob 6–14.

Yes, Mr. Rickey

Baseball's No. 1 Brain

Bless his nimble brain and all that went with it, by Judas Priest. Wesley Branch Rickey was baseball's front-office executive of the century. Mr. Rickey deserves standing applause for two accomplishments in particular—the birth of the farm system and the liberalization of black talent.

Mr. Rickey—even dear wife Jane addressed him formally in public—was a commanding person who well might have been a persuasive lawyer, a winning political personality, or a fire-and-brimstone preacher who could have swayed the sorriest of sinners.

But the farm boy from Ohio grew up with an athletic body, good enough to qualify him as a fringe big-leaguer, and as a mental giant happiest putting together a pennant-winning ball club. So baseball won Branch's heart and his nearly 85 colorful years.

Typically, working too hard as a player and then a college football and baseball coach while attending the University of Michigan Law School, B. R. weakened enough to require a western reprise in a successful fight against tuberculosis. Robert Lee Hedges, the man who had rebuilt Sportsman's Park for his Browns in 1909, lured him in 1913 with a combination business manager and field manager job.

Trouble was, when Hedges sold out to Phil Ball, the man who had financed St. Louis's entry in the two-year Federal League fiasco, the new owner didn't like the pompous, polysyllabic Rickey. If Ball had liked B. R., St. Louis's baseball future would have been drab brown rather than rich red. Ball disapproved of Branch's idea of developing one's own players to enable the poor clubs to compete with the rich.

When local fans loyally kicked in enough to keep the Cardinals in late 1916, area sports editors unanimously recommended Rickey to run the club. Petulantly, Ball sought to keep his unfavorable son, but he lost the suit.

Sam Breadon, an automobile operator, became Cardinals' president and sweet-talked Ball into letting the Redbirds rent Sportsman's Park. As a result, Sam sold the old National League park on Natural Bridge to the city in 1920 for Beaumont High School. Wisely, he fulfilled Rickey's dream with $300,000 seed money.

From 1926, for 21 seasons, the Rickey-built Redbirds won nine pennants and six world championships, a standard bettered only by the New York Yankees.

B. R. didn't share the last few bows. His Odd Couple relationship with Breadon ended. Branch was a psalm-singing, teetotaling Republican, his profanity limited to "Judas Priest." Singin' Sam, who knew all the words, was a Scotch-sipping convivial, a barbershop quartet singer—and a proud man. In 1942, Sam did not exercise Branch's third seven-year contract as general manager.

Moving to Brooklyn, threatening expensive scouting even when all others fled the war economy, Rickey followed his Christian conscience and shrewd baseball judgment. He tapped virgin talent—long-suffering blacks—quickly signing Roy Campanella and Don Newcombe after historic hero Jackie Robinson.

Rickey's bold move, originally criticized yet soon lauded, enhanced the Dodgers. It also enhanced the reputation and legacy of The Mahatma, as the New York press labeled Rickey when it wasn't angrily calling him "El Cheapo."

Rickey's color included his language. The gifted wordmaster best explained the elimination of an unnecessary player as "an addition by subtraction."

To the cigar-twirling executive, an athlete just good enough to hang on the roster was "an anesthetic player." A pitcher's screwball was a "reverse curve." An ability to change speeds was referred to as "variable velocities."

Himself a man of variable velocities, enjoying life "as a spirit of adventure," much as he did parrying comments with the press, Wesley Branch Rickey promised his dear mother he never would attend a Sunday ball game, but he always checked the house. For a fact, he was one of a kind, best described answering a question with delightful double talk as "possibly, probably, and in a given case, yes!"

THE MAHATMA: An apt late-year description of Branch Rickey. As manager (1919) of the ball club, he began to develop in '20.

★

Poetry in Motion

The Browns' George Sisler Was Labled Baseball's 'Perfect Player'

To Branch Rickey and many others, George Sisler was a picture-book performer, poetry in motion, the perfect baseball player, and a man who did the unthinkable. In 1920 for the old St. Louis Browns, Sisler got 257 hits!

Those 257 hits came in a schedule eight games fewer than now, just 154. So—fancy this!—that's an average of a hit and two-thirds for every game. And Sisler played every one, going hitless 23 games and twice two games in succession.

Imagine how he had to make up for those deficits to keep up that 1.66 average, a fabulous mark in a fascinating season in which he hit .407, not even his career best. In 1922, the year the Brownies lost the pennant to the Yankees by one game, Sisler hit .420.

But he always regarded as better the .407 season of the record 257 hits with 137 runs scored, 122 driven in, and 42 stolen bases. One thing more: although not a humorous man, George could say with a smile, "I finished second to Babe Ruth in home runs. He had 54 and [pause] I hit 19!"

Like George Herman Ruth, George Harold Sisler probably could have made the Hall of Fame if he never had swung a bat. Acquired from the University of Michigan for St. Louis by his former college coach, Branch Rickey, the 5'10" inch, 170-pound lefty came directly to Sportsman's Park in 1915. Fact is—twice as a gimmick Sisler didn't like—the team pitched him against his boyhood idol, Washington's great Walter Johnson, and Sisler won both, 2–1 and 1–0.

Sisler was converted to first base because coach Rickey had become business manager and field manager of the Browns. B. R. knew George's great all-around skills, manifested at bat, on the bases, and in the field, where he was perhaps the finest-fielding first baseman ever.

One year he executed 13 times the difficult and seldom-seen 3-6-3 double play, first to short and back. One time flipping a ball to a pitcher who had stumbled when trying to cover the bag, Gorgeous George leaped forward and caught his own throw! And on a squeeze play, anticipating, Sisler rushed in, snagged the batted ball, tagged the hitter, and threw to the catcher for a most unusual double play.

Sisler's great .340, 16-season career would have been longer and even better if he hadn't suffered a rare poisonous sinusitis in 1923. He was forced to the bench all season in '23 with double vision.

His three-season .400 average and total of 720 hits created a great St. Louis rivalry between The Sizzler and The Rajah, Rogers Hornsby. They had high regard for each other—"the rapier and the cannon," as Frankie Frisch labeled them.

Although a skillful place-hitter and bunter with a 42-ounce bat, Sisler proudly never bunted in his 41-game hitting streak, the league's longest until Joe DiMaggio's remarkable 56.

George Sisler, named to the baseball Hall of Fame in 1939 (three years earlier than Hornsby), reluctantly agreed to join old Coach Rickey—like most others, George still called him "Mr. Rickey"—for a 1965 induction into the Missouri Sports Hall of Fame at Columbia. After B. R. was fatally stricken during his acceptance speech, Sisler never attended another banquet.

Instead, he watched and glowed quietly over his three baseball-playing sons—George, Jr., president of the International League; first baseman–outfielder Dick; and pitcher Dave, later vice president at A. G. Edwards stock brokerage.

When Dick Sisler won the 1950 pennant for the Philadelphia Phillies over Brooklyn with a homer the last day of the 1950 season, George didn't know whether to laugh or cry. He was Rickey's favorite scout with the defeated Dodgers.

★

THE SIZZLER: Perfect player, in the estimation of many, George Sisler, the graceful first baseman too good just to pitch, was an all-around star with the St. Louis Browns, especially when he got a record 257 hits in a 154-game American League season, 1920.

1920

The Walker Cup

An International Amateur Donated by St. Louis's G. H. Walker

George Herbert Walker was the grandfather of a president—a pretty nice family tree contribution—but as G. H. Walker, golfer, golfing fan, and patron, he originated the game's international amateur trophy, the Walker Cup. And, like tennis's Davis Cup founder, he was a St. Louisan.

It's incredible that two of the sports world's most distinguished baubles were spawned by men from the old French fur-trading post, but, happily, it is so. Walker, who balked at having the annual U.S.–British amateur trophy bear his name, was president of the U.S. Golf Association when he proposed the contest in 1920.

The transatlantic tournament began in 1922 at Southampton, New York. The United States has played a heavy role in the 37 events, aside from a half-dozen years around World War II.

Although lured to New York from the firm he began—G. H. Walker Investments—Walker had lived nearly 50 years here, establishing himself as a golfing enthusiast at Washington University and as an amateur light-heavyweight boxer. He explored law and medicine but preferred neither as his life's work nor for that matter his father's old Eli Walker clothing establishments. Investments were G. H.'s ticket.

Investments and golf were games he admired with sportsmanlike conduct to the point that he once lectured an ill-mannered young golfing genius. Obviously, Bobby Jones listened to Walker's advice, because he became golf's greatest amateur and a model of decorum.

Back east, Walker lived in Connecticut and had a place at Kennebunkport, Maine, now a familiar address of his famous grandson, former President George Bush, properly, George Herbert Walker Bush.

G. H.'s son—George Herbert Walker, Jr.—became a baseball bug who contributed 10 percent of his stock purchases to the New York Mets in 1969. His father had died in '53 at age 79. The second Walker did more. He strongly recommended the Mets acquire Bing Devine, who for two straight years had been Baseball-Executive-of-the-Year with the Cardinals, then had been fired just before the Redbirds rallied to win the 1964 pennant.

Devine became assistant general manager, general manager, and president of the Mets before agreeing to return here.

St. Louis also is the home of the third G. H. Walker. G. H. the third—"Bert"—who is affiliated with Stifel, Nicolaus and Company investors. He has fond memories of both his father and Cup donor grandfather.

Bert can listen with amusement to tales of Dwight Davis, Jr.—Pete Davis—and Walker's uncle, Louis, both local baseball fans who carried their affection to New York, campaigning for the Cardinals and Mets to play in the same division.

Pete and Lou often played golf together. The younger Davis had formed a father-son tennis combination with Dwight, Sr. In the younger men's golfing days at a Connecticut country club course, Louis Walker walked happily into the 19th hole and told the bartender, "A beer for everyone, please."

Pete Davis interrupted. "Make that champagne," he said and, then addressing his friendly rival, "That's the difference, Louie, between the Walker Cup and the Davis Cup."

CUP DONOR: St. Louis's G. H. Walker of a distinguished family that even produced a president, George Bush, gave an international trophy—the Walker Cup—that has the prestige of tennis's Davis Cup.

1921

Big Time in the Humbling Game
Golf's U.S. National Amateur Came to Town

At a time when you had to see it or read about it—the National Amateur in golf, then virtually on a par with the U.S. Open in public opinion—St. Louis got the first opportunity west of the Mississippi to play host to the tournament in 1921. If you wanted to say three cheers and drink to it, you couldn't—prohibition, you know.

The thrilling tournament was won by Boston's Jesse Guilford over Chicago's Robert Gardner, seven up with six to play. A one-sided ending made the event at the St. Louis Country Club interesting.

To set the stage, this was the first year of the '20s that would roar with bootleg booze, speakeasies, and the money-making mob, with short skirts, women's liberation, and a fast postwar pace.

Why, that new thing called "radio" might soon be available in St. Louis. In 1920 at Pittsburgh, pioneer Westinghouse even had aired Warren G. Harding's presidential address on KDKA. Earlier, at a mid-September event in '21, a KDKG engineer named Harold Arlen had wandered into the Pirates' Forbes Field and broadcasted a ball game.

In St. Louis, station WEW was just a rumor, but among the four daily newspapers, the *Post-Dispatch*, which would come forth with KSD in '22, came up with a preview. The paper used wireless from fairway to clubhouse to downtown, faster for quick-changing stories.

By modern methods, extensive front-page coverage, hole by hole, would be overkill, but it was really the last gasp for the dailies to be first. They soon lost to radio and that picture-book marvel down the road called television.

At a time of end-of-the-century turmoil by public transportation, i.e. sophisticated MetroLink, the look back is interesting. With streetcars then labeled "trolleys," the recommended rail route was by the University-Olive car to Skinker Road, then a transfer to the Clayton line. With a Cella Avenue stop, the walk to the Country Club was four or five minutes.

The club offered parking for 800 automobiles in an area bounded on the east by Price Road. The price was right—nothing! Everything was available, open, and free except the private clubhouse. Special taxi rates from downtown hotels were $5 a car for six passengers and $3.25 for four in a Yellow Cab. Port-O-Potties were described delicately as "special booths." Stands offered "light refreshments and lunch."

The result was a rousing success to Doubting Thomases of the National Golf Association, impressed by crowds of up to 7,000. The president of the St. Louis Country Club, A. L. Shapleigh, was delighted, hailing the "sportsmanship of the spectators" and suggesting the tournament offered "more good publicity since anything since the World's Fair."

When the tournament came to town, the favorites were Boston's Francis Ouimet (we-may), former National Amateur and Open champion; Chicago's Charles "Chick" Evans; finalist Gardner; and a 19-year-old from Atlanta, Bobby Jones, who had been a prodigy from age 14.

A favorite was British champion Willie Hunter, a red-haired postal clerk, but the winner was big guy Guilford, from Boston by way of Manchester, New Hampshire, nicknamed, for obvious power reasons, "Siege Gun."

A first name sound-alike for Jesse Guilford was a kid from Yale, Jess Sweetser, actually a month younger than the other kid, Bobby Jones. Sweetser, like other stout competitors Jimmy Manion and Dick Bokelkamp, was from St. Louis with a New York address in 1921. A year later Sweetser would win the Amateur at Brookline in Boston.

★

"SIEGE GUN": Jesse Guilford's long-ball ability earned him not only that nickname based on an artillery unit, but also the championship to the 1921 National Amateur, held at St. Louis Country Club.

Close, but No Cigar

The Long Second-Guessed Near-Miss of the '22 Browns

If there's a royal second guess—the ability in hindsight to see clearly—it had to be at its majestic best in the last inning of the last 1922 game between the New York Yankees and, yes, the often lowly St. Louis Browns.

Barely a man is alive who can remember an event nearly eight decades earlier, but for years the "what-if" of the pennant series between the Yanks and Browns lingered on the last inning of the two contenders' last game against each other.

Past mid-September in 1922, the big Bronx Bombers, in the midst of a run to three pennants, came to Sportsman's Park for a showdown. Although handicapped by the absence of Babe Ruth, suspended by Commissioner Landis for 30 days, the Yankees got there with "only" 35 homers from the Babe.

By contrast, in a career year as a 30 homer, 30 stolen base player, the Browns' Ken Williams hit 39. Lean, lanky Williams was well up there in hitting, too, with the Browns' other outfielders, Bill Baby Doll Jacobson and hometown hero Johnny Tobin. And, of course, there was the perfection player, first baseman George Sisler. The Sizzler hit .420.

For the "Little World Series," as it was billed, the Yankees came to town leading by a half game. Railroad out-of-towners and wafer-thin roadway drivers paid scalping prices as more than 28,000 overflowed onto the field at Sportsman's Park, then only 18,000 capacity.

Critically, the Yankees won the first game 2–1, behind 20-game winner Bob Shawkey, a victor over spitballer Urban Shocker, who had won 24. Horribly, in the home ninth, as Yankee outfielders Bob Meusel and Lawton Whitey Witt converged on the ball, Meusel caught it as Witt collapsed. Whitey had been hit in the head with a thrown soda bottle. Fans were aghast.

Dr. Robert F. Hyland advised Witt not to play the second game. The great Sisler was in there even though

his right arm was so hurt that he had to help lift the glove on high throws. His record-tying 41-game hitting streak about to end, Sisler urged infielders to keep their throws down, but he played. So did Witt. Whitey led off, wearing a bandage around the head.

But the daring Brownie rookie, Hubert (Shucks) Pruett, a Mizzou medical student, kept his strikeout spell against Babe Ruth, throwing the left-handed screwball down and in. The Babe finally hit a slow curve for his only homer, but Pruett beat Waite Hoyt 5–1.

The showdown—and first place—was only three outs away from the Browns in the decisive third game, with Frank (Dixie) Davis against 26-game winner Bullet Joe Bush. St. Louis led in the ninth 2–1.

Yankee catcher Wally Schang singled off Davis's glove. Schang, who could run, took second on a passed ball. Here, Yankee manager Miller Huggins sent in left-handed-hitting Elmer Smith to bat for second baseman Aaron Ward. Brownie manager Lee Fohl counseled on the mound.

Fohl feared Smith against right-hander Dixie Davis. So, controversially, he took out Davis for the kid lefty who had pitched the day before, Pruett. Why not Shocker?

Huggins switched from Smith to right-handed-hitting Mike McNally. Playing it cautiously, Huggins called for a bunt. Fielding it, Browns catcher Hank Seversid slipped in making a low-tag throw to third.

When Pruett walked right-handed-hitting shortstop Everett Scott, filling the bases, Fohl turned to staff leader Shocker. Rival Bush, a good hitting pitcher, grounded into a force out at the plate, but then wounded warrior Whitey Witt, only 5'7", 150 pounds, drove in the tying and winning runs.

The second-guessing began before the pennant was decided by one game.

★

AH, SHUCKS: Which is the closest Hubert Pruett came to profanity, en route to a life filled with amazing strikeouts of Babe Ruth, a great medical career, and a valuable ragtime record collection, but even dear Doc couldn't help in the still-second-guessed critical 1922 final game against the New York Yankees.

1923

Iron Man

Johnny Stuart Was the Last Redbird to Pitch a Winning Doubleheader

To suggest at century's end that a pitcher went the distance in both games of a doubleheader would be both amazing and amusing, yet it was so when a Redbird rookie named Johnny (Stud) Stuart worked and won two games in one day.

The year was 1923, the date July 10, the place Boston, where the bumbling seventh-place Braves were worse off than manager Branch Rickey's Cardinals, who were backsliding to a poor fifth from a strong third and were ripped by injuries.

One troubled area was pitching, so Mr. Rickey decided he would use Stud Stuart or Johnny, as the field manager called him. An Ohio State football and baseball player, Stuart had started only one big league game, a year earlier. He hadn't done too well at Syracuse, then the Cardinals' top farm club, but he was a mop-up man in relief.

Manager Rickey didn't offer Stuart much help for the opener of the doubleheader. With Jim Bottomley hurt, batting champion Rogers Hornsby moved to first base. Specs Toporcer played second. The shortstop was Doc Lavan, and Milt Stock was at third base.

The Cards got off to a good start against the Braves, destined for a 54–100 coal hole. Outfielder Billy Southworth, playing second base, kicked Max Flack's leadoff grounder. Left fielder Jack Smith walked, and Hornsby, who would bat "only" .384, singled home the first run. Center fielder Hi Myers's fly ball fell in for a double, scoring another run, and Stock's outfield fly made it 3–0.

In Boston's second, Stuart gave up a run on a triple by Stuffy McInnis and an outfield fly, but a Redbird run in the third and four in the fourth, knocking out Boston starter David Fillingim, made it easier for Stuart.

With Smith, Hornsby, and Stock getting three hits each of the Cardinals' 15, the team breezed 11–1 with a three-hitter for Stuart. To beleaguered manager Rickey's delight, Stuart offered to work the second game too.

Off Joe Oescheger, famed for having worked the 26-inning tie against Brooklyn in 1920, the Cardinals ripped five straight singles. A three-run inning followed by three more in the second, in which Myers unloaded a long inside-the-park homer, left Oescheger relieved by Joe Genewich.

Stuart led by five into the eighth and began to weaken, but with two runs across, the third out was a sharp liner to Smith in left field. And after a hit and a second walk, a tiring Stuart won it, 6–3. He gave up 10 hits.

So it was two victories of what would become nine for Stuart in a season of five losses. The 21-year-old right-hander from Clinton, Tennessee, 5'11" and 170 pounds, would wind up in '25 with a career 30–28 record.

So John Davis (Stud) Stuart belongs in a book of brow-raising not only because no St. Louis pitcher has done it since, but also because no major-league pitcher has started, finished, and won both games of a doubleheader since Cleveland's Emil (Dutch) Levsen in 1926.

That's certainly longer ago than the day before yesterday, especially for now, when complete games are rare.

There's a footnote here. No, make it two. For one, in a depression gimmick, the Browns' colorful big Buck (Bobo) Newsom tried on a Sunday to go two in an advertised effort. Trouble was, Bobo barely staggered through a high-scoring, hot-weather opener. He didn't go far, troubled by too many walks and strikeouts.

In that 1923 game at Boston, working 18 innings, Johnny Stuart didn't strike out a single batter.

★

A ROYAL STUART: A name that wouldn't be remembered in a so-so career by a good college athlete leaps out only because in an emergency for the 1923 Cardinals, Ohio State's John Stuart pitched and won both games of a doubleheader, a feat last accomplished in 1926.

1924

The Rajah

Rogers Hornsby's Greatest Average, .424

Rogers Hornsby was a tough-talking Texan whose frank, profane opinions often caused him more trouble than enemy pitching because, to tell the truth, The Rajah had only sympathy for the guys who faced him. After all, they had to pitch to the greatest right-handed hitter ever.

There's really no question about Rog as "best" because, for one thing, his .358 career average is second only to Ty Cobb's .367. And he had the highest hitting season of the twentieth century—.424 in 1924—but, oddly, that really wasn't Hornsby's best.

For firepower, his .401 in 1922—the year rival George Sisler of the Browns batted .420—was The Rajah's most productive. Playing every game, the Cardinals' superstar got 250 hits, with 46 doubles, 14 triples, and 42 home runs. He led also with runs scored, 141, and driven in, 152. And in 623 at-bats, he struck out only 17 times.

Hornsby, averaging .400 over one five-season peak, was a positive menace. He stood deep in the far corner of the batter's box, bat silent on his right shoulder and strode into the ball so that the so-called perfect pitch, low and away, often was quite hittable. And, as he confessed with a slight wink after his 23-year career, which ended at age 41, he pulled back when lunging into high and tight pitches. Some could have been called strikes.

Rog had power to all fields, especially to right center, which made Sportsman's Park an ideal venue before a screen was put up to the 354-foot marker. But, heck, he could hit anywhere. As Casey Stengel sarcastically would remind hitters of his Boston Braves boo-hooing about the wind blowing in, "Yes, Mr. Hornsby played only one season here and hit .387."

That .387 in 1928 was the last of seven batting championships, but Rog batted .380 a year later when he led the Chicago Cubs to a pennant with his second MVP award. His first came in '25 when he hit .403 for the Redbirds, the year he became their manager.

As Mr. Blunt, Hornsby must have thought diplomacy was a respiratory disease. If he had been more civil with club owner Sam Breadon, doubtless he could have worn the bird and bat insignia longer. But after blistering proud Breadon late in the first championship season, 1926, he sought a three-year contract at $50,000, when only Babe Ruth made more. Breadon's cautious one-year offer of $50,000 merely agitated the red neck, though Sam had helped Rog buy Branch Rickey's Redbird stock.

The shocking Hornsby-for-Frisch trade late in '26 meant that Santa Claus had thrown Christmas coal into irate Cardinal fans' stockings. Fortunately, Frisch made fans remember Frankie if not forget Hornsby.

The Rajah, meanwhile, shot himself in his fleet feet, lasting only one year in New York even though he hit .361 for John McGraw's '27 Giants. Hornsby's merry-go-round moved faster, especially when his gambling on slow horses if not fast women got him in trouble with his Cubs' players and management, and with the commissioner, Judge Landis.

Hornsby managed moribund Browns teams early, 1933–37, and late, 1952, having been lured back by Bill Veeck in a boomeranging box-office experiment. Time had passed him by. No, Rog, you don't replace pitchers with a long vaudeville hook, just beckoning from the bench.

Mr. Blunt, baseball's greatest right-handed hitter, really had only one other weakness. Defensively, he was weak on pop flies because, obviously, Rajah Hornsby hit so few himself.

★

NICE LOOKING, BUT: Dimpled, good-looking Rogers Hornsby, shown at his playing peak, could turn as tough as he was to opposing pitchers.

1924

The Galloping Ghost
Red Grange Dedicated Illinois's Stadium Dramatically

Michigan, the "Valiant Victors" of song and annually one of the nation's football best, showed annoying arrogance that warm October afternoon in 1924, the day the University of Illinois dedicated Memorial Stadium. At the kickoff Michigan captain Herb Steger called out, "Where's Grange? We want to kick to him!"

The obliging Illini pointed to the goal line, where junior halfback Harold (Red) Grange of Wheaton, Illinois, gathered in the hand-off. Red loped upfield in long, sweeping strides until his interference formed, then cut to his right and was gone 95 yards—touchdown!

Under the rules then, the team that gave up the score had its choice of possession. Probably, Fielding (Hurry-Up) Yost, the longtime championship coach of the Wolverines, would have surrendered the ball because he believed in pressuring to make the foe make mistakes in its own half of the field. So interim head coach George Little ordered the Maize and Blue to kick off to the Orange and Blue, this time with no comment from Captain Steger, who never had played in a losing game, high school or college.

Fact is, Grange got back only to his 30, but, an exchange of punts later, the Galloping Ghost drove over the left end, cut back diagonally, and burst away for 77 yards.

Michigan did it again—kicked off this time out of their end zone—but shortly on the same play, Grange raced through the Valiant Victors for 56 yards and a third touchdown.

In the stands of the packed-house crowd of 67,000, Mrs. Yost tugged at the sleeve of the famed coach and inquired, "Fielding, why don't you do something about this?" Hurry-Up, named after what he constantly urged, was silent as he gnawed on his cigar. Silence was most unusual to the vocal Yost, but now he had no answer.

Before the first period ended, Grange slipped around left end, cut back to the right, and was gone for 44 yards—a fourth touchdown in 12 minutes!

Many a back has been hot before and after that warm afternoon at '24 in Illinois, but none can match the numbers alone of what Grange did in just part of the game. He didn't return to the lineup until the third quarter, and he scored his fifth touchdown from 11 yards out. And he flipped a short pass for the Illini's sixth score.

In the 39–14 Illinois victory, the off-season ice man from Wheaton had gone 95 yards . . . 67 . . . 56 . . . 44 . . . in the first quarter alone, then 11 for the fifth touchdown and a TD pass. His total rushing was more than 402 yards in 21 carries.

Grange's effort was regarded as the greatest ever by his wily coach, Bob Zuppke, and by the dean of college coaches, Amos Alonzo Stagg. The redheaded Grange had one remarkable encore in 1925 at Philadelphia's Franklin Field when Penn was an eastern giant. There, on a field muddied by snowy rain, Grange totaled 363 yards rushing on 36 carries and three touchdowns.

Eastern writers rhapsodized, led by the poet of the pressbox, Grantland Rice. The dean of American sports writers labeled Grange the Galloping Ghost.

Only injuries early in pro football kept the Galloping Ghost from an offensive career as noble as his defensive play for the Chicago Bears and his lifelong friend, former Illini George Halas.

When Halas turned Red pro for a full-house crowd Thanksgiving Day, 1925, when the Bears faced the rival Chicago Cardinals, the attraction proved the biggest boost for pro football until television much later.

Early in a schedule of exhibitions was a rainy, midweek afternoon game at St. Louis's Sportsman's Park. The event bombed at the box office almost as bad as Michigan's captain who had wanted to kick off to the Galloping Ghost the year before.

★

THE GALLOPING GHOST: On a warm windy afternoon in 1924 at Champaign, dedicating the University of Illinois's Memorial Stadium, Harold (Red) Grange had the greatest running day ever—four touchdowns in the first 12 minutes against mighty Michigan, later adding two more, one passing and another running. Total yards rushing were 421 in 21 carries—and immortality for old "77".

Jim's Sunniest Day

Sunny Jim Bottomley Drove in 12 Runs

A rare Redbird or bird of any color, Sunny Jim Bottomley not only was able to get six hits in a game—twice!—but also for 59 years he alone held the single-game major-league record for most runs driven in: 12.

Oddly, from 1924 to the time this century of sports was chronicled, the only other player ever to knock in 12 men in a game was another Cardinal. Playing for St. Louis at Cincinnati in late 1993, often-dealt Mark Whiten, whose fielding ability and strong throwing arm indicated that he should have lasted, hit four homers in a rain-delayed game.

Whiten, a big switch hitter who would dwarf the 6-foot, 180-pound Bottomley, became St. Louis's first player with four home runs in a game. And, of course, Mark's 12 ribbies tied Bottomley's untouchable total.

Whiten didn't last long in Redbird raiment or any other uniform, but James Leroy Bottomley, a farm kid from the coal-mining community of Nokomis, Illinois, became a fixture in the Cardinal lineup.

Naively writing manager Branch Rickey for a tryout, Bottomley was so green that when he first saw a slender bat in the rack, he asked pitcher Bill Sherdel politely, "Who's this Mr. Fungo?"

But he learned early and fast, taking over at first base late in 1922 at age 23. His .325 batting average prompted the sale of Jacques Fournier to Brooklyn. It was against Brooklyn—actually called the "Robins" then more often than the Dodgers—that Bottomley had the unforgettable 6-for-6 and 12 runs batted in on September 16, 1924.

Even though Rogers Hornsby hit a record .424 in 1924, the Cardinals finished sixth, in the beginning of the end for Rickey as manager. The Dodgers were managed by Uncle Wilbert Robinson, from whom they got the Robins nickname. They finished only a game and a half behind the pennant-winning New York Giants.

But the Robins had no chance against the Redbirds that September day; the final score was 17–3. In the first inning off right-hander Rube Erhardt, Bottomley drove in two of four runs with a single. In the second, Jim doubled in another run. In the fourth off right-hander Art Decatur, who walked Hornsby to fill the bases, Bottomley hit a grand slam.

Again off Decatur in the sixth, one on, the left-handed hitting first baseman hit another home run. Off rookie left-hander Tex Wilson in the eighth, Bottomley hit a two-run single.

The record for RBIs, oddly, was held by Brooklyn manager Robinson. Bottomley broke it in the ninth with a base hit off the fifth Dodger pitcher, Jim Roberts.

So the three singles, a double, and two homers totaled 12 RBIs, the record for nearly six decades, during which Sunny Jim Bottomley became a legend as a smooth-fielding, clutch-hitting Hall of Fame ball player.

As Sunny Jim, his cap perched rakishly over his left eye, Bottomley was a Ladies Day favorite, a longtime bachelor who walked with an undulating swagger. At the plate, he choked a heavy bat and used a slow wiggle-waggle in his stance; but he still hit a long ball, capped by a league-leading 31 homers in 1928, a year he was MVP. He had higher averages than his .325, but almost 50 percent of his hits were for extra bases, and he also led with 20 triples and with 136 RBIs.

By then the naive kid had become a cracker-barrel philosopher. When trainer Doc Weaver pleaded for a winning streak, ol' Jim drawled, "Naw, Doc, you win two, lose one, win two, lose one and, heck, you've got 100 and a pennant."

With four pennants, Sunny Jim would know.

★

SUNNY JIM: Ladies Day favorite Jim Bottomley, swaggering Cardinal first baseman, had a record 12 RBIs in one game in 1924—"6 for 6"— using a choked grip and mild preliminary swing most deceptive to his long-ball results.

1926
Alex the Great

Old Pete Alexander Was Cards' First Series Hero

Grover Cleveland Alexander was epileptic, alcoholic, his own worst enemy, and one of the greatest pitchers ever. And in the sunset of an incredible career, Old Pete, as they called him, created a sunrise for the Cardinals with one of baseball's most distinguished relief roles.

Over the years Alexander the Great won a record-tying 373 National League games, and his corner-cutting control was as famous as when he was a kid back home in St. Paul, Nebraska, bringing home a rabbit or squirrel for dear mom by plunking them dead with a rock.

As an unsuccessful telephone lineman, Dode Alexander, the neighborhood nickname for the sandy-haired kid, turned pro for $100 a month at Galesburg, Illinois, in 1909. Barely a year later, he broke in sensationally for the Philadelphia Phillies, posting a 28–13 record.

By 1915, the first of three straight 30-plus seasons, Alexander pitched the futile Phillies into their only pennant until 1950. In 1916, his dazzling 33–12 record included 16 shutouts, still a major-league record. Shrewdly, with young Alex at draft age, the Phillies unloaded him to the Chicago Cubs' William Wrigley, who allotted $500 a month for Alexander's bride when the pitcher was away in World War I.

By the time Alexander had returned, shell-shocked from artillery pounding in France, his incipient epilepsy surfaced. Now, John Barleycorn became his best batterymate, as dear wife Aimee explained over the years, particularly when she acted as advisor for a movie in which Doris Day played her and a young actor with a date with destiny—Ronald Reagan—played her fairy-tale hero in *The Winning Team*.

When Alexander came over to the Cardinals on waivers for $4,500 in mid-season 1926, he still could pitch. With a livelier ball, he had added a screwball to go with his pinpoint fastball and short, sharp curve.

But new Cubs manager Joe McCarthy didn't like the old-timer's conduct, and though teetotaler Rogers Hornsby could hit Alex about as well as any pitcher, The Rajah wanted Old Pete to join the Cardinals. Alexander's 11 victories helped the Redbirds to their first pennant.

Twice against the heavily favored Yankees, Alexander won Series-tying games, the second, 6–2, with 10 strikeouts and the sixth again at Yankee Stadium, 10–2. Manager Hornsby asked him to take it easy tonight "just in case." Alex nodded, "But don't ask me to warm up more than once."

Curiously, he never warmed up except on the mound for his historic appearance. Dozing, sitting cross-legged in a busy bullpen, he slowly removed his red woolen sweater and, knock-kneed, sauntered slowly in the raw rain. Hornsby met him near the mound, "We're up 3–2, Pete, bases loaded, two out."

The thin man with the turkey-wattled neck smiled, "Guess, there's no place to put him, eh Rog?"

On four pitches, Grover Cleveland Alexander, at age 39, brought sunrise for the Redbirds. He struck out Tony Lazzeri.

★

ALEX THE GREAT: Grover Cleveland Alexander—"Old Pete"—was his own worst enemy as well as the hitters', a record 373-game winner and hero of the Cardinals' first world champions, 1926. Here, in 1927 with a colorful uniform symbol of redbird circled by black lettering, the 40-year-old master won 21 games.

1927

As Quick as a Flash

Frankie Frisch Was at His Finest His First Season Here

Sixty-three years after he last left his feet for a diving stop or knocked down another with a thick chest, Frankie Frisch lives in many ways, including a revealing statistic. In 1927, the year the Fordham Flash made St. Louis remember Frisch if not forget Rogers Hornsby, he handled 1,061 fielding chances, still a record.

From Abner Doubleday until now, no infielder other than a first baseman, of course, has ever handled as many plays, putouts, and assists as Frisch in '27, the year he took himself and owner Sam Breadon off the spot.

Always capable in the clutch, hailed as a "money player," Frisch was a whirling dervish the year he replaced superstar Hornsby, naturally a future Hall of Famer. Afield, the Flash was like a stocky Ozzie Smith spectacular, especially going to his right at second base. So when shortstop Tommy Thevenow broke a leg and a nervous "Class B" kid named Heinie Schuble tried to fill the breach, Frisch, in effect, told Heinie to worry about his right; the Flash would take care of Schuble's left.

With control pitcher Grover Cleveland Alexander, Jesse Haines's hard knuckler like a sinker, and lefty Wee Willie Sherdel not striking out many, either, Frisch was as busy as a cat on a hot tin roof and just as hot himself.

Overall, Frankie had batting averages higher than .337, including 1923 with the old New York Giants, when he wrested the total base title from Hornsby, but the switch-hitter never was more timely than his 208-hit season. His 48 stolen bases led the league, and he struck out only 10 of 617 times at bat, a Redbird record.

When young Paul Waner nosed him out for the MVP award after a .380 season for pennant-winning Pittsburgh, it was injustice even more than Frisch's

getting the award in 1931, a championship season. Heck, Frisch exceeded that season's .311 mark nine times in 19 years.

Frank Francis Frisch, son of a wealthy German linen manufacturer, was born in the Bronx, a few miles from what is now Yankee Stadium, but the Giants were the kings when he joined them in 1919.

He brought with him an athletic background matching Jackie Robinson's. He captained Fordham's baseball, basketball, and football teams, and was a second team All-American in football. He was an excellent skater and challenged bobsledders during winters at Lake Placid, New York, frolicking with U.S. Olympic performers.

Unwilling to be farmed out, Frisch uniquely never saw a day in the minors as player, coach, manager, or broadcaster. He was an intellectual roughneck who knew the difference between Richard Wagner and Honus Wagner. He had a horticulturist's green thumb and a librarian's love of books, but he was above all a leader.

The Old Flash, as he labeled himself, played on a National League–record eight World Series teams, four of them winners, two with the Cardinals. By 1934, a year older than the 37 listed, he was a tired gaffer who didn't do well in the rough-and-ready World Series against the Detroit Tigers. He saw his career Series average dip below .300, but he had one last golden moment.

With the Series tied and scoreless in the seventh game, the pilot light of the old Gas House Gang glowed. Frisch, fouling off several pitches, hit a bases-loaded double that triggered a seven-run inning, en route to an 11–0 cakewalk.

Frisch, funny and fiery, and often profane, had a typical reaction. "I'd rather have that hit than hit .800," he said. "But you know what? I really tripled into a double. Skylarking, watching those guys score, I should have been on third base. Hell, if one of my buzzards had done that, I'd have fined him fifty bucks!"

★

TEACHER'S PET: Frankie Frisch (right), pilot light of the Gas House Gang, was owner Sam Breadon's favorite player. Breadon (left), whose Cardinals won nine pennants and six world championships, praised the Fordham Flash, a fellow New Yorker acquired in the controversial trade for hitting hero and first title manager Rogers Hornsby. In a dying Breadon's last interview, unwilling to pick an All-Star team, Singin' Sam said, "The best player I ever had for one season was Frank Frisch in 1927."

Pigskin Peter Pan

Long-Lived Bert Clark of Ol' Mizzou

If there's one man to whom the unfolding of a new century and millennium would seem almost as impossible as beating Nebraska three years in a row in football, it would be Ol' Mizzou gridiron David who slew Goliath—little Bert Clark.

Little and durable, Bert Clark was a longtime football coach at Principia College, then athletic director, business manager, and treasurer. At this writing and reading, the waspish little guy was heading toward age 95, a spry guy older even than his old friend and teammate, the late Don Faurot.

Clark, whose painting hangs as a Mizzou Hall of Famer in Columbia's Hearnes Center, was the son of a Chillicothe hotel operator, a track man who could swivel his hips with the best of them, and yes, star in three straight football victories over Nebraska. Then and now, the Huskers were kingpin of the conference and the midlands.

In 1923 Nebraska beat Notre Dame's Four Horsemen their junior year, and two years later the Huskers topped Red Grange and Illinois. In Gwinn Henry's first year as Missouri coach, 1923, Nebraska was held to a 7–7 tie and then was upset three straight years by Missouri when both were in the old Missouri Valley

Conference. And 5'8", 153-pound Bert Clark scored all the Tiger touchdowns.

In the 1925 game, marking Nebraska's first defeat ever by a Valley foe, Clark caught a running pass from Ted O'Sullivan and scored from 50 yards out, the difference in a 9–6 game.

When Nebraska controversially was stopped at the MU goal line, a steaming Husker coach wanted to know how far the blankety-blank back had to cross the goal line? Noting a fumble, the head linesman Warren Giles had a snappy answer, "With or without the ball, Coach!"

The '26 game at Lincoln had an interesting footnote, too. The night before, Tiger players had been taken to see a hokey silent film in which recent college super-great Grange, kidnapped, had escaped to score the winning TD in the movie, *One Minute to Play*. On screen, Grange made a nifty move.

Next day, characteristically hiding out close behind the line, Clark slipped out late for his second scoring pass from Abe Stuber. Hemmed in at the sideline, Bert

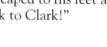

remembered Grange's clever film stop-and-go. He stopped, the Husker back went by him, and it was a 14–7 final.

The '27 game at Columbia's new Memorial Stadium lingered long because Nebraska won everything except the scoreboard. Injured backs George Flamank and Bert Clark limped in for one play, a touchdown pass that produced a 7–6 victor and created a Mizzou legend. Flamank to Clark!

A spectator that day in '27 was Faurot, then coaching Kirksville Teachers College in Friday night games. Forty-six years later, the longtime Tiger coach and athletic director, for whom Memorial Stadium had become Faurot Field, watched Al Onofrio's Tigers avenge a 62–0 lacing at Nebraska.

In Tom Osborne's first year as Nebraska's head coach, Ol' Mizzou's outplayed team managed a harrowing 13–12 upset. Faurot leaped to his feet and shouted, "1927 all over— Flamank to Clark!"

★

HAPPY COPY CAT: Gritty little Bert Clark, pint-sized Bert Clark, was not only alive in the millennium year, but he could remember his three touchdowns that upset Nebraska, 1925–27, one of them inspired by what he had seen the night before in a Red Grange movie.

1928

Mat Marathon

Meet the Man Who Won It, Ed (Strangler) Lewis

St. Louis' best, or at least best-remembered, wrestling match lasted three and a half hours back in 1928, but it lasted for many years as an excuse for father's late-night out on a Friday.

Back in February 1928, Ed (Strangler) Lewis, recognized as wrestling champion, met Joe Stecher of Nebraska, an old nemesis. The match was at the Coliseum, the Washington and Jefferson indoor amphitheater used before the Arena and Kiel Auditorium.

The main event went on at 9:55 P.M., best two out of three falls, and ended about 1:30 A.M., providing one heck of a fine excuse for many spectators, who received a built-in alibi for a long night out. For years thereafter, at the newspaper and radio offices, women would call and ask not the night before's results but what time the match ended.

Was the match fixed? Well, let's put it this way: Sam Muchnick, a young baseball writer with a boxing and wrestling column, was in the dressing room after the first fall of the three-hour tug o' war between big Lewis, who used a bear hug, and lean, lanky Stecher, who had the best scissors since Abe Lincoln quit popping grain sacks when training to wrestle. Twelve

years earlier in Omaha in red-hot weather, Lewis and Stecher struggled for an exhaustive five hours to a draw.

That night in '28, Muchnick heard Lewis, winner of the first fall, suggest he didn't want to humiliate Stecher. "So, Joe," said the Strangler, "you take the second one quickly and I'll take the third." Said and done.

Lewis, born Robert H. Friedricks at Nekosha, Wisconsin, became a quick-footed brawling bear and an intellectual, once one of the top 10 bridge players in the United States. He had a rich, sonorous voice and a grasp of religion, politics, and other diverse subjects. Over the years he became best described as a "lovable fraud," able to win at all costs if necessary.

The deft grappler could get up before the Third Baptist Church and deliver a temperance lecture that would have done Branch Rickey proud, but as he did at one St. Louis Elks sports dinner, he would put away three carafes of wine at the head table and sleep through his introduction.

The way Ed looked at it, after battling John Barleycorn and 6,200 other guys for more than 44 years, wine probably didn't count.

A charming man, that Lewis. Twice he was blinded by trachoma, a dreaded disease caused by dirty mats and

...WRESTLING...

'Strangler' Ed Lewis

World's Heavyweight Title Claimant

— *vs.* —

'Tiger' John Pesek

Formidable Championship Contender

— *AT THE* —

NEW COLISEUM

Thursday Evening, April 7th

Two falls out of three to a Finish

SANDY McDOUGAL *vs.* **TONY CATILINO**
SCOTLAND ITALY
One fall

Special Semi-Windup To Go on After Lewis-Pesek Match
PAUL JONES *vs.* **JOE ZIGMUND**

Under the direction of Thomas N. Packs

Prices: $1.65, $2.20, $3.30, $4.40, $5.50

Tickets at COLISEUM, RED BALL GYMNASIUM, MARYLAND HOTEL,
NATIONAL A. A. GYMNASIUM

'STRANGLER'
ED LEWIS
In Action

unsanitary wrestling conditions of early days. Working his way through five wives and $3 million, big Ed groaned and grunted for his cakes and ale until he was an overstuffed, squinting 58.

Before life's end in 1966, that former sportswriter, Sam Muchnick, president of the National Wrestling Alliance, had the old champion on the road as manager of the new champ, Lou Thesz. Both Muchnick and Thesz contended that, on the up-and-up, Lewis was at his best putting other guys down.

Loyally, Lewis never rapped the old sport, not even, in effect, having to stand still in 1929 so that former Dartmouth football star Gus Sonnenberg could flying tackle-and-butt him out of the ring for his questionable title. You see, four years earlier at Kansas City, another transplanted gridder, Wayne Munn, had thrown him out of the ring.

Said Lewis late in life, "I guess you can date the 'end' of wrestling as I knew it from that match."

But not the end of those repeated phone calls from the dear ladies after that mat marathon with Joe Stecher 72 years ago.

★

THE BEST BY TEST: Ed (Strangler) Lewis, shown here demonstrating his powerful headlock, was the top wrestling attraction in the minds of the late Sam Muchnick, current Lou Thesz, and many others. The old bridge champion, who saw the beginning of wrestling circle circus to keep up his lifestyle, is best known in St. Louis for having won a three-and-a-half hour marathon at St. Louis's old Coliseum in 1928, which ended at 1:30 A.M.

1928

Beau James

Colorful Jim Conzelman, St. Louis's Football Finest

Once upon a time the professional football Cardinals—Phoenix, by way of St. Louis and Chicago—were champions of all they surveyed, and Washington University was good enough on the gridiron to lose by only one touchdown to Illinois and to Notre Dame. The reason? A once-upon-a-time guy named Jimmy Conzelman.

Jim Conzelman was born James Gleason Ryan Dunn, which is about as Irish as the shamrock, but young Jimmy's father died when he was an infant and, with gratitude, the kid took the name of his stepfather, a doctor.

When good doctor Conzelman died at a time when his young stepson was a Roaring Twenties riot, having fun running up touchdowns and scores for old McKinley High School and Washington U., young Jim Conzelman stepped out to help mom with her larger, young family.

So, the ruggedly handsome, broken-nosed young man, a wartime contributor to the 1919 Rose Bowl team and middleweight boxing champion of the Great Lakes' naval station, became a pioneer player in the National Football League. It was so informal then that one day when he was playing quarterback for the Milwaukee Badgers, a sub came in to tell Jimmy that the club owner just had fired the coach and that Conzelman would replace him now.

Because over the years he was good at everything he tried, Conzelman soon managed the Providence Steamrollers to the NFL championship and earned the MVP as a player in 1928.

Restless, James-of-all-games decided to return home and publish a weekly newspaper in Maplewood. But soon alma mater Washington U. lured him to coach football, and using the gift of gab he had developed, Conzelman raised the money to raise the team's sights.

After World War II, Washington University de-emphasized sports, but they really had cut back when they dropped the hometown hero who won three Missouri Valley Conference championships and in 1936 narrowly lost to Illinois and Notre Dame, using just 11 players in one game and 15 in the other.

With a drinking buddy named Charley (Blue Shirt) Bidwill in Chicago, Jim soon put in two terms coaching the Cardinals, steering them to their one and only NFL championship in 1947. Quarterback Paul Christman remembered Conzelman as the best coach at relaxing a squad. Said Christman, "In a tough week, Jim would blow a whistle and we'd all have a Coke."

A year later the Cardinals lost a chance at a second title in a blizzard aftermath at Philadelphia, but Conzelman lost something—heart—after punter Jeff Burkett was killed in a plane crash and all-league tackle Stan Mauldin died of a heart attack.

So the white, shaggy-haired coach came back to St. Louis as an advertising executive—a little tired from too many nights as James-of-all-games—as author, after-dinner speaker, commencement orator, actor, sculptor, band leader, songwriter, piano player, and radio commentator.

St. Louis properly has to remember James Gleason Ryan Dunn Conzelman as a premier player and coach, the city's first member of the National Football League Hall of Fame—the wittiest, too. As Hollywood's Pat O'Brien put it, following Jimmy at a Chicago Quarterback's Club luncheon, "Speaking after Conzelman is like following *Gone With the Wind* with a magic lantern!"

★

BEAU JAMES: Colorful, capable Jimmy Conzelman (left), a great pro player, good coach, and sparkling entertainer, took alma mater Washington University to scheduling heights in the depression, aided by Gale Bullman (right). "Gloomy Gale" would win a strong affection in years following at Rolla when coaching its Missouri Miners.

1930
The Joker in the Deck
Flint Rhem's 'Kidnap' Story Takes First Prize

Moonstruck or moonshine, bottled in bond, Charles Flint Rhem—they called him Shad back home in Rhems, South Carolina—could have been one of the Cardinals' best pitchers if not the thirstiest. But he figured in a rare episode when he was "kidnapped" in a close pennant race.

You might not believe that gunmen would hold a pistol to a guy's head the night before he was scheduled to pitch a key game, but that's what Flint Rhem "convinced" manager Gabby Street of when he showed up that next morning in 1930, tired and disheveled. "Cups of raw whiskey, Sarge!" Rhem drawled to old soldier Street in an accent so thick it was difficult to figure whether he was drunk or sober.

Rhem, you see, was an imaginative man and a pretty good pitcher. At age 25 in his second full season, 1926, he won 20 games for the Cardinals' first championship ball club, but he never really came close again until traded six years later; on the other hand he usually toed the mound as a break-even pitcher.

In 1930, for instance, he was 12–8 as the Cardinals came back from 12 games out in early August. The Cards were only one game over .500, and then they won 39 of their last 49 games. The finish probably ranks second only to the 1942 St. Louis Swifties.

In '30, the season with the highest league batting average in history, the Redbirds averaged a record 6.5 runs a game and used the June 15 deadline acquisition of bulldog veteran Burleigh Grimes to help their surge.

So, with clubs ahead of them waffling, first Brooklyn and then New York and Chicago, the Cardinals climbed from fourth to just one game out for a late-September showdown at Ebbets Field. Recovering, Uncle Wilbert Robinson's Dodgers—or "Robins," as they called them in tribute to the old manager—had won 11 games in a row.

Gabby Street, managing the Cardinals, would have preferred Wild Bill Hallahan to face Brooklyn's great red-faced ace, Dazzy Vance, but Hallahan's middle finger on his right hand was smashed in a taxicab door. So Street figured on an extra day for Hallahan, but then Rhem showed up claiming to have been "kidnapped."

So Gabby went with Hallahan, a big-game guy, and in that crazy high-scoring era, Wild Bill turned out to be Sweet William. And Vance, as always, was a dazzler.

Before a packed house of 30,000, the game was scoreless into the 10th, just after a second-base collision between Cardinal shortstop Charley Gelbert and Dodger infielder Mickey Finn. With Gelbert limping, Street called on little left-handed-hitting Andy High, a reserve infielder, to pinch hit.

High would recall that Vance blazed two fastballs past him, then hung a curve. Eyes bulging in gratitude, High pulled it for a double. With two out, he scored on a single by center fielder Taylor Douthit.

In the home 10th, with Sparky Adams moving from third base to short, High played third. With the bases loaded and only one out, the Cardinals played back at double-play depth. Catcher Al Lopez's sharp grounder bad-hopped and was juggled by Adams, but money-player Frankie Frisch, pivoting, reeled off the DP that represented a 1–0 victory and a tie for first place.

Next day, High did it again as Handy Andy in a pinch-hitting rally, and when the Cardinals swept the three-game series, they were home free. They would lose a good six-game World Series against Connie Mack's great Philadelphia A's.

Flint Rhem? Well, Ol' Shad told many such tales. For instance, the time he alibied to the manager that he had drunk the most one night with loner Grover Cleveland Alexander because, shucks, Sarge, Old Pete was more important to the ball club.

The "kidnap" story, which, of course, nobody believed, lasted until Fred Saigh, as owner, threw a 25th anniversary party for the 1926 champions. Bless his guilty old heart, Rhem confessed the hoax and then, too loaded to take the field, took his bow from the press box.

★

FAMOUS FIBBER: *Charles Flint Rhem—"Flint" to the public, "Shad" to his teammates—came from a town named for his family, Rhems, S.C. Rhem could have been a great pitcher except that his talent couldn't keep up with his thirst. Flint's tale of his "kidnapping" the night before a critical game in a comeback season for the Cardinals, 1930, lingers long—and amusingly.*

1930

Zup

Famed Illinois Coach Was a Master of Deception, Upsets

Bob Zuppke, for whom the football field at Champaign is named, had a perfect six-for-six record against St. Louis–area teams in his 29 years as coach of Illinois, but the little legend did much to attract our town's football fans.

Zup, as he was called, would have been a box-office smash if the folks who paid their way into Memorial Stadium heard him speak. He was—for a truth—almost as funny as the actor/columnist he resembled, Will Rogers. Zuppke and Notre Dame's Knute Rockne formed an amusing combination when they appeared often on each other's platforms.

At South Bend, for instance, Rock might suggest modestly, "My assistants do all the work. All I do is blow up the balls." To which Zup, on cue, would counter, "I haven't that much wind."

For years, a great rival for Illinois was the University of Chicago, then a powerhouse coached for 41 years by immortal Amos Alonzo Stagg. Lonnie Stagg was proud that he didn't cuss.

Zuppke agreed. "No," Zup said, "Coach Stagg never swears at his men because he doesn't have any. He'll call this one a jackass, another, another, and by the end of the workout, there are no men playing, just jackasses grazing!"

For all his quips and quotes, Robert Carl Zuppke was a philosopher in canvas pants, born in Berlin and moved to Milwaukee at age two. He had a slight Germanic accent that made his favorite—Red Grange—come out as "Grainch."

When Red had his incredible five-touchdown, 402-yard game at Memorial Stadium's dedication in 1924 against Michigan, Zuppke set up his longtime foe, Michigan's Fielding (Hurry-Up) Yost, then on a coaching sabbatical as athletic director at Ann Arbor. With Yost in the stands at Nebraska, Zuppke set up an outside running game for Grange, certain Hurry-Up

would hurry up and tell his interim coaching successor.

When Red came out exhausted against Michigan after scoring four times on long runs in the first quarter, Zuppke said, "Nice going, Grainch, but you should have scored five if you had turned to the right."

Red, of course, was the old man's favorite. Zuppke, who was a colorful painter, had given Grange a prized painting of him in action. His work was displayed on exhibit, usually featuring raw landscapes—deserts, forests, and oceans.

In football, he was an exception, too, from his first season in 1913. Hired from Oak Park High School in suburban Chicago, he handed Missouri its only defeat, 24–7, in a game where the Tigers saw a trick play that later enabled them to beat Oklahoma.

Trick plays and upsets marked much of Zuppke's career at Illinois, which included seven Big 10 championships won or shared and an overall 131–81–12 record that would have been better had he stayed abreast in the more aggressive recruiting era that followed his last title in 1927. He retired in 1942 at age 63 and was elected to the college Hall of Fame in '51.

In the twilight of his coaching career, Zup's Illini were too much for Saint Louis University in 1931 and for Washington's Bears four times through '36, but, of course, he'll be remembered most for his upsets and innovations.

The Dutch Master invented the spiral snap from center, the on-side kick, the screen pass, the technique of pulling back the guards on offense to protect the passer and, defensively, the dropping back of the guards into the secondary. Remarkably, Zup invented the huddle, too. And he was number one as a psychologist.

That was manifested in 1939 when Michigan's great coach, Fritz Crisler, expressed the thought that his current Tom Harmon was better than Illini's Red Grange. Zup's use of that indiscretion created a frenzy and a stunning Illini upset 16–7.

★

ZUP: A magic word depicting the University of Illinois's famed football coach of unexpected plays and unexpected victories, Bob Zuppke, the masterful tactician for whom the playing field at Champaign's Memorial Stadium is named.

1931
Wild Horse of the Osage
Colorful Pepper Martin Was Wildest in '31

When a depression-shocked nation, sinking into the financial doldrums, needed a national hero, it got one in 1931 in the form of a wide-shouldered, hawk-nosed, grinning ball player named Pepper Martin.

Actually, the full name was Johnny Leonard Roosevelt Martin—the "Pepper" was properly applied by a Redbird farm-system man and his descriptive nickname, the Wild Horse of the Osage, by a sportswriter in Rochester.

Life was a bowl of raspberries—with some occasional bourbon thrown in—for the Oklahoma Irishman with a touch of Indian blood. Later, his Mudcats, a band of cacophonic Cardinals with Pepper playing the guitar (to him the "git-tar") would be as famous as his aggressive play and belly-busting slides. But by 1931, up with the team a couple of times primarily as a pinch runner, the 27-year-old leap year baby had other ideas—and complaints.

To general manager Branch Rickey, whom he admired, Pepper poured out his frustration. "John Brown, Mr. Rickey," Martin drawled in his nasal twang of the Southwest, "if you can't play me, trade me."

Mr. Rickey, who liked profits as much as he did Pepper's spirit of adventure, soon unloaded Taylor Douthit, a master center fielder making $14,500, in favor of young Mr. Martin's $4,500.

The rest of the season Pepper hit .300. Early, he made doctors and others wince the way he thundered down to first base and then, rather than running through the bag, stopped with a screech that would pop viewers' hamstrings. Pepper was so good that when the Cardinals won easily and sought to end the bid for a third straight championship by Connie Mack's Philadelphia Athletics, the *Post-Dispatch's* J. Roy Stockton suggested the rookie retread might be the Series hero. In a word—wow!

First day, facing the great Grove, a 31–4 fireball left-hander, the right-handed-hitting Martin prayed quietly, "Please, God." He doubled, singled twice, and stole a base in a 6–2 loss.

The second game, 2–0 Cardinals, was a classic Pepper Martin one-man show with a bow to Cardinal left-hander Wild Bill Hallahan. Off George Earnshaw, Martin stretched a second-inning single into a double, then stole third and scored on an outfield fly. In the seventh, Martin hit another single, stole second, took third on an infield out, and scored on a squeeze bunt.

Back in Philadelphia, even A's fans cheered Pepper in a 5–2 victory over Grove when, backing Burleigh Grimes's two-hitter, the Wild Horse got two hits, a stolen base, and two runs. Next day, Earnshaw allowed only two hits, but Pepper got them both, one a double.

Again putting the Cardinals ahead in a series won in seven, Pepper beat out a bunt, hit a homer, singled, and drove in four of the runs in a 5–1 victory.

Going 12 for 18, Pepper Martin was "too hot not to cool down," but at Series end he had a .500 average with 12 hits, including four doubles, a homer, five runs, five RBIs, and—because nobody must have run in the American League then—five stolen bases.

They never forgot Pepper Martin.

★

SECOND THOUGHTS: Big Al Todd might have thought he could intimidate fist-clenched Redbird rookie Paul Dean the way Todd did older brother Dizzy, but the bulky Philadelphia backstop was interrupted by a mild-mannered man who was all right except when he got mad—Pepper Martin.

1934
Dizzying Heights

'Me 'n Paul,' Dizzy Dean's Greatest Season

Dizzy Dean wasn't always as modest as when he allowed that if they gave the ball often enough to his younger brother, "Me 'n Paul" would win 45 games for the St. Louis Cardinals in 1934. Heck, they won 49 and four more, two apiece in a rowdy World Series with the Detroit Tigers.

The colorful Gas House Gang prevailed in a series so rough that commissioner Landis, who knew all the words himself, even fined umpire Bill Klem for using the wrong words in an elevator altercation with the Tigers' Goose Goslin.

The Tigers got into the World Series with a breeze, hitting .300 as a team for future Hall of Fame catcher Mickey Cochrane. By contrast, the Cardinals' Frankie Frisch, himself Hall of Fame–bound, got there only because the New York Giants collapsed in the final week.

Old Flash Frisch, a fading age 38, was a player-manager whose best days were behind him, but switch-hitting first baseman Rip Collins had a career year—.333 with a league-leading 35 homers and 126 RBIs— and Muscles Joe Medwick was almost as tough with his bat as with his tongue.

A rookie power-hitting catcher, Bill DeLancey, was even sassier when catching the Great Dean, who liked the kid's guts. DeLancey was the batterymate, too, for rookie Paul Dean, two years younger than the lean, lanky guy who at only 23 called himself Ol' Diz.

Ol' Diz, correctly Jay Hanna, won 30 games and brother Paul 19, including a late-season no-hitter at Brooklyn just after Dizzy had pitched a three-hitter. They figured they had to be good against Detroit's G-Men, a play on words for FBI men, meaning Gehringer, Greenberg, Goslin, and Gee Walker.

For underpaid Redbirds, a $6,000 World Series share loomed like a pot of gold at the end of the rainbow. In tough times, manager Frisch, who had made $28,000 as a player, was down to $18,500 as the pilot light of the Gas House Gang.

The old Dutch Master, playing his eighth World Series, contributed a clutch three-run double in the final game. Medwick, ousted by the commissioner for his own good after a savage slide infuriated hard-losing Detroit fans, had 11 hits with a .378 average. Collins averaged .367 with 11 hits, and Wild Horse Pepper Martin, .355.

In that Series, Pepper put manager Cochrane into a hospital overnight with a hard slide, the Tigers' JoJo White roughed up Frisch on the bases, and Detroit shortstop Bill Rogell plunked Dizzy Dean on the head with a throw when the pinch-running pitcher didn't slide.

But it really was the Deans' Series, Dizzy and Paul. Dizzy won two out of three—Paul won two— aided by his own bat and a base hit by All-American Leo Durocher.

For game seven, Dizzy psyched opposing pitcher Eldon Auker, warming up with a submarine delivery. "Gee podnuh, you don't expect to win that stuff," said Dean, using a four-letter vulgarity.

Dizzy broke it open with his bat in the scoreless third, stretching a single into a double and setting up a seven-run inning in which he also singled.

The cakewalk, ultimately 11–0, was a depressing nine-run rout when Medwick got into a sixth-inning kicking contest with Tiger third baseman Marv Owen. Angry hometown fans threw everything at Medwick

except a fit in a 20-minute delay.

Commissioner Landis could have ordered a forfeit, but he was charitable. During the delay, watching Pepper Martin, he had learned to spit chewing tobacco through his teeth. Then he told Medwick to get lost.

★

HOLD THAT TIGER: Dizzy Dean, at the 30-game peak of his pitching career, plays with a toy on the eve of the 1934 World Series to the delight of many, including his admiring friend, talented Will Rogers. Cowboy-humorist Rogers, then turning out a daily bit of national journalistic wit, was number one at the box office in Hollywood as an actor. Ol' Diz mourned—as did the nation—when Will was killed a year later in a plane crash in Alaska. Paul (left, above) did, too.

1935
Boxing's John Henry
Lewis Won Title and Admiration Here

For a guy born in Los Angeles, reared in Phoenix, and fighting out of Pittsburgh, St. Louis was Home Sweet Home for John Henry Lewis, who not only won his championship here, but also used our hometown as a favorite place to box as king of the light-heavies.

St. Louis saw John Henry for the first time when he challenged New York's Bob Olin for the 175-pound title on Halloween night, 1935, at the Arena. At the time, both the big dirigible oval on Oakland and the Kiel Auditorium downtown were virtually new.

The sleek, handsome Lewis, just 21 years old, actually came to the Big One after having lost successive decisions to Slapsy Maxie Rosenbloom and Abe Feldman, but earlier he had won a non-title bout with champion Olin at San Francisco.

Here, championship fights were unique, and this was the first since the onerous bar against mixed-race matches had been lifted by the state legislature. Times were tough, so the presence of 9,219 spectators who paid an average of less than two dollars a ticket was a featured footnote.

So, of course, was John Henry Lewis, after Olin won the first two rounds. John Henry almost put away the Fordham graduate in the middle rounds, then hung on for a 15-round unanimous decision.

Lewis was good enough, a good champion, and obviously well liked, enough that his manager, Pittsburgh's Gus Greenlee—also a promoter in black league baseball—brought him to town often, almost always to Kiel, which opened in 1934, spic and span.

In 1936, Lewis returned in non-title bouts to knock out a longtime well-regarded St. Louis light-heavy, Al Stillman, who had beaten Jimmy Braddock. That one lasted only four rounds in January. In March, John Henry outpointed Eddie Simms. In June, he kayoed Tony Schucco in the eighth. And in August he went 10 to beat George Nichols.

Truth is, money obviously wasn't big enough to permit Lewis to put the title on the line. In '37 after knocking out Donald Barry in five in April and decisioning Emilio Martinez in May, promoters set up a championship return bout here with Olin. John Henry put away the former champ in eight on June 3.

In the hungry era between the world wars, the double decade to the '40s, the way to make a buck was to box. After losing a heavyweight fight to Spain's Isadore Gastanaga at Detroit in October 1937, John Henry got sweet revenge here. On December 12, he knocked out Gastanaga in nine.

Seeking bigger money against bigger opponents, just five days later Lewis outpointed an aging, well-regarded heavyweight, rubbery Johnny Risko, at Cleveland.

In February 1938, Lewis made his 11th and last St. Louis appearance, stopping one Fred Lenhart in eight. That October at New Haven, he outpointed Al Gainer in a title bout.

Even more than famed namesake Joe Louis, John Henry Lewis could box and hit. For instance, in a career of 105 bouts, he scored 54 knockouts and lost only seven decisions. He was never knocked out until . . .

Joe Louis, a personal friend, granted him the bigger payday of heavyweight championship fights, January 25, 1939, at New York. Mercifully, Joe put him away quickly in the first round. The fight was John Henry's last. Joe Louis knew a well-kept secret. His old friend was going blind in one eye!

★

THE REAL JOHN HENRY: John Henry Lewis was a nimble, nifty light heavyweight, a St. Louis favorite over the years before and after winning the 175-pound championship from Bob Olin at the Arena in 1935. The grinning Lewis, shown that title year, held the crown unbeaten through 1939. He retired after a quick first-round kayo by heavyweight champ Joe Louis in 1939. Virtually blind in one eye then, John Henry died in 1974 at age 60.

1936
Dee-Lightful Dee

Beckmann Pioneered as Woman Athlete, Coach

An international women's pioneer as player and coach, she was called The Duchess when she coached men's athletic teams in World War II. That's right—men!—but then, Dolores (Dee) Beckmann was always special even before she went into track's Hall of Fame and Missouri's, too.

Just 20 years have passed since Dee was named to the Missouri Sports Hall of Fame, two years after one of her pet projects, Helen Stephens, inducted her into the national women's track Hall. And 70 seasons have passed, after Dee's heavy campaigning for American women, since she and others sang a song-list favorite en route by ship to Amsterdam.

The favorite song in 1928 was "You're the Cream in My Coffee," and like cream rising to the top, that was Dee, physical education graduate of St. Louis's Loretto Academy. At age 16, she had held all the Ozark AAU records simultaneously—nine firsts and a second.

She was the first woman to win international acclaim in four sports—track, fencing, basketball, and hockey. Denied victory at the Amsterdam games while bucking a tradition—a misplaced shot put paralyzed an arm—she became the first U.S. women's track coach in '36, the first woman elected chairman of the AAU's committee, and the first woman of St. Louis Parks and Recreation.

Yes, and in 1942 she was the lady who coached American GIs located in Iceland, but then, that was just the beginning of the intriguing trek that took her to coaching jobs in England, India, and Japan.

Tall and statuesque, she met emperors, statesmen, and dictators, so The Duchess label fit, though Baroness might have fit better if she hadn't changed her name.

To avoid conflicts, she simplified her surname by dropping the "o" before the "e" in the German umlaut. As one with the same problem, author Broeg understands. So Dee became just Beckmann. "Which," she would relate merrily, "gave my old friend, J. Edgar Hoover, a fit with my passport problems."

Big names were commonplace to the world-traveling athlete with a pursuit of the unusual. General Douglas MacArthur, head of the U.S. Olympic team in '18, charmed the ladies, Dee included, but he was married then to a Wannamaker, of the wealthy Philly Wannamakers. Later, as five-star general, MacArthur persuaded Beckmann to coach the Japanese track-and-field team for the Asian games in New Delhi.

This was a far cry from the kid who got into the games because, as she put it in her soft, melodic voice, her father wanted a boy. Ultimately, she left St. Louis, but St. Louis never left her. Educated at Harris Teachers College and Washington U., she had enough credits for a Ph.D., but the road was s-o-o interesting.

As far back as '28, she dazzled Russians with her speed and personality, sorry that the United States had eliminated the 800 meters for women—considered too strenuous for 32 more years. The Duchess's friends and acquaintances are names written brightly in the pages of the twentieth century.

At Germany, she dined with propaganda hound Joseph Goebbels and corpulent Herman Goering and found them heel-clicking sycophants to Adolf Hitler, who stood aloof and alone, mumbling.

Dee was a weekend guest of the Prince of Wales, before marriage and divorce left him as the Duke of Windsor. She later sipped tea with the real Duchess and dined at the White House with Eleanor Roosevelt.

By the time she made her last return to St. Louis for the Missouri State Hall of Fame award—no longer running, but walking regularly at her retirement home in Sun City, Arizona—Dee Beckmann was a legend of women's athletics.

★

DEE-LIGHTFUL: Dolores (Dee) Boeckmann, shortened by dropping the "o", was a pioneer performer, coach, and champion of women's athletic privileges, a lady legend—Beckmann.

Dee Beckmann
Olympic '28 '36 '64

1936

Right in Der Führer's Face

Helen Stephens's Famed Olympic Efforts Frustrated Hitler

Someone or some several tried to tell that tall teenager from Fulton, Helen Stephens, that if she kept up that heavy exercise and running, she'd be crippled by 40 and unable to walk by 45. The Fulton Flash, the golden girl of the 1936 Olympics, could have laughed in their faces, as she almost did in Adolf Hitler's.

No, Miss Stephens, twice a gold medal winner with a record 100 meters then and on a championship 400 meter team, didn't have the rudeness to insult or upstage Hitler, dictator of host Germany in '36, but she came close.

Over the years, 75 of them, mostly spent in sports in one form or another, Helen had to recount often her brief encounter with Der Führer. After all, no other American athlete met him, most certainly not the black man, Jesse Owens, who romped to record after record. After all, for a man who used Aryan supremacy as a springboard to his hateful success, Hitler couldn't acknowledge a man of a different color, even a superstar.

Jesse was, of course, a many-splendored man and a good friend of Stephens's. Before turning to a World War II stint in the Marines and a long career as a research librarian for government here, Helen did a natural thing, briefly turning professional.

As a result, a great admirer of Babe Didrikson, she traveled with baseball's semi-pro team, the bearded House of David, and also played women's pro basketball and participated in exotic 100-yard sprints, once against a midget auto. And in races against the gifted Owens, she once lost just barely.

That, figured because her 100 meters at Berlin was only a second slower than Jesse's 10.3, and her 11.3 lasted until Wilma Rudolph 24 years later.

This was, you can see, a great stride for the hick from the sticks, as they liked to label her and which, cunningly, she used on a rare sly occasion. She really was a razor-sharp student as well as a speedster who made her Fulton coach do a double-take when she broke the world record unofficially at age 17.

For her first trip to St. Louis, the 1935 national indoor meet at the Arena, she had to borrow track togs, including shoes. So she spun international heads when she beat Poland's 1932 Olympic champion, Stella Walsh.

They hawed-hawed afterward when she asked innocently, "Who's Stella Walsh?" but, of course, knew. Off the record, she cracked, "I could beat her barefoot."

At age 18 in Germany, the cocky kid with the casual air and embarrassing male voice really wanted no part of Hitler, though obviously none then knew the depths of the dastardly dictator. So she stalled with fellow Olympic relay winner, Harriet Bland of St. Louis.

First, she retired to the dressing room to freshen. Then, urged by a second messenger not to insult Hitler, she emerged to see Der Führer kick at an unauthorized photographer as one of his Black Shirt elite smashed the poor man's camera.

Face to face, towering at six feet over Hitler, she declined to Sig Heil or to Nazi salute, held out her hand, and, accepting congratulations, gave him, as she put it, "a good American salute."

For a time afterward, Helen coached the women's track team of alma mater William Woods College at Fulton, where much of her memorabilia is housed. Then, between accepting repeated Halls of Fame honors—nationally and locally—she bowled and competed in the St. Louis Senior Olympics as an enthusiast.

Helen Stephens got one last reward before her death from a stroke and heart attack in 1994. The National Women's Hall of Fame at Seneca, New York, inducted her with Gloria Steinem, Rosa Parks, and Georgia O'Keefe—pretty fast company, almost as fast as the Fulton Flash.

★

FULTON FLASH: Helen Stephens, the small-town mid-Missouri girl, ranked second only to Jesse Owens in the 1936 Olympic Games. With Adolf Hitler in the stands at Berlin, Helen sprinted to the 100-meter victory, as shown here, and anchored a winning 400-meter victory for the United States, too.

1936
Buddy's Finest Hour
Ticker Tape for Table Tennis

If at age 16 you had a ticker-tape parade down Broadway—New York's Broadway, not ours—life thereafter would have to be downhill, but not if you're a multi-talented man with a good voice and big heart—Buddy Blattner.

Robert Garnett Blattner—Bob to few, Bud or Buddy to many—headed toward 2000 a handsome, silver-haired 80 after a many-splendored career that also produced a worthwhile charity for kids nearly 30 years ago—the Buddy Fund.

That resulted when friend Ben Kermer and others wanted to honor him with a night of gifts for his contribution as broadcaster of the old pro basketball Hawks. Blattner liked the gesture but not the idea. He asked that all potential gifts be given to needy kids.

The committee accepted the challenge. Through members and Rawlings Sporting Goods, it came up with the slightly flawed sports equipment at a 3-to-1 dollar value. The thought was so good that they formed a continuing club of goodwill, now totaling millions over the years for distribution annually. Appropriately, the broadcaster's nickname was a 7-come-11 natural.

So Buddy Fund Blattner, ensconced down at the Lake of the Ozarks and spending winters in Florida, served as a cheerleader and participant, even happier than when he had that New York ticker-tape parade at just 16.

St. Louis's Blattner and Indianapolis's Jimmy McClure teamed in 1936 to travel to Prague and win the world's table tennis title from the Czechs, then dominating the sport derisively called Ping-Pong. More recently, China has flourished in the sport.

A year later, Blattner and McClure repeated as champions, assured of election later when the Table Tennis Hall of Fame was formed. Buddy, meanwhile, demonstrated further the hand-eye coordination for which his father merits credit.

A physical fitness man at the North Side "Y", the senior Blattner played games with son Bud. One included stringing a rope across the kitchen, draping a bed sheet over it and then, standing behind it, using a rapidly moving flashlight to require hand coverage the kid darting back and forth on the other side.

It worked great. In high school, a basketball and tennis star, a member of the junior Davis Cup team, young Blattner turned baseball pro with the talent-rich Cardinals in 1938. By '41 he was a regular infielder on their Sacramento Pacific Coast championship team.

Two things hampered him then, as he would relate: World War II and the competence of the '42 Cardinals, a great championship club with 106 regular-season victories.

Service bound, he was sold to the New York Giants. Afterward, as a rookie in '46, first time back home, he beat the champion Cardinals with a game-tying double off Harry (The Cat) Brecheen and a winning homer off Blix Donnelly.

By '49 at age 29, he faced a crisis. He quit as a utility infielder with the Phillies and pursued an off-season television job in the medium's infancy, as a game-show participant and script writer. Privately, he honed baseball-broadcasting skills for radio.

Hired by Bill DeWitt in 1950 to assist Dizzy Dean with the Browns, he soon joined Ol' Diz on the national TV Game-of-the-Week for seven years. He spent one season with the Cardinals and seven years each as radio voice of the California Angels and Kansas City Royals.

Meanwhile, nine winters he traveled with the basketball Hawks, designing clever nicknames and coining an unforgettable line when an official whistled an infraction.

Intoned Buddy Fund Blattner cheerfully, "They're walking the right way." Or, sadly, "They're walking the wrong way."

★

SMILE, BUDDY BOY: Unusually sober-faced, Robert (Bud) Blattner, age 17, fourth from the left, gathered with other table tennis champions at a dinner early in 1937 at the former New Yorker Hotel, just after teaming with Jimmy McClure to win the world's double titles. Not even the photographer could identify all. Players with paddles from the left, Sandor Glanez, Standa Kolar, Laszlo Bellak, and Sol Schiff, all international stars.

SELFISH WITH THE BELTS: *Tireless Henry Armstrong, probably St. Louis's most gifted fighter ever, is shown just after he won the featherweight championship in 1937. Armstrong soon gained the lightweight and welterweight titles as well—at the same time.*

TWIN TALENTS: *Two of the finest fighters ever, pound for pound, St. Louis's Henry Armstrong (left) and Sugar Ray Robinson met in New York City, 1941. Hammering Hank, just one year short of retiring, lost a 10-round decision.*

1937

Perpetual Motion

Henry Armstrong, Three-in-One Boxing King

Pound for pound, bell to bell perhaps boxing's most exciting fighter, perpetual-motion Henry Armstrong came off the streets of St. Louis to unprecedented success. He was the only man to hold three professional weight-division championships at the same time.

Most startling, there were only eight fighting divisions when Armstrong won those three titles over a two-year period, 1936 to 1938. And he might have won a fourth if an alleged financial "fix" hadn't sullied another chance.

The story of Armstrong, boxer and Baptist minister, high school poet and class valedictorian, is an amazing one of a little man's cream rising to the top.

Born Henry Jackson in Columbus, Mississippi, in late 1912, the kid moved at age five to Papin Street on St. Louis's near south side. There, you had to be able to fight to survive.

Still, he well might have fulfilled that ambition of grandmother Henrietta to become what she wanted—a minister. But tough depression times, requiring him to work a man's job after his father's crippling rheumatism, hit Henry full in the face like that fluttering newspaper sports page.

Pulling it off his face in Carondelet Park, where he was working as a railroad gandy dancer, he noticed the headline—Cuba's Kid Chocolate just won $10,000 in a fight.

That night he ran—he always ran home, to school, and to his odd jobs—but he ran harder. He had to tell dear Henrietta that the ministry would have to wait. The grandma, who had grown up in slavery and once saw Abraham Lincoln, was understanding.

That's when Henry Jackson met Harry Armstrong and became Henry Armstrong, to protect his eligibility when he boxed both amateur and pro. His first ring name was Melody Jackson because Harry Armstrong heard him cheerfully sing.

Boxing 62 amateur bouts, of which he won 58, the stocky little kid began to build his incredible endurance, but it didn't happen soon enough to avoid a three-round kayo loss in his first pro bout on July 27, 1931. But from that knockout at age 19 until he lost to Pittsburgh's Fritzie Zivic 14 years later, unsuccessful in seeking to regain his welterweight crown, he never was stopped.

His fabulous title success began in October 1936. Working out of Los Angeles, Henry Armstrong caught and collared featherweight champion Petey Sarron in six rounds in New York City.

A year later, hopscotching the lightweight title when holding the 127-pound crown, he outpointed veteran welter king Barney Ross. A knockout was imminent in round 14, but close up, the proud Ross mumbled, "Don't put me away, Henry."

Six months later, Hammering Hank stepped back to the 136-pound lightweight division and dethroned Lou Ambers, again in New York.

Unable to get back to the featherweight limit, Armstrong vacated the title, but then, in defense of the 147-pound welter, he outpointed the Philippines' Ceferino Garcia, meaningful because by early 1940, already with Armstrong having lost the lightweight honors back to Ambers, Garcia had won the middleweight division.

Fleshed up, Armstrong met Garcia for the 160-pound championship in March 1940. Before the fight, heavy mob men made him an offer he refused, $75,000. The courage didn't help. Henry got only a draw. He would insist, smiling, "I suspect they got to the referee instead."

Fighting as many as 29 times a year, the human buzz saw lost twice to Zivic. No longer managed by famed jazz singer Al Jolson, he continued to Valentine's Day 1945 after 175 career fights, of which he lost only 21.

Caught up in the fast life of Hollywood and an alcoholic, Henry Armstrong saw the religious light. He moved into the ministry in 1951 and played himself in a movie on his life. He wrote his autobiography, then returned in triumph to St. Louis as assistant director of the Herbert Hoover Boys Club. The old champion, a boxing Hall of Famer, led the kids in inspiration and the city in dinner invocations.

★

1937

Have Trunks, Will Travel

Durable World-Traveling Wrestler, Lou Thesz

At a time when, as Casey Stengel put it, most guys his age are dead, Lou Thesz sniffed recently at the roses, presumably a climax to a career in which he claimed a wrestling championship at 21 and at 74 nearly beat a guy half his age.

Son of a St. Louis cobbler who was an amateur middleweight wrestling champion in Hungary, Thesz has spread the good word about the old hometown and received reciprocal honors. For instance, the latest in 1999 was his induction into the International Wrestling Hall of Fame and Museum.

Newton, Iowa, is near the University of Iowa, longtime king of NCAA wrestling champions, formerly led by Dan Gable, Olympic winner and longtime coach of the Hawkeyes in tights.

Gable, director Mike Chapman, and associates honored Thesz and three other professionals even though pro wrestling long was suspect before the modern burlesque hit the circus. Named with Thesz were an early century legend from Iowa, Frank Gotch, fabulous Ed (Strangler) Lewis, and Minnesota's highly capable Vern Gagne.

Said Thesz, "I'm sure Gotch and Lewis would be as honored as Gagne and I are. After all, we did know how to wrestle even if some matches were pre-determined."

In the eyes of Thesz, 83, Lewis was the best and also a topflight bridge-playing internationalist. Ability in and out of the ring is important to Thesz, who helped Pop in the shoe-repair shop and pursued night school with a thirst for knowledge. As he put it frankly, "If you didn't waste all your off-hours doing what you shouldn't do, there are public libraries in every town."

Articulate, Lou also represents the decades of 16 million miles of travel for matches. He's especially esteemed in Japan, where he's still invited often to foster freestyle and teach martial arts. In his judgment, British fans are the most appreciative.

With some 6,000 matches—often four, five, and six nights a week when a wrestling buck or any dollar was hard to find—he had to learn the skills to win and, if necessary, the restraint to lose. Beginning in St. Louis in December 1937, he held the National Wrestling Alliance championships a record six times.

"In our trade," he put it, "I was a 'hooker,' a guy who could win through his skills. Now, Hulk—or Handsome—Hogan has added extra shtick with the WWF, but as a wrestler I'd have to give Hogan a zero or a '1'. I don't think he'd know a half-nelson from Lord Nelson."

Among Thesz's coaches, his father was first. Included was Lewis, whom he most admires, and Greek import George Tragos, later University of Missouri wrestling coach. Said Thesz, "To my surprise, George taught me to hurt my opponent, in effect, to let him know who's boss."

Thesz's own worst injury was a broken knee suffered when football's Bronko Nagurski dropped him over the top rope for a nine-foot fall to a concrete floor.

In his career oddities, he stepped back 30 years ago to play bruising comic Big Julie in Frank Loesser's *Guys and Dolls* at the St. Louis Muny. At Memphis, he participated in the first mixed match—white against black, wrestler against boxer—when he met former heavyweight champion Jersey Joe Walcott. Lou won in a fourth-round takedown.

Years later in Tokyo against a young Japanese wrestler to whom he had taught freestyle, increasingly popular in the land of the sumo, Lou Thesz suddenly lost. When he attempted a bridge for a back body trip, a hip collapsed—his artificial hip!

★

GLOBAL GRAPPLER: Lou Thesz, the son of a St. Louis shoe cobbler from Hungary, was acclaimed champion of the National Wrestling Alliance six times in 6,000 matches around the world. At 74, despite an artificial hip, Thesz went 12 minutes in a match in a country where he is a favorite, Japan. The articulate world traveler was 84 in the millennium year.

1939
One of a Kind

Missouri's Pass-Pitching Pioneer, Paul Christman

Sixty years ago on an Indian summer afternoon in November 1939, the University of Missouri–Columbia climaxed its centennial celebration by putting a cherry on the birthday cake. Paul Christman beat Nebraska in one of the most significant games in Tiger football history.

Most old enough remember that '39 Orange Bowl season, Missouri's first, as a result of a nail-chewing 7–6 victory over Oklahoma on a rainy late November afternoon before 28,000, then largest in the first 13 years of a smaller stadium.

But the anniversary celebration game, capping off a week of ceremonies and distinguished speakers, was more important if only because it was the only defeat Nebraska suffered until the Rose Bowl a year later.

Actually, in a 13–10 upset in '38, Ol' Mizzou had beaten the Cornhuskers for the first time in 11 years. The hero then was a cocky, tow-headed sophomore quarterback from Maplewood High School, Paul Christman. Soon, Pitchin' Paul was a strong contender for the Heisman Trophy his junior year.

Christman, tagging along late to Mizzou behind his Orf twin passing targets, Bud and Bob, had failed to impress as a freshman at Purdue and dropped out and reported to Missouri. Reflected coach Don Faurot, the man for whom the field is named at Columbia, Christman's arrival was the "most significant" in football at Ol' Mizzou.

Before that big one in bluebird weather in '39, Christman prankishly stage-whispered to a student reporter, "Here, kid, a scoop for you. I'll pass those bums out of the stadium by the half."

He did, with three touchdown passes in the first half, en route to a 27–13 upset and, as mentioned, Nebraska's only defeat until the 1941 Rose Bowl game. In '39, the week after MU scraped by Oklahoma for the Big Six championship and first bowl bid, the Huskers shut out the Sooners, 13–0.

Christman was one of a kind, a refreshing kind. That '39 game against Nebraska, roughed up out of bounds at the feet of the Husker coach, Major Biff Jones, Pitchin' Paul brushed himself off and quipped, "What do you teach these guys, Major? Touch Football!"

Years later he would apologize to Jones, but the old army officer laughed it off. He must have known that Christman was a humorous leader. In the huddle, addressing Bob Steuber, he might say, "Hey, Stu, your zipper's open." Or, to the squad before calling signals, "Hey, have you seen that Marx Brothers movie downtown?"

Christman finished third in the Heisman race behind Iowa's Nile Kinnick and Michigan's Tommy Harmon. Hurt a year later with a hamstring injury, he was good, but not great. Then he went into the Navy and came back as quarterback of the Chicago Cardinals. He led Jimmy Conzelman's Cards to the NFL title in 1947 and a division championship a year later.

A manufacturer's agent in Chicago, he became outstanding on radio and television, first on Notre Dame's network, then usually with Curt Gowdy on whatever network paid the most. Jack Buck, for one, thought Christman was the best color analyst ever—humorous and quick to get in and out.

In 1970, he accepted a new assignment, but, at age 51, he suffered a fatal heart attack. So the first Monday night color commentator became Dandy Don Meredith.

Said Don Faurot, who outlived Paul Christman by nearly 45 years, "He was a good kid, a fine man and a coach on the field. I gave him more authority than I did any other quarterback even when I had to swallow hard when he'd throw three straight passes out of the end zone, but he was one of a kind."

Yeah, coach, the very best kind.

★

PITCHIN' PAUL: A snub-nosed, cotton-top Maplewood boy, Paul Christman, gave Missouri what it needed most—a box office performer and bowl player, 1937–40. Later, after quarterbacking the Chicago Cardinals to the 1947 NFL title, he was a topflight television color commentator, his career cut short by death at only 51.

A Hot Time in the All-Stars
Memories of Four from '40 to '66

The tip of the iceberg—ah, that's a pleasant thought especially at sweltering-hot all-star time in baseball—to the Grand Old Game's midsummer classic played four times in St. Louis over 60 years.

St. Louis, meaning essentially the Cardinals, really ought to shame itself for dragging webbed feet in seeking the summer inter-league show. The Gateway City got an early look the year Busch Stadium opened, 1966, as part of St. Louis's bicentennial celebration.

But difficulty getting back into the batting order made the next one likely closer to the time of the World's Fair centennial, 2004.

Of the games played here, the National League and American split. The NL, obviously inferior to the muscular AL those early years, fashioned a shutout here the first time, 1940, 4–0, with the Cardinals as host.

In '48 with the old Browns the guest ball club, the Americans won, 5–2. With the Redbirds as the only major-league franchise, the Americans won again in 1957, 6–5. And the year the Cards moved downtown 11 games late in May, they had shining jewel Busch Stadium ready for a 10-inning contest won by the Nationals 2–1, with Cardinal catcher Tim McCarver scoring the winning run.

The game really wasn't a thriller despite the low score, partly because of the tedium of 12 singles from men of muscle watched by a capacity 49,936 crowd. In concert the fans must have appreciated when Los Angeles's Maury Wills bounced a single up the middle that scored McCarver.

You see, it was so hot that colorful Casey Stengel, just retired at 76 as manager of the New York Mets, best assessed the new stadium. Asked about it, Ol' Case said, "Why, it holds the heat quite well."

It isn't that St. Louis's park is the hottest. In '54, Cleveland's heat rivaled our town's all-time record of 115 degrees for a high-scoring game won by the Americans 11–9. And in '60, Kansas City's revamped Municipal Stadium was hotter than Stan Musial's typical all-star hitting, as the NL won 5–3.

That day, pinch-singling as the Comeback Man, Stan led to part of the legacy about all-star game history. Just think, when the first all-star game was played here back in '40, a crowd of 32,373 at the smaller old ballpark saw Max West hit a three-run homer and Paul Derringer, Bucky Walters, Whit Wyatt, Larry French, and Carl Hubbell blank the muscle men on three hits. Musial, just 19, kept score by radio in Daytona Beach, Florida.

Eight years later when the game returned to St. Louis, Musial was an established star. That day before 34,008 happy fans, Stan hit his first of a record six all-star homers, a two-run shot off Washington's Walt Masterson. But when the American League manager cockily letting Vic Raschi bat for himself with three on in the fourth, the Yankee's two-run single off Cubs' lefty Johnny Schmitz broke a two-all tie.

About icebergs, that All-Star game saw Boston Braves' repeated 20-game winner Johnny Sain threaten a sitdown strike if he didn't get a new contract after they gave a kid, Johnny Antonelli, a $65,000 bonus. Johnny got it, too, topping Dizzy Dean's league high for a pitcher, $25,500. Bob Hannegan also called in Musial to make good a salary adjustment to $36,000.

Brooklyn boss Branch Rickey sweet-talked Giants' owner Horace Stoneham to replace his manager, Mel Ott, with Leo Durocher. And B. R. brought back Burt Shotton from his front porch in Bartow, Florida.

Shotton, B. R.'s "Sunday manager" when Rickey was St. Louis skipper, had won in '47 when Durocher was in commissioner Happy Chandler's sin bin. He did it again in '49.

About the all-star games in St. Louis, Minnie Minoso starred at bat and in the field for the AL in a 6–5 win in 1957, and as mentioned, McCarver wobbled in with a 2–1 NL winner in '66, the year the good ol' hometown tried to prove John McGraw correct when he used to say that—for the Cardinals to win in St. Louis heat—they had to be 25 percent better!

FOUR OF A KIND: Researcher Jerry Vickery offers a look at scorecards for the four All-Star games played in St. Louis, 1940 with the Cardinals as host, '44 Browns, and Redbirds again in '57 and '66.

★

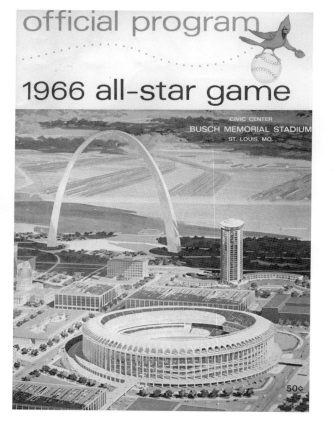

1942
St. Louis Swifties
The Incredible 43–8 Finish of the Redbirds

Nationally known New York sports cartoonist Willard Mullin portrayed the 1942 St. Louis Cardinals as the "Swifties," caricatured by a top-hatted, swirling mustached dude, a slick riverboat gambler—most apt because the St. Louis Swifties did everything in an incredible year except steal first base.

If there's any ball club that hasn't said "uncle" to the New York Yankees, kingpins of World Series play, it's the St. Louis Nationals, who have won three out of five classics from the Bronx Bombers, none more amazingly than in '42.

The Yankees had won eight straight Series since Grover Cleveland Alexander shut them down in relief in 1926. Fact is, they had lost only four of 36 Series games and, heavily favored, figured to do more of the same after Red Ruffing held the Cardinals hitless into the eighth inning of the first game at Sportsman's Park.

But manager Bill Southworth had put together Branch Rickey's dream team in the last year of the old master's long career as general manager. The prize was defense and pitching depth, highlighted by incredible speed, reflected more in how many bases they took audaciously than in stolen bases.

Actually, among the regulars, only young veteran Enos Slaughter hit .318 and rookie Stan Musial .315. The difference was that from top to bottom, from little Jimmy Brown at second base to catcher Walker Cooper, then rangy and rawboned, they all could pressure opposing infielders in handling slow-hit balls and enemy outfielders, too.

Their defense everywhere was A-1, especially up the middle with two all-time glove greats, Mr. Shortstop Marty Marion and the inspirational captain and center fielder, Terry Moore. From having seen the Chicago Cubs nip the Cardinals with 21 straight in 1935, his rookie year, Tee Moore was a bear cat on beardown baseball.

Despite the great club's early wins, they were second most of the season to Brooklyn's Dodgers, their hated Hatfield-and-McCoy rivals, but the St. Louis Swifties won 43 of their last 51 games and wound up two in front with a 106–48 record. Joe McCarthy's Yankees made it the first World Series between 100-game winners.

And New York won the opener, 7–4, but not before the Cardinals knocked out Red Ruffing in the ninth, a springboard to the impossible. Behind handsome rookie Johnny Beazley, the rapid-winning Redbirds won the second game 4–3, thanks to a great outfield throw by Slaughter in the ninth inning.

At New York, the circus came to town. Or, at least, the Swifties. Behind Ernie White, pitching the first Series shutout against the Yanks since Jesse Haines in '26, the great Redbird outfield prevailed—Tee Moore took away a probable inside-the-park homer from Joe DiMaggio with a diving catch, Musial leaped at the left-field fence for another, and Slaughter skied high to pull down a 2–0 game ender.

Running the bases like scalded cats in a 9–6 slugfest, the Swifties successfully challenged the great DiMaggio in game four. Next day, through coach Art Fletcher, manager McCarthy objected to little equipment manager Butch Yatkeman being on the noisy Cardinal bench.

Taken aback, captain Terry Moore told coach Fletcher at home plate, "Listen, Chisel Chin, tell Mac there ain't going to be no tomorrow in this Series."

There wasn't. Thanks to Beazley's second big-game performance and Whitey Kurowski's two-run homer, the Swifties closed it out in five games, 4–2, handing the proud champions as many defeats in one Series as they had suffered in the last eight!

★

OUTSTANDING OUTFIELD: *One of the best ever, centerpiece of the Cardinals' spectacular 1942 St. Louis Swifties, was captain and center fielder Terry Moore flanked by future Hall of Famers, Enos Slaughter (left) and Stan Musial (right). The Man was 21, Country 28, and Terry Moore 30.*

1944
Brownies' Biggest Day
Little Chet Laabs Won Famed Showdown

The old St. Louis Browns' one and only pennant, achieved in, of all things, a four-game sweep of the New York Yankees, was climaxed by the greatest final-day reversal of any player. Chet Laabs, who once struck out five times in a final game, clinched the Brownies' 1944 Cinderella season with two home runs.

Typical of the makeshift situation in World War II, when just about everyone including most GIs wanted the game to continue, some served outside the military as if in it. For instance, Laabs, a sawed-off slugger best known for his ability to strikeout often and to hit the long ball occasionally, worked in an armory factory.

With the stubby blond outfielder spending more time in a Detroit war plant than in a St. Louis uniform, manager Luke Sewell wanted Laabs' potential power in the lineup for the showdown series with the Yankees, not of prewar prowess, but—still!—New York. And the Browns hadn't swept the Yanks four straight since 1929.

In a season in which the Browns opened with a record nine straight victories, their early foot narrowed to a point in the final week where, trying to keep up, Sewell forced the Boston Red Sox to play a nasty night game in the rain. "Luke," said rival manager Joe Cronin, "you'll be sorry."

Defeat forced a showdown with the Yankees or a one-game playoff at Detroit. Dramatically, that last day at Tiger Stadium, Washington's knuckleball right-hander Emil (Dutch) Leonard brushed off a bribed hotel-room phone call and beat Detroit 4–1.

So the Browns could win if they could beat Joe McCarthy's depleted troops one more time. Some of the oldest in a local American League record of 37,815 shoehorned into Sportsman's Park could remember back to 1922. That's the year the Yanks nosed out the Browns by one game.

For the showdown, Sewell gambled on an alcoholic character named Sigmund (Jack) Jakucki. Jack, age 35 with a record of 12–9, exhibited baseball's worst. At a national semi-pro game at Wichita, angry Jakucki had dangled an umpire atop a river bridge.

Drunk or sober, big Sig was competitive, and after he yielded a first-inning triple to Hector Martin, followed by a throwing error by shortstop Vern Stephens, he limited the Yankees to only one run, also unearned.

Still, it was 2–0 New York in the home fourth when thick-necked Laabs stepped in there with a man on against right-hander Mel Queen. Now, as mentioned, this was the same Laabs who, facing fast-firing Bob Feller in a 1938 Detroit windup at Cleveland, was five of Feller's record 18 strikeout victims.

This time Laabs lofted a game-tying two-run homer, bringing down the house. Later, Laabs would hit another two-run homer, giving him two for the day and five for the season in 35 games. And Junior Stephens also hit one in the 5–2 game that brought with it a pennant, the Browns' first since they were an American Association ball club managed by Charley Comiskey in 1888. Despite only 88 victories, the 1944 Brownies deserved it because they lost no season's series to any competitor.

There's a tendency, then and even now, to deprecate as underachievers the '44 Browns—put together shrewdly by general manager Bill DeWitt of 4-F's, castoffs, cutthroats, and over-aged gaffers—but they epitomized team play, forced a much better and deeper Cardinals' team in a six-game World Series they almost won.

Besides, they had a guy named Chet Laabs, who would recall, "Don't call me a dumb Polack. I'm smart enough not to let Bob Feller skull me on the day school is out and, later, to spoil my only crack at a World Series."

HAPPIEST HOUR: In the crazy aftermath of the Browns' only pennant, 1944, club owner Don Barnes shakes the hands of (to his right) big Sig Jakucki and Mike Kreevich. From the left, first row, manager Luke Sewell, Barnes, Jakucki, Kreevich, Vern Stephens, and Al Hollingsworth. Second row, Floyd Baker (between Barnes and Jakucki); over Kreevich's shoulder, Tex Shirley. Grinning at top row left, coaches Fred Hofmann and Zack Taylor, arm raised.

★

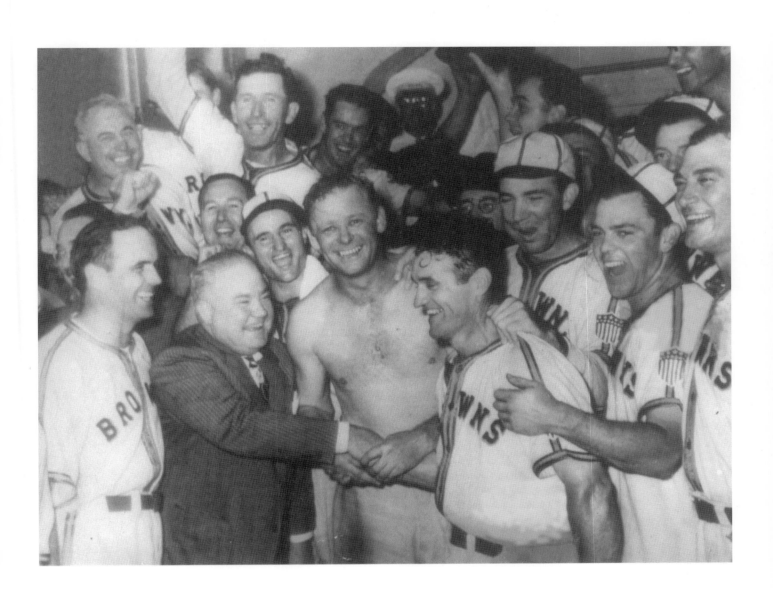

1944
Streetcar Series

Mr. Shortstop Marion Capped MVP Season

Appropriately, in a year when the Most Valuable Player award went to a defensive genius, shortstop Marty Marion, the Cardinals used an incredible fielding play to avoid an embarrassing upset from their local-rival Browns in the one and only Streetcar World Series, 1944.

At a time when travel was limited and frowned upon, the all–St. Louis Series at Sportsman's Park was as cozy as the Redbirds winning a second championship in a three-year pennant run. They again had won 105 games, and the makeshift Browns, Bill DeWitt's 4-F's and castoff cutthroats, barely had finished one ahead with only 88 victories.

Fact is, the Brownies needed a four-game sweep over the war-weakened Yankees to qualify for their one and only Series in the 52-year history of American League baseball in St. Louis. The biggest question was: Who would get to use the Fairground Hotel suite shared alternately by the managers, the Redbirds' Billy Southworth and the Browns' Luke Sewell?

The Series proved the value of defense even on a weary field, used by both St. Louis major league clubs and not nearly so well kept because of manpower shortage. Still, the Cardinals' long-legged shortstop, Marty Marion, who spread his arms like an octopus's tentacles, sucked up so many unlikely plays that he was the Nationals' MVP even though he hit only .267.

The Browns' hard-hitting young shortstop, Junior Stephens, committed three of the Brownies' 10 errors in the Series to the Cardinals' one, but the Redbirds needed one exceptional play to avoid likely defeat.

The Browns won the opener 2–0, when Denny Galehouse out-dueled big Mort Cooper and George McQuinn stroked a two-run homer. The Americans also had the Nationals on the ropes in the second game. The Browns overcame a damaging error by pitcher Nelson Potter, and with the score tied they knocked out Max Lanier in the eighth. But stocky Redbird reliever Blix Donnelly, taking over with Mike Kreevich on second and none out, held the Browns from scoring.

Donnelly appeared not so lucky when McQuinn, a hot .438 Series hitting hero, opened the eleventh inning with a double. Next up, bunting, Mark Christman dropped down a perfect roller toward third.

Donnelly, leaping off the mound, raced to his right, fielded the ball, and throwing blindly, delivered the ball to third baseman Whitey Kurowski on the sliding McQuinn's spikes.

Reprieved, the Cardinals won in the home half, 3–2, on a pinch-hit by Ken O'Dea, but no club ever has come back from a 3–0 start in games, where the Cards would have been after the Browns' Jack Kramer won the third one, 6–2.

With Stan Musial homering and Harry Brecheen beginning his World Series success, the Cardinals tied the Series at two games apiece with a 5–1 victory.

Then, on a warm Sunday with white-clad fans blurring the batting background, Cooper struck out 12 and Galehouse 10 in a reprise of the opener. This one was taken by the Cards 2–0 on homers by Danny Litwhiler and Ray Sanders. So the wrap-up came in the sixth game, when Stephens made a damaging error and Ted Wilks saved Lanier, 3–1.

But at the millennium, the what-if still exists. What if, in the year of defense, as portrayed by Mr. Shortstop Marty Marion, the Cardinals hadn't salvaged that second game on Blix Donnelly's great glove play? As old Brownie fans still say, "Down three-to-oh, no way!"

★

MR. SHORTSTOP: Or Slats or the Octopus, as they called him in awe, was the key player of the Cardinals' wartime success. A youthful, injured athlete who was rejected for military service, he became the first defensive player to win the Most Valuable Player award in 1944.

Race to Remembrance

Enos Slaughter's Run Made Brecheen a Series Winner

They called him "Country," but Enos Slaughter was a city slicker when he stole the 1946 World Series from the Boston Red Sox with the greatest ride since Paul Revere.

By '46, like many major leaguers, Country Slaughter had missed three solid seasons in service, where he entertained troops in the South Pacific; he played every ball game as if it were the last. Sliding on sharp coral fields in the islands, he got enough painful abrasions, but he felt he owed it to men who might die.

Slaughter, returning, hit his lifetime .300 and a league-leading 130 RBIs, but the big man was THE Man, Stan Musial, a .365 hitter. And in Boston's first World Series since Babe Ruth, Ted Williams topped a heavy-hitting club with 38 homers and 123 ribbies.

With the Sox breezing to a pennant, the wobbly-legged Redbirds needed the first historic playoff against Brooklyn and were 7–20 underdogs.

Boston beat freshman manager Eddie Dyer's meal-ticket in the opener, aching-backed Howard Pollet, on a tenth-inning homer by Rudy York. Briefly, the Redbirds pulled even, winning 3–0 with a scrawny little left-hander, Harry (The Cat) Brecheen, who, like Slaughter, would have a date with destiny.

Behind Dave (Boo) Ferriss, with the Series moved to Fenway, the Sox used a three-run homer by York in the 4–0 third game. Momentarily, the Cardinals had target practice in the following day's 12–4 victory, with 20 hits that included four each by 20-year-old catcher Joe Garagiola, third baseman Whitey Kurowski, and Slaughter.

Country's number one man, Musial, was having trouble at .222, but Stan's six hits were good for 12 bases and four runs batted in. Ted Williams, frustrated by a tender right elbow suffered in a practice game and St. Louis's strong infield shift, got only five singles and one RBI. In desperation, at .200, Teddy Ballgame bunted, a banner headline in a Boston tabloid.

When Slaughter was forced out of the fifth game, hit on the elbow by Joe Dobson in a 6–3 Sox win, St. Louis appeared to have little chance back home. En route, up all night with hot-and-cold pads to his elbow, Slaughter insisted he would play despite doctor's orders. They feared a clot could move to his heart.

The Old War Horse was never better. In Brecheen's Series-evening 4–1 win, Slaughter got a base hit and took an extra-base hit away from Williams. And then there was in game seven his famed first-to-home run on a king-sized single.

Earlier, Enos groused to manager Dyer that he had been held up unwisely once by third-base coach Mike Gonzalez. Weary of the veteran's constant bitching, the manager told him, all right, all right, if it happened again, go, and Dyer would take the rap.

So with a lead-off single in the home ninth, tied 3–3, Slaughter impatiently watched Bob Klinger retire two batters and then was off-and-running when left-handed-hitting Harry Walker, a .412 batter, arched a long high fly to medium left center.

By the time Slaughter reached second, aware that Leon Culberson had replaced brilliant Dom Dimaggio in center field, Country knew he would go all the way. At third, he roared past Gonzalez, retreating with hands winging in despair. Sox shortstop Johnny Pesky, taking the throw in with the crowd roaring, saw only a blur in the low late afternoon sun.

Off balance, Pesky didn't get much on the throw. As catcher Roy Partee came out to smother the ball, Enos Bradsher Slaughter scored the winning run that made Brecheen, in relief, a record-tying three-time winner. The only spoil-sports were unromantic official scorers who called Walker's saggin' hit a double.

★

RACE TO REMEMBRANCE: *Enos Slaughter's daring dash, shown here in his slide home, decided the seventh game of the 1946 World Series. It became a play that will be remembered. As a result, the War Horse was able to buss the other Series hero, three-game winner Harry Brecheen. Manager Eddie Dyer lets it all hang out.*

1946
'Cool' as in Papa Bell
A Lithe Hometown Legend and Hall of Famer

The real monument to Cool Papa Bell isn't the lavish $15,000 slab in a St. Louis cemetery, it's the tales of accomplishments by a dignified man who lingered too long out of the limelight but wound up in the baseball Hall of Fame.

Cool Papa Bell—officially James Thomas Bell—survived a career of exclusion from the "bigs," as black players called baseball's major leagues, but he prevailed when the gates of Cooperstown were thrown open to all men.

Bell, a wafer-thin, switch-hitting outfielder, was a swift superstar in the Negro Leagues from a kid of 19 in 1922 until he bowed out at age 47 in 1950, then too arthritic to win a spot in the majors and also the money denied him.

Bell escaped Starkville, Mississippi, for a job in a St. Louis packinghouse. He found baseball as a miniature oasis and finished his life as a night janitor and then security guard at City Hall, but he never lost personal charm or class, not when forced by Jim Crow to long baseball bus rides, side-door bologna sandwiches, and rundown hotels.

The hotel fleabags were so bad that once when rooming with the fabulous Satchel Paige, his biggest booster, he flipped a faulty light switch with a temporarily delay. Gravely, Cool assured Ol' Satch that Paige had been right—Bell could get into bed before the lights went out.

Cool Papa, married to a St. Louis woman for 60 years, never left the Gateway even though the St. Louis Stars left as 1931 champions during the depression.

Following the sun winters—Mexico, Cuba, and the Dominican Republic—for the hard-to-get Yankee dollar, Bell built a legend with his bunting, batting, base-stealing, and ball-hawking.

If some stories are exaggerated, many hold up, as for instance when Cool Papa singled and stole three bases on the next three pitches by Pittsburgh's veteran Heine Meine in a post-season exhibition. Or, when facing Cleveland's Bob Lemon in another October exhibition, Cool scored from first on a sacrifice bunt.

Elected to the Hall of Fame in 1974—he never missed Cooperstown functions until his death in 1991 at 87—the trim, erect man impressed many, including the chairman of the Hall of Fame, Ed Stack. Stack, who rarely attends funerals, came here for Bell's. Said Ed, "I loved Cool Papa."

So did St. Louis, at least belatedly. Bell's street, Dickson, where he lived in a well-kept two-story home on the near north side near Martin Luther King, Jr., Boulevard, was renamed Cool Papa Bell Street.

Many owe something to the retired man. His base-running tips helped both Maury Wills and Lou Brock. And when Cool was a veteran, he twice beat out grounders to Jackie Robinson's right and told the future big-league pioneer that his future wasn't at shortstop. Robinson made the Hall of Fame at second base.

For Bell's Negro League years in St. Louis, the Stars played at a rickety wooden park, now occupied by Vashon Community Center at Market and Compton, actually the campus playing field west of Harris-Stowe College.

With a looming car barn just north of the playing field at Laclede—drives off the beckoning left-field carrier often were ruled doubles—the 260-foot distance ran out of real estate when Market was widened to its present dimensions.

Creaking depression financial shorts not only forced St. Louis to lose Stars Park and the Stars, but also made St. Louis a two-team town. Cities with one major league team could rent out the big park when the major league clubs were on the road.

So we lost sight of the rapid-running Slim-Jim. They say not even Olympic sprint champion Jesse Owens wanted to race the baseball man. Cool did break the base-running record of 13.5 seconds set by Evar Swanson in 1931.

"But just barely," recalled James Thomas (Cool Papa) Bell in a rare display of ego. "It was raining. On a dry field, I once did it in 12 flat."

COOL PAPA: James Thomas Bell, one of the swiftest ball players ever, a converted pitcher and switch-hitting outfield ballhawk, played with such relaxed skill that he long was known as "Cool" before his Hall of Fame induction and, as a noble person, Cool Papa.

★

Weeb

Washington's Ewbank Used Hilltop En Route to Pro Hall of Fame

The hobgoblins pulled a dirty trick on Washington University that Halloween night in 1946 at old Francis Field House. At a party put on by the chancellor to honor a new secret addition—the football coach—they stole away the guest of honor.

If ever there was a situation as embarrassing as the red in the university's athletic colors, it was at the party new chancellor Arthur Holly Compton put on for students, alumni, and friends of the battling Bears. Already one year tardy at getting back on the gridiron among teams that gave up the sport in World War II, Washington had named and would present their football coach, whose identity had been guarded almost as big a secret as chancellor Compton's wartime contribution, the atom bomb.

But when it came for athletic director Blair Gullion to interrupt the apple-dunking, doughnut-nibbling, cider and coffee sipping of the pranksters' holiday, he had an embarrassing private message for the chancellor. The coach hadn't come. At the last minute he had turned down the job.

Stuart Holcomb, hired off Army's coaching staff as an assistant to Colonel Red Blaik, had agreed to the job and motored west, stopping at West Lafayette, Indiana, where he obviously had made previous inquiries. He got the Purdue job and would coach the Boilermakers for nine years. Then Stu Holcomb became a good will ambassador for baseball's Chicago White Sox.

So—here, meanwhile—how now, brown cow, or, rather, battling Bears?

Gullion, a big bald man and a heckuva good basketball coach, knew a few things, obviously among them those who could coach football. Shortly after that October 31 disaster, he brought in a stubby assistant coach from Brown University. The runty man came from Providence, Rhode Island; by way of Richmond, Indiana; Miami University of Oxford, Ohio; and wartime assistance on Paul Brown's coaching staff at the Great Lakes in Illinois. His name was Wilbur Charles Ewbank, but only his dear Mom called him "Wilbur." Most knew him as "Weeb."

Cheerfully, here, the coach showed his sense of humor. As he put it, most often folks put a "u" where the "w" belonged in Ewbank, and they pluralized the surname. Or, as he added merrily, they got it all mixed up and even called him "Heeb Weebanks."

But he was a tough little guy. Most had known him as a pugnacious, pug-nosed, three-sport player at Richmond and as captain at Miami, aptly known as the cradle of college coaches.

First day here, he advised his players he didn't want any of them messing around with his daughters, but one, a little transplanted halfback from New Jersey, Charley Winner, got close enough to marry Nancy and father Ewbank's grandchildren.

Even though Washington had de-emphasized football under chancellor Compton's direction, GI Bill scholarships brought in experienced players who found Ewbank strong, firm, yet fair. His Bears lost their opener in 1947 to Missouri Valley College, then carving out a small-college dynasty at Marshall, Missouri.

But the Bears lost only three more games out of 17—just one in 1948—and then Ewbank quit. He knew the GI Bill would run out, and he wanted a chance. As he put it that last night at dinner, "I want to work a couple of more years for Paul Brown, a genius, and then I'll be ready."

Indeed, after coaching the guards for the Cleveland Browns for two seasons, Ewbank became head coach of Carroll Rosenbloom's Baltimore Colts and a Super Bowl coach. Then, as the only coach to win the old American Football Conference, he took Sonny Werblin's New York Jets to the top.

En route to great success, including election to pro football's Hall of Fame, Weeb Ewbank did everything except openly decide between his two great quarterbacks, John Unitas and Joe Namath.

★

A DATE WITH DESTINY: Weeb Ewbank (second from the left) took the Washington University head football coaching job in an emergency opportunity, posted a 14–4 record in two years, 1947–48, and went into pro football as an assistant to Paul Brown at Cleveland. Before his career ended, with championship seasons at Baltimore in the NFC and New York Jets, Ewbank was a pro football Hall of Famer. With him in his years here were (left to right), Frank (Red) Cummiskey, Les Avery, and Irv Utz. Avery and Utz stayed for years on the Hilltop.

Dandy Man

Dukes Duford: Good Coach, Better Man, and Pioneer Promoter

If the ancient and honorable remember an old St. Louis Thanksgiving Day tradition, Washington University meeting Saint Louis U. in football, it might be the way to introduce Dukes Duford. The Bears could beat the Bills, but they couldn't beat Dukes.

Actually, the Turkey Day rivalry between Washington and St. Louis wasn't as long as it might have been, but it had romantic asides, including the ability of Dukes Duford to do what no other coach on either side had done. That is, win three in a row.

For Wilfred J. Duford—no wonder Dukes liked his nickname—the three straight over Washington when both the Bears and Bills were in the Missouri Valley Conference was merely part of his accomplishments for the Grand Avenue gang. For himself, the greatest accomplishment probably was using his vision as athletic director to take St. Louis big time in basketball.

Duford, who grew up in Wisconsin's cold upper peninsula, came to town as a shy, smiling, warm-hearted man who had been an athletic triple threat at Marquette, good enough to briefly play professional baseball, football, and basketball. Yes, and to win lifetime regard from two Marquette classmates with names better-known than old W. J.'s—Spencer Tracy and Pat O'Brien.

Coaching nine years at St. Ambrose College in Davenport, Iowa, Duford put together a 31-game winning streak and won appointment at Saint Louis U. as coach and athletic director in 1940.

Here, upgrading Billiken scheduling and handicapped by a couple of years without football in wartime, he was only so-so as reflected in six seasons, 23–33–2. But Dukes came within a late 95-yard interception return of an upset over Missouri in 1946.

As athletic director, he first pinpointed Billiken potential with a 1945 freshman kid named Ed Macauley. He even persuaded the reluctant Arena to book a Valley doubleheader between Saint Louis and Oklahoma A&M and Washington versus Tulsa. The big attractions were the Aggies' seven-foot center from Jennings, Bob Kurland, en route to two NCAA championships for Hank Iba's team, and the Bears' Dr. Stan London.

The double dip nearly filled the Arena, then seating 14,000, but when Dukes's puppy-dog relations with Notre Dame got the Irish to agree to come here, the Arena balked at a $7,500 guarantee. Boldly, Duford booked Kiel Auditorium himself. The game was a sellout, and the basketball Billikens forgot their vest-pocket gym.

For that alone, Duford should have stayed AD, but when they canned him as coach, they removed him as director, too. Professionally quiet, the old coach spent 17 years as director of the city's sensitive Human Relations Council, then was asked to return to the campus as AD when director Larry Albus was called to service.

Later, relieved of the ulcer of coaching, he worked with friend Bob Hellrung and his medical collection business, traveled to football games, and salted down his beer. He was 82 in '81 when the big heart gave out.

About coaching, he accomplished a coup winning those three straight over Washington in a series dominated by the Bears, 15–9, with three ties.

Impressed by Don Faurot's brand-new split-T formation in 1941, Duford borrowed the basics, practiced secretly for a few days, then surprised the old rival. Washington, changing policy, dropped St. Louis after the war. Three years later, Saint Louis U. dropped football.

Duford's last victory over Duquesne on Thanksgiving Day, 14–13, in his last game, was typical of the old coach. En route to the game-winning score, quarterback Fred Broeg suffered a broken nose for the second straight week. As he ran off bleeding, commiserating coach Dukes Duford asked, "Was that the same one you broke last week, kid?"

★

DUKES: Wilfred J. (Dukes) Duford at Saint Louis University couldn't compete against a big-name football schedule, but he pushed Billiken basketball successfully.

1947
Roses for the Orange and Blue
Illinois Won the Bowl's First Big One

The University of Illinois began the half-century television tie-up with the Pac 10 Conference unforgettably in 1947. Ray Eliot's Illini stuffed UCLA's press clippings down the Bruins' throats, 45–14.

The memory of Illinois' clobbering of a favored West Coast champion, beginning a five-year pact that lasted until nearly the millennium, lingers long for two reasons—too many Illini didn't want to make the Rose Bowl trip, and too many more were offended by the rude reputation of the event's atmosphere.

At the time, gifted Jim Murray of Pulitzer Prize fame hadn't brought his biting, humorous touch to Los Angeles newspapers. L.A. press could be tough; so could the cocky coast team.

Crowed UCLA, "We want Army"—then the unbeaten Black Knights of the Hudson. The Bruins were not excited by the fortunate box-office link between the West Coast's conference and the Midwest's best, the Big 10.

Many players from both teams probably were finishing their first postwar season, eager to spend that first Christmas at home in three or four years. So only after the persuasion from Eliot, a persuasive coach, did the Orange and Blue give a favorable vote. En route by train, by way of New Orleans, the hard-bitten Illinois team stopped for workouts twice on the three-day trip.

Discreetly, they kept coaches out of a club car, where, as men 24 to 26 years old, they drank beer. Pasadena's Huntington Hotel, traditional for visiting Rose Bowl teams, was isolated from excitement, but the scorn in the media caught the Illini's eyes—the coach's, too.

At game-time, Eliot told his awakened giants that even hulking Wilfred Smith of the *Chicago Tribune*, accompanying them, had picked UCLA.

Although basically a defensive team, led by chew-'em-up All-American guard Alex Agase, quarterback Perry Moss poured Ruck Steger, Julie Rykovich, and Buddy Young around and through the stunned foe.

Rykovich and Young averaged better than five yards each, and Buddy, a bouncing five-by-five at 5'6" and a chunky 165 pounds, darted for many long gainers.

A crowd of 93,083, more pro-home-team because of limited travel opportunities, watched Illinois drives of 60, 77, 51, and 86 yards in their surge to six touchdowns, two of them by Young.

Even UCLA's second touchdown, a Rose Bowl record 103 yards by 143-pound UCLA scatback, Al Hoisch, had touches of the Illini's dynamic little man.

Afterward, Hoisch confessed, yep, he had been tired, but concerned most whether Young was in the lineup.

Typically a defensive safety—there was no two-platooning then—Young had retired to the bench, where athletes in the Orange and Blue could chant to UCLA, "We want Army. . . ."

On the rather wet merry trip back to Champaign—and loyalist Ruck Steger of a million-dollar gift to the alma mater athletic department is the authority for this one—crestfallen football expert Smith saw angry scowls and locked himself in his compartment.

In response, the Illini locked the car's outer door. Cross-country, Smith wanted to know what it would take to win his release. The chorus was simple:

"Pay the bar bill. . . ." He did.

★

TRAILBLAZERS: When the Pacific Coast and Big 10 Conferences began their glamorous half-century Rose Bowl pact in 1946, Ray Eliot's war-returnee Illini set a savage pace. Among the orange and blue in the top row from the right is St. Louisan Russ Steger.

From the left, first row, scout Lee Johnson, head coach Eliot, Alex Agase, Julie Rykovich, Buddy Young, Captain Mac Wenskunas, Lou Agase, Ralph Serpiro, Ike Owens, line coach Tony Blazine, and trainer Matt Bullock.

Second row, line coach Burt Ingwersen, Bob Prymuski, Sam Zatkoff, Lou Donoho, Mike Kamp, Bill Huber, Bill Heiss, Herb Sweigert, Al Mastrangali, Bill Franks, backfield coach Ralph Klaherty, and manager Bill Buchanan.

Third row, Tom Gallagher, Tom Stewart, Gene Kwasniewski, John Wrenn, Les Bingaman, Ray Florek, Bob Dunx, Chick Maggioli, Jim Valek, Vern Seliger, and trainer Ike Hill.

Fourth row, end coach John Marwain, Paul Patterson, Chuck Gottfried, Bert Piggott, Art Dufelmeier, Steger, Don Maechtle, Joe Bucconi, and Frank Bauman.

Profile of a Winner

Basketball's Colorful Ken Loeffler

When St. Louis won its first professional basketball championship, back when the nation's big arenas decided they needed something other than a hockey tenant, the local Bombers' best performer was not a player, but a coach—Ken Loeffler.

To be accurate, Kenneth Diethelm Loeffler was not only an intellectual snob, but also a no-nonsense guy from the mining country of western Pennsylvania, Beaver Falls. He was quick-witted, a warrior with a sarcastic edge so sharp it didn't draw blood. But my, how he could coach!

Before World War II, in which he served as a judge-advocate attorney, Loeffler was a brilliant football and basketball player at Penn State with dual degrees in engineering and law. He preferred coaching, however, and led teams for years at Geneva College and then at Yale. His roommate at Yale was an assistant football coach named Gerald Ford.

When head football coach Ducky Pond wanted to substitute for glamorous Heisman Trophy winner Larry Kelley in 1936, the player would wave off the sub. When the flaming redhead tried that on Loeffler in basketball, Ken called time and walked off the pet by the elbow. Yeah, Larry was the president's wife's favorite, too.

When the big arena bosses decided on the Basketball Association of America in 1946, St. Louis was one of a dozen major cities. Loeffler, serving on a dude ranch in Wyoming, forded a stream to install a phone line, awaiting a favorable reply.

At the Arena, using an effective weaving offense, Loeffler split two units into man-to-man and zone defenses. The zone was so good that the BAA soon barred it.

Loeffler's team, led by two-handed set shooter Johnny Logan from Indiana, lost the first western championship on a last-second basket by the Stags at Chicago. A year later, same site and same situation, the Bombers trailed by 15 points in the fourth period with no 24-second clock to help.

The bow-tied coach was rewarded by an incredible 23 straight points, the 1947 Western Division championship, and a playoff lost to the highly favored Philadelphia Warriors. Back in college, poet and pianist Loeffler coached LaSalle University to an NCAA championship.

★

GENIUS AT THOUGHT: Ken Loeffler had only a couple of sensational seasons in St. Louis as coach of the professional basketball Bombers. The intellectual roughneck by way of Penn State engineering and Yale law school was a most interesting coach and conversationalist.

The Little General

Saint Louis U.'s Greatest Success Came Under Eddie Hickey

Saint Louis University's Billikens, back in the big leagues of college basketball, had their finest seasons in the mid-years of the century—Eddie Hickey's years.

Hickey, sawed-off at 5'5", a dynamic chunky man who had quarterbacked Creighton University football in the Roaring '20s, was a master of the fast-break and winning. He posted a 36-year college career of 570–268, including the Billikens' best—an 11-season 211–89 and the University's only championship.

The Bills of 1947–48, remarkably recruited from the sidewalks of St. Louis and many with war experience, were 24–3. Captained by a former military pilot, Danny Miller, they also were led by a gifted hometown All-American, Easy Ed Macauley.

With Hickey's flair for run-sheep-run basketball, the Bills made a show at winning the National Invitation Tournament championship, then played entirely at New York's Madison Square Garden. Thereafter, in regular-season New York and six more NIT tournament visits, Hickey and his teams were a good show in the Big Apple.

Despite successful showmanship, Saint Louis's record in the Missouri Valley Conference included only three championships. Oklahoma A&M's Henry Iba had a hex on Hickey with his slow-down, ball-control play. The Little General won only seven of 22 from the Iron Duke, winding up often as second fiddle to the czar. But, oddly, Hickey had a similar whammy over Kentucky's Adolph Rupp, beating the famed Wildcats three straight times.

With the Billikens, at first with a light touch because Hickey's military discipline annoyed the players, the little coach tightened thereafter with almost Napoleonic rule, and his teams responded as well schooled. Their fast break—"controlled fast break," Eddie would emphasize sarcastically—featured an explosive movement that required the ball not to hit the floor. Rebound, quick pass, break down court to the middle! Shoot! Score!

Hickey took his high-wire act to Marquette in a change-of-scenery move after a 16–10 record in 1958. Marquette just had suffered its worst season. Immediately, the Little General posted a 23–6 record and gained an NCAA berth and Coach-of-the-Year selection by the nation's writers.

Six years later at the age of 62, after a sorry 5–21 season, he was asked to step down, but he left Marquette with a 92–60 record and future Basketball Hall of Fame recognition—and a special fondness for his '48 NIT St. Louis champions.

"The Paddycake Boys," he recalled, smiling. "They hummed the ball around so fast, folks thought they were playing paddycake."

Edward Sylvester Hickey, reared in small-town Nebraska, graduated from Creighton in law in 1926, but he was enamored more by the game he could teach if not, obviously lacking size, play well. He head-coached both football and basketball at Creighton Prep for eight winning years, then moved to the university in 1935 and immediately led the Blue Jays to the Valley title.

After service in World War II as a navy lieutenant, Hickey bypassed Creighton, where he had two more Valley titles, an NIT appearance, and one in the NCAA. His 132–72 record for nine seasons at Omaha was followed by his success in St. Louis. Here, he took over a team recruited by ex-Billiken star and coach John Flanigan.

Little Eddie's tenure saw three 20-game seasons, a second All-America, Dick Boushka, and a perfect three-for-three against Missouri before he dropped the state rival for what Hickey regarded as excessively rugged play by Sparky Stalcup's teams.

MR. BASKETBALL: Although Bob Pettit with the champion basketball Hawks was the best player to wear a St. Louis uniform, the century's number one award to the player who did the most for the hometown in Doc Naismith's game was No. 50—Easy Ed Macauley, first hometown All-American linchpin of Billikens' National Invitation Tournament champions and star with the Hawks' 1958 title team. Later, he coached for Ben Kerner and performed on radio and television.

★

1948

The Natural

Red Schoendienst Was the Natural Before Robert Redford

For one magic moment back there in June 1948, Red Schoendienst must have thought he was roommate Stan Musial, "filling the room with base hits," as Stan the Man always cracked. The willowy young redhead broke two batting records and tied four.

By '48, Schoendienst, then a freckled and almost frail 25 year old, hadn't yet proved that he would hit well enough—to go with his skill at second base—to earn Hall of Fame recognition.

But in an unusual switch-over of foes on a weekend, Red the Head tattooed the right-field screen at Sportsman's Park as if he were Stan the Man, his road roomie.

Batting left-handed and using a choked grip, though not nearly so shortened as later, Schoendienst smacked three doubles and singled in a June 5, 1948, game with Brooklyn.

Next day with the Phillies in town, Red drilled three doubles off the right-field screen, a barrier put up by owner Phil Ball of the landlord Browns in 1929. Reaching the heights, Schoendienst hoisted another onto the pavilion roof for a home run.

Second game that Sunday, Red hit the screen twice more for two base hits, giving him a record eight doubles in three straight games and a new standard of seven long hits in two successive games.

Even with that savage weekend, often out of the lineup, the Cardinals' second baseman played only 118 games and hit just .271. Averages then, generally, were based on a little higher standard than now, and after hitting .278 as a rookie in 1945 and a more promising .281 in a '46 pennant season, he had faltered. Schoendienst's average dipped to .253 in 1947, Sam Breadon's last season as owner.

To manager Eddie Dyer, Breadon, accustomed to Hall of Fame hitting heights from Rogers Hornsby and Frankie Frisch, grumped and wondered how the heck Dyer expected to win with a ".250 hitter" at second base.

Dyer knew better. As a rookie manager in '46, Eddie had earmarked the baby-faced 23-year-old kid as "my number one utility man," bringing from Red a throaty, profane beeswax response—privately.

That's the year Red filled in for holdout Whitey Kurowski at third base and the injured Marty Marion at shortstop. So second baseman Lou Klein saw the handwriting on the outfield wall. Klein jumped to Mexico with pitchers Max Lanier and Fred Martin, leaving Red behind with a new job, a note, and a new roommate.

Explaining to roomie Red where they had gone, veteran pitching ace Lanier concluded, "And keep hitting those line drives, Red." Because Musial tired of having a road roommate who wanted too many beers before dinner, the great combination was formed.

When Stan would quip later about filling the room with so many hits, "he wasn't just a woofin'," as Dizzy Dean would say. With Musial getting 3,630 hits and Schoendienst 2,449, that totaled 6,079!

It well could have been more if Red hadn't been saddled with a form of low-grade tuberculosis detected in early release from the army. He virtually collapsed 13 years later after leading Milwaukee to a second straight pennant.

By then, with a timely rest after an accident one summer, 1953, he had hit as high as .342 and seven times batted over .300. By then, Mr. Breadon, he most certainly wasn't a ".250 hitter" at second base. Still, he could have made the Hall of Fame earlier.

And, who knows, that 7-come-11 natural from Germantown, Illinois, might have matched that remarkable hitting weekend of 1948.

★

ADHESIVE HANDS: *Red Schoendienst, relaxed, a loosey-goosey player, fielded spectacularly and, though handicapped, hit enough to win Hall of Fame recognition.*

1950

The Impossible Dream

St. Louis–Led U.S. Upset England in Soccer

At that time a half century ago, the parallel would have been if Oxford University's baseball team had beaten the world champion New York Yankees. In mid-July 1950, playing the game invented by Britain, the United States beat the English in soccer—World Cup soccer—and with a majority of St. Louis players.

If the upset doesn't seem quite so shocking now, it's only because in recent years, better coaching and better preparation have enabled America to qualify for the World Cup, not merely to be invited as in '50 in Brazil.

Now, Uncle Sam might tweak John Bull's nose in the number one international game, most certainly everywhere, including host country Brazil. Heavily favored against tournament favorite England, Brazil assigned the Brits' game with the United States to Belo Horizonte, a small mountainous town with a large 30,000-seat stadium.

America's hopes lay in a 17-man squad, coached by Bill Jeffrey of Penn State, with six players from St. Louis, including five starters.

Those five and reserve Bob Annis will live brightly in St. Louis sports history. They were led by a curly haired, stoop-shouldered goalkeeper, Frank Borghi, a ham-handed former minor-league infielder who would play the best game of an outstanding career.

Also, close up was Charley (Gloves) Colombo, the ball-dogging, relentless center halfback who wore kid gloves even on the hottest day.

On Colombo's right side as a defensive back was stocky Harry Keough, who would become the best known of the group because of his international play

and as a championship coach at Saint Louis University.

The other two red-white-and-blue guys from St. Louis were the wing men, Gino Pariani and Frank (Pee Wee) Wallace. Wallace came closest to scoring a second goal for the United States.

The game's only goal came reasonably early—in the 37th minute of the 90-minute game—and Keough as right defensive back saw it unfold. A throw-in from his side was moved up field by easterner Walter Bahr, whose shot probably was from too far out, but, trying to head the ball, forward Joe Gaetchens misdirected it. Gaetchens was an American citizen from Haiti. He nudged it just to the opposite side of the British keeper. Goal!

Keough, still coaching Washington University's women's team, remembers so well.

"That was no 'neutral' field," recalls Harry. "To a man, the Brazilians rooted for us as underdogs. Other things linger; for instance, Colombo's great tackle from behind, probably illegal, but a potential game-saver, and Borghi with those large hands repeatedly intercepting crossing patterns."

Borghi, a recently retired undertaker, still is smiling shy about his greatest game. Fans carried him off the field. Gloves Colombo and Wallace are gone. Pariani defensively handcuffed a Spanish goal-getter in an earlier 3–1 loss.

The third tournament game, following the win over England, was a loss to Chile, 5–2. By then, the walking-on-air Yanks had achieved their remarkable day in soccer's sun and in the history of the great quadrennial. Internationally, the World Cup was—and is—the Super Bowl, World Series, and Final Four combined.

Only recently has America even qualified for the Cup, but that wonderful 1–0 win back there a half century ago even inspired a recent book. It still looms as Uncle Sam's soccer highlight and most certainly for his proud St. Louis players:

Borghi . . . Colombo . . . Keough . . . Pariani . . . and Wallace!

A DISPUTE IN BELO HORIZONTE: Defenseman Charley (Glover) Columbo (4), goalminer Frank Borghi (1), and England's Stanley Mortensen dispute a cross. Bahr, Pariani, and McIlveney look on.

(bottom left) THE HOPELESS HEADER: Gino Pariani (right) and Joe Maca (center) look on while England's Mortensen fails to get one past Borghi.

(bottom right) FRIENDLY RIVALS: Kutis star Harry Keough (left) and Simpkins' goalminer Frank Borghi, hometown foes, solidified the U.S.'s defense against England.

★

Baseball's Littlest Man

The Day Midget Eddie Gaedel Pinch-Hit

Unfortunately for St. Louis's baseball fans, the American League's last best hope, Bill Veeck, was disappointing with the Browns before the sport-shirted promoter and the ball club both left town. But the fella with the furrowed forehead left behind a lovely legacy—the midget!

A prankster as well as a promoter (Veeck drew 2.6 million at Cleveland in 1948 when many clubs barely drew a million), Bill loved to surprise, but also to annoy. He knew that starchy-collared American League president, Will Harridge, would never permit use of a midget.

Bill had one. Secretly, drawing a line from novelist James Thurber in 1951, he sneaked into town a 26-year-old man, perfectly proportioned, who was trim and handsome, but only 3'7", 65 pounds. Beforehand, Veeck preached to the little guy that he would orchestrate the show from the Sportsman's Park rooftop. As a former Marine expert rifleman, he would shoot the midget if he dared swing at a pitch.

Eddie Gaedel understood. Dressed in former owner's son Billy Dewitt's uniform, he was hidden in a giant paper-mache cake. So far it was fun for the Chicago advertising agent during delightful half-time ceremonies honoring the 50th anniversary of the American League.

A sizable 25,000-plus crowd—of course, many more say they saw it—were given free ice cream and trinkets as they came in. Before the second game of the doubleheader with Detroit, baseball double-ugly Max Patkin did his gig at first base, trampolinist Willie Keo soared at second base, and at third Satchel Paige, Al Widmar, Ed Redys, and Hollywood Johnny Berardino entertained as a band.

Finally, that giant cake was wheeled out. Eddie Gaedel jumped out and hurried to the Browns' dugout as the surprised crowd laughed, applauded, and giggled at his uniform number—"1/8."

Upstairs in the privacy of the absentee Cardinals' clubhouse, the short snorter needed help. Manager Zack Taylor sat Eddie on his knee, tied the shoestrings, and suggested that he didn't think Detroit would be angry enough to throw at the little batter!

Little Eddie did a double take, leaped down, and headed for the door, only to run into the massive arms of traveling secretary Bill Durney. Big Bill repeated Veeck's shooting threat.

Leading off the home's first, field announcer Bernie Ebert intoned, "And for the Browns, batting for Frank Saucier, number 1/8—Eddie Gaedel."

The little guy came out swinging two toy bats. Now, would plate umpire Ed Hurley spoil the show? But, wait, out with a telegram from the league, approving the contract of Edward C. Gaedel, came Brownie manager Taylor. Bless the tough Boston Irishman, Hurley motioned lefty Bob Cain to pitch.

Catcher Bob Swift rushed out to confer with Cain. Swift wondered if he could lie down to create a better target? Naw. And Cain wondered if he could pitch underhanded as in softball? Naw. So they walked Eddie on four pitches and when Gaedel got to first base, safe and in one piece, he gave pinch runner Jimmy Delsing a grandiose pat on the fanny and fled the field to applause.

Afterward, dressed neatly, the midget gave a bit of canned prattle until it was suggested that he had become what all others dream of. He was an ex-big league ball player!

Chest thrust out, he hurried to a cab for the plane to Chicago. Three nights later at Cincinnati, intoxicated, Eddie was arrested for having abused a cop.

Ten years later, in 1961, at age 36, Eddie Gaedel was badly beaten at a bar near the home he shared with his mother and died of a heart attack. One baseball man showed up at the funeral—the pitcher who walked him, Bob Cain!

★

PROOF POSITIVE: Yes, a midget really did bat for the St. Louis Browns in a major-league ball game, August 1951. Owner Bill Veeck leaked his secret of the surprise package pinch-hitter in time for Post-Dispatch *photographer Jack January to kneel at the first-base batter's circle at Sportsman's Park and record this you-gotta-believe-it photo.*

1952
A Paige of History

Black League Baseball's Best Legend, Satchel

Anything was possible in the incredible pitching career of Satchel Paige. So why wasn't it possible for the 46-year-old, stork-legged master of the mound to go 17 innings in relief and then win it with his own bat past midnight?

That's exactly what happened the night of June 3, 1952, at Washington's Griffith Stadium, where the old Browns beat the defunct Senators, 3–2, on a base hit by Paige. Ol' Satch got only five hits that season, three of them that night.

Paige's appreciative boss—Bill Veeck—had drawn the long-legged legend from black-league baseball to the majors in 1948. At Cleveland, Ol' Satch contributed a 6–1 record in the pennant season.

With the bashful Browns the great Veeck sought to tease out of mediocrity, Ol' Satch was more box office than talent, attractively seated in a rocking chair his promoter friend had stored for him in the Browns' bullpen.

For Paige's five-plus innings of scoreless relief, Veeck advised traveling secretary Bill Durney to buy Satch a suit "not for his pitching but for his hitting."

When the future Hall of Famer singled in Joe DeMaestri with the winning run in the 17th—after neither team had scored since the Browns tied in the eighth—the weary old warrior bent over at first base.

Paige, 12–10 in 1952, was used ordinarily in relief, but he still managed three complete games in six starts, two of them shutouts. Even without his old pinpoint fireball, he still had corner-cutting control and a hesitation pitch off his windmill windup.

Although he didn't last in the bigs after buddy Bill was frozen out by the majors in 1953, Satch went back to his profitable barnstorming. Satch got a welcome relief from another admirer, Charley Finley, then at Kansas City.

To upgrade Paige's position in the pension plan—and to put a few folks in the stands—Finley signed Ol' Satch to pitch a game in 1965. At age 59, the grand geezer of the game pitched three scoreless innings against the Boston Red Sox, walked none, struck out one, and gave up just one hit—to future Hall of Famer Carl Yastrzemski.

The tales of Leroy Robert Satchel Paige are taller than the willowy wonder, though not the stretched story that he got the last hit in 1952 to enable the Browns to catch an overnight train to St. Louis.

Not that time, anyway, though as trainer Bob Bauman would relate, Paige was as rare as his long, supple arm, "The most velvet I ever touched."

Doc Bauman, stationed across from Paige in cozy rail roomette cars, was amazed how train galley crews would work late for their favorite to prepare the fresh catfish he would bring aboard. Refreshed, Satch would type portable notes overnight.

In tough times Paige would go it alone as, for instance, in 1935 when he hooked up with a Bismarck, North Dakota, team called the "Coloreds." At a time $1,000 was worth robbing a bank, as many depression desperadoes did, Satch took Bismarck to Wichita for the first national semi-pro tournament and won it. His record 60 strikeouts still stands at the new century.

With the Browns, the easy-does-it veteran liked to tease young catcher Clint (Scrap Iron) Courtney. Satch bet Clint in batting practice that he could throw out the catcher from deep short; wearing catcher's gear, he could gun Courtney trying to steal; and playing left field, with his playmate tagging up at third, he would throw out stubby exasperated Scrap Iron at home plate.

He did—all three. Hmm, maybe Ol' Satch could have pitched forever!

OL' SATCH: Leroy Robert (Satchel) Paige was the featured alumnus of the long-neglected Negro major-league ball clubs, given his chance at age 42 with Bill Veeck's Cleveland Indians. He helped win the 1948 pennant then joined Veeck here with the Browns in 1952 and '53. When the lanky legend pitched three no-run innings in 1965, to boost his pension benefits, it looked like it might be as Satch and Dave Lipman wrote— "Maybe I'll Pitch Forever."

★

The Old Mongoose

Happiness Came Late for Boxing Great Archie Moore

If Archie Moore had been as colorful in the ring as he was out of it, the capable old light-heavyweight boxing champion would be recognized even more for what he really was—a legend of the ring.

After chasing the title chance many of his 30 years boxing professionally, Archie got his long-awaited opportunity in his adopted hometown—St. Louis—and he relieved Joey Maxim of the 175-pound crown at the Arena on December 17, 1952.

At that time, the Old Mongoose, as they called the strict-striking enemy of king cobra, was old—all right, 39—but amazingly, he held the title until he nearly tripped over his beard eight years later.

Also in that period, Moore fleshed out into a heavyweight, fighting at 200 pounds, then shriveling back to reach the 175-pound limit. His tales of his diet were typical of the roughish rascal.

Moore said, for instance, he had discovered weight-reducing brew in a secret potion given him by an Australian aborigine. Truth is, drinking orange juice to retain his strength, the Mongoose would chew up a steak, then spit out the meat so that his body got only the valuable juices.

Sure, that regimen took discipline, but Archie had learned patience in those years when he fought out of an unattractive peekaboo stance. Ultimately, Moore would put his foe to sleep—he has a record 141 knockouts in 229 bouts—but he wasn't good box office.

So he was on the exotic move seeking foes and dates—from Australia to Argentina—putting together impressive winning streaks. One long streak was stopped by his first knockout defeat, to Cleveland's Jimmy Bivins in six rounds in 1945. Poor Jimmy got the Mongoose mad. Archie went on to beat Bivins three times, twice by kayos.

For years, christened Archibald Lee Wright, Archie insisted he was born in December 1916, in Collinsville, Illinois, but dear mom, who was there too, suggested that it happened December 1913, at Benoit, Mississippi. At his death in late December 1998, Moore conceded his mother's age estimate—84—but still held out here for St. Louis suburb Collinsville.

Here, meaning St. Louis, Archie was managed by George Wilsman and Eddie Vandeventer, who fought as Kid Bandy, but after three fights early his first year, 1936, including two knockouts and his first loss, he hit the home sod seldom, following the fleeting buck transcontinental and post-Pacific. It wasn't until Archie was under the direction of flimflam man Jack (Doc) Kearns that he got his title chance against Maxim near birthday time in 1952. Joey, a master of defense and pretty good against heavies, couldn't handle the determined Mongoose. Maxim also lost two return bouts.

Archie fought often, but risked his title infrequently, fighting Bob Olson, Yolande Pompey in London, and Yvon Durelle in Montreal. The Mongoose's gutsy efforts, surviving early knockdowns to stop the Canadian champion, was his finest hour, and he did it again at the same site.

Meanwhile, fighting for the bigger buck, the venerable warrior tried and failed for the heavyweight honors against Rocky Marciano, Floyd Patterson, and Muhammad Ali.

With 199 victories in 229 bouts, Archie Moore retired at age 50 for movie roles in which he was almost as cute as his lower-lip mustache tuft. He was engaging as raftsman Jim in a well-received *Huckleberry Finn*.

Then he retired to his ABC's—Mongoose Moore's camp for which the initials spelled out the message he had proved—any boy can.

★

HIS FINEST HOUR: Thirty-seven by his calendar, 40 by his dear Mom's, Old Mongoose Archie Moore had his finest hour in 1958 when, knocked down early and often by Yvon Durrelle in a light heavyweight title bout, he stopped Durrelle in 11 rounds in the Canadian's home city, Montreal.

1954

The Man's Finest Hour

Stan Musial's First Ever—5 Homers!

One of Stan Musial's greatest days—maybe the greatest—was the May day in 1954 when Stan the Man hit five home runs in a doubleheader, a record that stood uncontested until, curiously, a kid who saw it from a bleacher seat hit five himself.

The tale of Stan Musial—a tall tale when you consider how fast and far he came from the minors to the majors—has fewer bright moments than Sunday, May 2, 1954, when he teed off on New York Giant pitchers as no man ever had homered against any big-league staff.

Musial, by the way, never had hit three home runs in a game except for 1941, his rags-to-riches season. He did it at White City Park in Springfield, Missouri, where—to her great annoyance—his number one fan, wife Lil, was diapering infant son Dick in the restroom every time Musial homered.

Before the first game that Sunday 45 years ago, a New York sportswriter asked Cardinal manager Eddie Stanky his choice as the best player in the National League. That season Willie Mays, still a big-league stripling en route to greatness, had returned from military service. Stanky, pointing to Musial, answered simply, "Number 6!"

First time up that warm, rainy Sunday, Musial walked. Next time, facing left-hander Johnny Antonelli, Stan timed a slow curve and hit it to the right-field roof at Sportsman's Park. In the fifth, Antonelli fired a fastball down and in, but Musial got out in front of it and hit another onto the pavilion.

In the sixth, Musial singled off former Redbird right-hander Jim Hearn. When Stan batted in the eighth, score tied, the crowd roared in excitement. Musial hammered Hearn's inside slider to the roof for the third homer that won the game, 9–6.

After the game, nibbling a ham sandwich with milk in the clubhouse, Musial got a call from wife Lil, understandably upset. She had missed this three-homer game, too, because second daughter Janet was ill with a sore throat.

Second game, lights on, Musial walked in the first inning, and the crowd booed. Second time, with perhaps his best swing of the day, he hit a 420-foot shot collared by Mays at the center-field fence, another homer if the wind had been blowing from left field instead of right.

In the fifth, facing knuckleball artist Hoyt Wilhelm, headed for the Hall of Fame as primarily a relief ace, Stan hit a slow curve clear over the stands onto Grand Avenue. The fifth is the one Stan the Man remembered most. It was against Wilhelm's dancing knuckler, hit even higher and farther over the roof in right center.

At nearly 8 P.M. in the rain-delayed doubleheader, lost 9–7, Musial tried too hard against right-hander Larry Jansen. He popped out, and most of the crowd fled as if someone had yelled "fire!"

Among those taking it on the lam was a young St. Louis high school kid named Nate Colbert. The name should be familiar. Colbert went on to a big league career, and on August 1, 1972, playing with San Diego, Nate tied Musial by becoming only the second major leaguer to hit five home runs in one day.

★

THE FAN'S MAN: Stan Musial, team player and durable, played often silently when hurt. He was an all-around player at any outfield position or first base, though he preferred right field, but played most of it in left. He was voted—hands down—St. Louis's number one ball player of the century.

1957
Kutis Soccer
Harry Keough and Company

In the twentieth-century history of St. Louis soccer—Muny League, CYC, and Khourys—international recognition came seldom here. But, curiously, just about every time Uncle Sam and the hometown proved it belonged, one man was involved—Harry Keough, not to be confused with Bobby Kehoe, the local star who led the Catholic Youth Council All-Stars to the famed 1–1 tie against Britain's professional champions in 1964.

It was all Harry Keough—from the time he played right fullback in America's astonishing 1950 World Cup upset over England, 1–0, until his own son, Ty, also an international player, worked later global cups as a television broadcaster.

If college soccer had been available, Harry Keough and older brother Bill would have taken advantage of scholarship opportunity. Their father, Pat, best known for an encyclopedic baseball memory and a collection of Irish tenor John McCormack records, didn't have then the money he earned on the "$64,000 Question," a television contest craze of the 1950s.

The midnight-to-dawn gas company employee scrambled with a sizable family in the Spanish Society community south of Carondelet Park. First son Bill,

nifty with a soccer ball as with his W. C. Fields juggling act, played soccer briefly in Chicago, en route to a traveling career as a professional trampolinist—oh, my aching back!—until age 65.

Brother Harry, praiseworthy in a delightful mutual-admiration society with Bill, started for Kutis, sponsored by a sportsman undertaker. The Kutis banner, improved briefly by short-lived coaching contributions of a former German pro, Hans von Strandl, produced six successive U.S. national amateur championships and the Open in 1957.

Included in that period when, in effect, the Muny League was really glorified organized soccer on a sandlot basis, Kutis beat three touring first division professional German teams—Eintracht-Frankfort in 1951, Nuremberg in 1955, and Schaben-Augsburg in 1956.

But always a realist, Keough recalled, grinning, "Then they brought in Kaiserslautern, which had six of the players who won the '56 World Cup for West Germany. My, wouldn't you rather me talk about my boy, Ty, named for his Grandpa's favorite player, Ty Cobb?"

★

A BATTLE FOR THE BALL: *Kutis and St. Engelbert vie for position in a Muny match-up.*

POETRY IN MOTION: *A stripe-shirted Kutis player disputes a pass with two St. Ambrose players at a league game at Fairgrounds Park, Field #2. With baseball as the primary professional sport, amateur soccer once lured large crowds.*

KUTIS KINGPINS: *National Champions, 1957: Front row: Fred Vasquez, Ruben Mendoza, Bob Rooney, Jim Murphy, Bill Looby, Tom Murphy, Dick Meismann. Back row: Bob Burkard, Butch Cook, Bob Whitehead, Val Pelizzaro, Tom Julius, Harry Keough, Joe Carenza, Bill Eppy, Russ Murphy, Leroy Franks.*

1958

Southern Comfort

The Hawks' Bob Pettit Starred in Two of Three NBA St. Louis Classics

Robert E. Lee Pettit's grandfather taught Bob early the principles of unselfish play, demonstrated in St. Louis's first National Basketball Association All-Star Game.

The first NBA All-Star game here in late January 1958 didn't fill up the Arena, then smaller until the enlargement by hockey's Salomon family, but the 12,854 fans saw hometown star Bob Pettit shine even though on a losing side. Bob was the MVP in a game won by the East over the West, 130–118.

Pettit not only set an all-star scoring record—28—but he also broke the rebound record, his own! Pettit had pulled down 24 rebounds his second year in the league, 1956. With an encouraging hometown crowd, he hauled in 26, working backboards at both ends.

Given the opportunity to present the game's trophy to her son, Mrs. Pettit lingered to tell about the 6'9" star's fabulous grandfather, Albert, who ran away from home at age 14 to fight for the North in the Civil War, yet named his son Robert E. Lee in memory of the South's statesman soldier. A member of the University of Michigan's first football team, Albert Pettit went west to Colorado for a fortune in silver and real estate, then moved to Dixie as a man of peace.

Grandson Pettit, reversing family direction, became a man of ability and character, a first-round basketball draft choice from LSU and a standout of disciplined, principled play despite handicaps.

In the '58 game, he was handicapped like the attendance, which was limited by heavy snow and curtailed plane travel. Pettit played with his left hand in a cast and suffered on a play when the East broke an 82–82 tie in the third period.

For the first half, Pettit eluded great the intimidator, Boston's giant defensive wizard Bill Russell, scoring 17 points. Overall, with Bob Cousy starring with 20 points and the veteran Dolf Schayes showing his back-court ability for the East, Pettit earned post-game tribute, which eased the pain of a collision that gimped his knee.

After all, Robert E. Lee Pettit had it a lot nicer than Hawks' teammate Slater (Dugie) Martin. Dugie limped off with an injury that would bench him, allowing him to receive further bad news. Someone had stolen his car.

St. Louis's second pro basketball contest of stars was played January 15, 1962, before 15,112, and Pettit emerged with his third MVP.

In a game where the West outrebounded the favored East—after all, Red Auerbach had both Bill Russell *and* Wilt Chamberlain—the underdog won handsomely, 150–139.

It took a football coach, Missouri's Dan Devine, then with nationally ranked teams, to sum up the why and the wherefore of the win. Said Devine, "They wanted it more—at least Pettit did, the most unselfish great player I ever saw."

Gathering in 27 rebounds—corraling many off the defensive board and high-tailing it to the far end—Pettit scored 25 points, including some off offensive rebounds.

For the West, magnificent Oscar Robertson was second in MVP voting. He scored 26, and Private Elgin Baylor shed his army uniform and scored 32. For the East, Wilt the Stilt was number one overall with 42 points, but the East succumbed to a second-half surge. The intimidating Celtic, Russell, was limited to 12 rebounds, only half of rival Chamberlain's.

Big Russ's favored East would win the third and final NBA All-Star game here in '65, 124–123. For 16,713, then the largest All-Star crowd in history, that one came in the sayonara sundown for the hero of the Hawks, Bob Pettit.

★

CHAIRMEN OF THE BOARDS: *Only Bill Russell stands between Pettit and two points. The third rebounding maven Wilt Chamberlain moves into position just in case. Russell, Chamberlain, and Pettit pounded the boards nearly every All-Star game.*

1958
Hawks Topple Celtics

Bob Pettit

They laughed back home when the lanky neighbor's kid, awkward as well as gangling, tried to play one-on-one basketball, but years of rigorous practice turned that slim-jim into a superstar as St. Louis's best-ever pro player, Bob Pettit.

And Robert E. Lee Pettit, en route to the role as the game's first 25,000-point player, hit his peak in the clutch with the 50 points that beat the Boston Celtics in the sixth game of the 1957–58 playoffs. The Hawks' 110–109 thriller at old Kiel Auditorium was the only championship the Celtics didn't lose for a decade.

Pettit, handsome and humble, never talked much about that one, but one of the St. Louis area's greatest all-around players, prep to pro, Ed Macauley, rhapsodized about it. Said Easy Ed, "Pettit not only hit 50, including the clincher, but he hit 19 of our last 21 points."

The one NBA championship in a period of five division titles in 13 years kept the series from going to Boston's home court.

Without Pettit, Cliff Hagan, and local hero Macauley, attendance flagged to the point that owner Ben Kerner, unable to find a hometown owner, sold the franchise to Atlanta for three million dollars after the 1967–68 season.

Said Kerner later in his mid-80s, "I couldn't have competed with the staggering financial changes. I got Pettit up to $70,000. Now, why, even the ball boy makes more money."

At age 32, after 11 professional seasons, Pettit retired on his terms, financially fixed through good investments, to a career in banking at his hometown, Baton Rouge, Louisiana. The player and boss Kerner retained a strong business as well as personal friendship.

Having passed Dolph Schayes's previous pro record of 19,115 points, Pettit retired when still scoring at a 22.6 rate, his lowest average, but his pride told him it was time to go. Annually, he had been 1-2-3 not only in scoring, but also in corralling rebounds at both ends of the court, a tribute to his talent, hustle, and determination.

That determination was manifest under special night-lights in the backyard when the awkward, skinny kid fleshed out physically and honed his skills. He grew like Jack and the Giant killer's beanstalk between his sophomore and junior years of high school. At alma mater Louisiana State, he learned from LSU's Olympic trainer the importance of upper-arm strength for shooting and rebounding.

From 195 pounds when finishing college to Rookie of the Year with the Hawks in their last season at Milwaukee, Pettit stoked up to 235 pounds, eating four full-sized meals every day except when playing, then just three.

"I've been lucky," he said, "not lucky to have a large body, but to have had the mind to convince myself that I could make it only if I worked out three hours a day, 12 months."

A selfless team player at 6'9", Pettit converted himself from a back-to-the-basket hook-shot pivot man to a face-front forward who used the jump shot almost exclusively.

Pettit needed only an adequate dribble to be a perfect player, but he was true blue, a polite, genteel southern gentleman except on the court. "Big Blue" became a tender nickname when imaginative broadcaster Bud Blattner saw him wear a long blue topcoat on the road.

When "Big Blue," the Hawks' number 9, was at his very best, owner Ben Kerner would lament, "I don't know why anyone except Pettit ever shoots!"

That was obvious the night of the nifty, title-winning 50.

★

C-H-A-M-P-E-E-N-S: *That's how Hawks' owner Ben Kerner doled out praise for the team that was effective for 13 seasons, led by number one scorer Bob Pettit (9). Others from the left include Walt Davis (12), Captain Charley Share (13), Ed Macauley (20), and Clyde Lovellette.*

BOMBS AWAY: *The Hawks' big three gunners were (from the left) Bob Pettit, Clyde (Boom-Boom) Lovellete, and Cliff Hagan.*

1958

3,000

Stan Musial's Dramatic Arrival at a Magic Number

One of the golden moments in a golden career was achieved when Stan Musial reached the magical 3,000-hit plateau in May 1958, at Chicago, capping an interesting, even amusing, climb.

Back 10 years earlier at the same Wrigley Field, then age 28, Stan got his 1,000th hit. A photographer was taking a corny picture of Musial kissing his bat when Bob Broeg, traveling with the Cardinals, walked into the clubhouse and scoffed.

"Heck, Stan," he said, "I once saw a man get his 3,000th hit!"

Musial's brown eyes widened. He did quick mental arithmetic and said, "Man, that's 15 years of 200 hits."

Uh-huh, Broeg agreed, unless a guy could play longer. Six years earlier at Boston's Braves Field, working for the Associated Press, Broeg had seen Paul Waner, longtime Pittsburgh standout, become only the seventh player to reach 3,000.

Musial, asked to identify Waner's predecessors, knew Ty Cobb, of course, but he suggested Rogers Hornsby and Babe Ruth and Lou Gehrig and Al Simmons. Wrong, wrong!

Then he heard the actual names. Aside from Cobb, they were Cap Anson, Tris Speaker, Eddie Collins, Napoleon Lajoie, Honus Wagner, and Waner. Gravely, Musial said: "You know, you play this game to win and you play it for money, but it helps to have incentives on hot days and when your ball club is not winning. Keep reminding me."

So 10 years later, nearly age 39, Musial was two hits shy when the Cardinals took what amounted to their last train trip in the new era of the plane, round trip to Chicago for a two-game series. Stan had hoped to do it in St. Louis—incredibly he'd had 43 hits in the first 22 games—but . . .

When he doubled the first game against the Cubs, he suggested wistfully to coach Terry Moore, "Gee, Tee, I'd like to walk four times tomorrow and save 3,000 for that big crowd at Sportsman's Park."

Moore told manager Fred Hutchinson. Hutch agreed with Musial. He announced he would use Stan only if necessary. Relaxed from a night out, Musial was also weary. He had been up most of the night, calling the police and hospitals, trying to locate a dear friend's wife, Molly Pizzica. She had been missing because a helpful hotel bellman had let her into a wrong room.

So, now it was the sixth inning, Cards losing 3–1, when Hutchinson beckoned for Musial to pinch-hit for Sam Jones. Off Moe Drabowsky, The Man sliced a breaking ball deep into the left-field corner, doubling to set up a winning inning, 5–3.

That last train ride was historic in the first season the West Coast made flying necessary. An Illinois Central rail chef whipped up a "3,000 Hit" cake. Broadcaster Harry Caray presented Musial with appropriately engraved cuff links. Winning pitcher Toothpick Sam Jones cradled a bottle of champagne Stan bought for him.

En route, the train stopped at Clinton and Springfield, Illinois, permitting Musial, as if on a political bandwagon, to get off, sign autographs, and speak briefly.

Almost two hours late, near midnight, the train moved into crowded Union Station, where Musial said from a platform that he now knew how famed pilot Charles Lindbergh felt. A fog-horned fan roared, "What did he hit?"

Musial ended the ceremonies merrily to many young well-wishers up too late. "Hey, kids," Stan the Man laughed, "no school tomorrow!"

And in his first home game the next night with Sportsman's Park packed, Stan (The Man) Musial hit number 3,001, a home run!

★

"AS IF THE COPS WERE COMING": That's the amusing accurate way Hall of Fame pitcher Ted Lyons described Stan Musial's stance. Coiled, he peeked over his right shoulder like an errant kid serving as lookout, seeing if John Law was coming. Although he had five full seasons before he developed his full swing, Stan the Man uncoiled to hit 475 career homers—and a record six in All-Star games.

1959
Daddy's Delight

Judy Torluemke Rankin Became a Golfing Great

At age six, daddy put a golf club in her hands and promptly quit playing to become her first coach. At only 14, she became the youngest winner of the Missouri State Amateur in 1959. At 15, she became the youngest to finish as low amateur in the U.S. Women's Open. She's Judy Torluemke.

From the pretty little princess of pro play, traveling the roads alone at age 19, Judy Torluemke emerged overnight from a slight, freckled kid to a mature woman, a mighty mite who blossomed as Judy Rankin.

By her admission and recollection, Judy owes much to father Paul Torluemke and not only because the well-traveled advertising executive quit his game to help hers. After all, he also toted her to Miami for expert instruction from golf doctor Bob Toski, but Paul showed a side many didn't expect.

Many figured Torluemke would be like a stage door momma, buttinski clinging only to her life on the links, but daddy urged her to marry. As she put it back in 1964, as a kid touring those some 30–35,000 miles for 35 sanctioned tournaments, "My father said that if I played until 40, he'd come back to haunt me. He expects to have grandchildren."

By the time she married Texan Yippy Rankin in June 1967, she had managed only a couple of second-place finishes in 112 tournaments, but marriage to the man from Midlands worked wonders.

From 1968, she began to win regularly, finishing first 11 times, capped by seven tournaments in 1976 and a record $150,734, a sizable difference a quarter-century ago and, yes, much different from the 701 bucks for 15 tournaments when she was that blonde, green-eyed kid back in '62.

With a bow to those who helped back home with dear dad—Bob Green, Jeannie Dobbins, and Eddie Held—her greatest thanks went to Toski for help at her father's insistence.

Toski told her not to worry about her unorthodox left-hand grip, which many had urged her to change. From a flat grip, she had been unable to fade the ball from left to right, but Toski showed her how to do it— and with control. Said Judy, "He helped my short game, too, and my mental approach."

He also helped her line up a winter job playing and teaching at Ocean Reef, a resort at North Key Largo. After all, something had to help pay for those gargantuan meals the 5'4", 115-pound little lady ate to boost her strength.

Marriage and maturity did the rest. Judy and husband Yippy had a son, Tuey—hey, they sure use funny names down there deep in the heart of Texas!— and Tuey became a football player at Texas Tech and a coach in Lubbock.

By 1976, LPGA Player of the Year and low-score winner, mom set a record for most top-10 finishes in the season with 25. But daddy's little darling, Missouri women's amateur champion a second time in 1961, has traveled as far as she did behind the wheel of fortune. The first woman to break the $100,000 barrier with a career $887,858, she's still active as a television commentator and captain of U.S. women's Soldheim Cup team.

Judy Torluemke Rankin is in the college women's Hall of Fame and Texas Golf Hall of Fame. Hey, to the Missouri Sports Hall of Fame at Springfield, how about a nomination for the former princess of the playing pros?

★

GIFTED GAL: Judy Torluemke, better known as Judy Rankin lifted up to her father's wish when he gave up his own game to devote time, attention, and better teaching to her. From a teenaged start, she became a great golfer, a winning pro and organizer of the LPGA, and what Paul Torluemke wanted—married and a mother.

The Old Master of Ol' Mizzou

Don Faurot, a Legend for Whom the Football Field Is Named

During the 1999 football season, the University of Missouri erected and dedicated a larger-than-life statue to Don Faurot, the man for whom the stadium is named—and a guy so old he could remember when future Highway 40 was gravel with wood planks.

That's the way Faurot, who died a few years ago at age 93, remembered bumpy transportation when he was a kid, but the narrow two-lane road wasn't much better when he began to recruit St. Louis heavily as head coach. The date was New Year's Day, 1935.

Many of the "M" men who played for Faurot from 1935 to 1956, plus others before and since, contributed to the statue at Faurot Field, which the Thin Man from Mountain Grove helped build. Actually, Don spent most of his boyhood in Columbia, sneaking into old Rollins Field to see the Tigers play, but in his later youth his father was a state experimental agriculture agent at Mountain Grove.

Old Fred Faurot, a French-derivation Yankee, had played college football at Nebraska and Iowa State. Whenever he saw son Don's teams play, he would send the coach a long note that always wound up the same: "Better get back to the fundamentals. . . ."

"F. W." . . . as they called old Fred W., helped his kids put up all kinds of athletic equipment and offered each of his four sons a gold watch if they didn't drink or smoke. All collected.

When Don Faurot was a 148-pound senior at Missouri—fullback, linebacker, punter—the 1924 team played Southern California on Christmas Day at the Coliseum in Los Angeles. The Tigers' captain, Art Bond, father of Senator Kit Bond, had to help beat the drums for funds for new Memorial Stadium. It would be built between two bluffs south of the campus. Trouble was, one blast catapulted a rock crusher and truck into the valley, where it's still a steel-covered dinosaur.

One of Faurot's jobs as a paid student was to help lift and grade the field that eventually would have his name.

One of Faurot's accomplishments is obvious. Recruiting virtually all of the Missouri players, largely from the St. Louis area, helped him turn around a team that had gone 2–23–2 in three seasons under Frank Carideo. Faurot's first team had an odd record—3–3–3—and the second one was 6–2–1. By 1939, he had the first of five bowl teams.

Trying to pay off deep stadium debts, he scheduled tough teams on the road for better attendance, losing more than he might have. Next, he scheduled tougher teams for play at the stadium, originally sunken with a 28,000 capacity, then began to build the super-structure that three times has exceeded 70,000.

Finally, stepping down gracefully under pressure after losing seasons, he hand-picked two coaches who followed him into the college football Hall of Fame—Frank Broyles at Arkansas and Dan Devine at Arizona State, Missouri, and Notre Dame.

He also had created one of football's best offensive formations. Both pro football's Jim Conzelman and college's Bud Wilkinson were ecstatic about the Split-T formation, featured by the keep-or-give option of the quarterback and also the halfback option pass.

To Faurot, as an athlete even better in basketball despite the loss of right-hand fingers at the joint, "The option is like the 2-on-1 fast break in basketball."

The Split-T feature is still a play of impact in '99. No wonder they put up that statue to the man for whom Faurot Field is named.

★

BRONZED IN BRONZE: Don Faurot, trim and bronzed late in his 93-year life, was a smiling football legend at alma mater Missouri from 1935 to 1996—and beyond.

1959
Tradition Trailblazers
Saint Louis U.'s First National Champions

Missouri's loss was Saint Louis University's gain. As far back as 1939, Ol' Mizzou turned down a suggestion to field a soccer team. Belatedly, in view of early recommendations, the Billikens did, too. When they approved it 40 years ago, virtually overnight Saint Louis became the Yankees of baseball, Notre Dame of football, and Kentucky of basketball.

Until the rest of the country caught on and caught up with St. Louis, recognizing that the old riverfront town was a fountainhead for soccer talent, the Bills' Blue and White prevailed in NCAA play.

Oddly, the national tournament began in 1959, the year after Saint Louis U. organized a club team and spent only $200. When the NCAA championed the cause officially, Saint Louis U. went directly to the top.

At that time, the university had no scholarships for soccer. As envisioned for years by many, including the *Post-Dispatch*'s Dent McSkimming, the *Globe-Democrat*'s Bob Burnes, and finally the Catholic Youth Council's Monsignor Louis F. Meyer and Bob Guelker, the kids on campus would come running.

That's what, back in 1939, Bob Broeg had envisioned after inviting fellow students at Columbia, many of them Don Faurot's Orange Bowl football team, to play a Sunday soccer exhibition against a Jefferson City church team. Faurot, understandably, feared NCAA disapproval. As athletic director, despite suggested automatic strength with so many St. Louis kids there, he declined even to support a club team.

Missouri, with women's soccer, still had none for men. Meanwhile, as mentioned here, Billiken athletic director Bob Stewart, who had played soccer at Syracuse, listened. He established a team and brought Guelker aboard as coach.

Most of Guelker's players were from the CYC program he had administered for Monsignor Meyer. As one who never had played the sport, the 35-year-old Guelker became a good student, teacher, and organizer.

Those 1959 pioneer Billikens of the little round ball reeled off an 11–1 record, marred only by a late-season loss to Wheaton, 2–1, a record that included decisive victories over Illinois, Indiana, Michigan State, and Purdue.

In the playoffs, they knocked off San Francisco 4–0, and falling behind City College of New York by two goals at the half, they were bribed by Guelker. The coach promised them that if they got through to the finals, he would provide a sightseeing trip en route to New York. St. Louis prevailed 6–2.

So it was to Connecticut for the finals at Bridgeport. Kim Tucci, a good eyewitness as the team's assistant trainer and now a local prince of pizzas and politics, smiled in recollection. He recalled a reception that was rude at best. The Bridgeport campus was closed for the holidays so, though able to arrange a room elsewhere for coach Guelker and his wife, the rest slept on cots in the visitors' clubhouse dressing room. As Tucci cracked, "Amid orange peels."

After a scramble for breakfast, St. Louis was led by All-Americans John Dueker, Tom Tost, and Jerry Knobbe to the championship, won decisively 5–2.

★

FIRST IN SHOES: Bob Guelker's 1959 Billikens led the championship parade back in 1959. The head coach, later even more incredible at nearby Southern Illinois–Edwardsville, is light-suited second to the left in the second row.

1960
The Devine Decade
Dan's Masterpiece at Ol' Mizzou

Of all the games Ol' Mizzou has won in football since they bought their first lopsided ball back in 1891, the one that probably lives longest was the highlight of Dan Devine's career as the Tigers' winningest coach. It was the late November day, 1960; they beat Oklahoma in Norman.

Over the years, using the formation Bud Wilkinson had learned from Missouri's Don Faurot, the Sooners' graying Galahad had ruled the roost in the expanded Big Six, once winning 31 in a row, then 47 and—finally—73 straight in the conference.

So, most certainly, as nicknamed by longtime Tiger assistant coach, Hoot Betty, Norman was "the snake pit." Missouri hadn't won down there in the red clay country since Faurot's first trip, 1936, and now it was 24 years later. And the Tiger players had not only a championship ambition, but also a secret.

Two years earlier in Dan Devine's first trip to Norman, the fast-striking Sooners had embarrassed the Tigers 39–0. Devine's Irish surfaced. The little coach leaped onto the training table and, trembling, addressed his seniors. "I promise you," he said, "that two years from now, the sophomores will win down here and dedicate the game to you!"

And many of those '58 seniors were in the stands that day in '60, just about the time the secret leaked. Beforehand, that first unbeaten season, including a victory at Penn State, Devine had privately told those sophomores-now-seniors that they had four goals.

Missouri's first opening game victory since 1947—that first win at Norman since '36—the first conference title since '45, and Ol' Mizzou's first bowl victory ever in seven tries.

A tall order from a short coach indeed, and on Oklahoma's first series the Sooners' Mike McClellan broke a 70-yard scoring run for the first rushing touchdown the Tigers had yielded all season.

Devine's offense featured a power sweep so effective that as Air Force's Ben Martin cracked, "It was student body, left—student body, right."

Swift St. Louisan Norris Stevenson swept 77 yards for one first-half touchdown and—on a special draw play Devine had devised—Donnie Smith scored from 30 yards out. But a 12-point Tiger lead at halftime was down to five near the end of the third quarter when All-America Danny LaRose shanked a punt to his 40. Oklahoma had the ball and momentum!

Here, Devine's defensive genius Al Onofrio switched to an odd-man line, a penetrating defense he had put in just the day before. Missouri held, forced a fumble, and recovered. And on the first play of the fourth period, entering the lineup fresh, Stevenson took a pitchout left off the steeply crowned Bermuda grass and turned the corner. Sixty yards later, that score was a backbreaker in what became a 41–19 victory.

With only one week to go in the season and the national polls—bowl games didn't count then—Ol' Mizzou was number one for the first time ever. It didn't last because of a 23–7 loss to Kansas's sleeping giant. The game soon was reversed because the Jayhawks had used an ineligible player.

The top ranking was lost, even though in the Orange bowl, winning more impressively than the 21–14 final score, the Tigers held Navy's Heisman Trophy winner Joe Bellino to just four yards.

Disappointment, sure, but not when the coach's clean sweep of predictions included that wonderful win in the Oklahoma snake pit.

★

DEVINE DECADE: Led by Dan Devine, Missouri in the 1960s had the steadiest winning college team, the only major university not to exceed three losses in any season, 1960–69. Devine, who left for Green Bay in 1971 and then Notre Dame, won two conference championships and four bowl games in six tries.

NORMANDY'S NORM: Norm Beal (21) of suburban St. Louis turned around the first bowl game Missouri ever won, running back an intercepted pass against Navy in 1961.

THE GRIN: *Even so serious Sonny Liston had to chuckle after his second one-round kayo of Floyd Patterson, 1963, in Las Vegas. Advisor Jack Nilon shares the occasion.*

THE GLARE: *Or glower or stare of Charles (Sonny) Liston was enough to scare most, more certainly Floyd Patterson from whom Liston took the heavyweight title in one round and then did it again—in one!*

1962
Seldom Funny Sonny
Scowling Charles (Sonny) Liston, Champion

For a year and a half, St. Louis had the distinction of having an adopted son as the area's first heavyweight boxing champion, but the period was only a reprise in the ill-fated life of Charles (Sonny) Liston.

On September 1, 1962, at Chicago, at least 31 years old, Liston knocked out champion Floyd Patterson in one round. Nearly a year later at Las Vegas, big Sonny did it again, brutalizing the gentle Patterson in Round One.

After a fawning exhibition tour of Europe, where he didn't have jailbird stigma and happily avoided trouble, Sonny put the title on the line February 25, 1964. The site was Miami Beach, and the opponent was a handsome, gifted, glib, poetry-rhyming kid from Louisville name Cassius Clay.

One thing for sure, Liston's big, penetrating eyes and scary scowl, which intimidated many, in and out of the ring, didn't bother Cassius. Mr. Clay, of course, would win a century's reputation as one of the most influential athletes—Muhammad Ali.

But in a pretty good bout, suddenly big, bad, and portrayed as ugly, Liston couldn't come out for the seventh round, sidelined by a limp arm injury, a mishap that drove his kid conqueror into boastful, triumphant sounds of joy.

Until, unfortunately, spirited ability to take punishment as well as give it left middle-aged Ali virtually silent as an amused saint, the new champion went on to win fame and fortune with guts enough to buck the wartime draft. Muhammad Ali became a classic symbol internationally.

En route, he won a repeat victory over Liston in a one-round fiasco at Lewiston, Maine, one of the few communities that would see Liston take what seemed a dive job.

If Ali's cult following or the mob that apparently controlled Liston's life had a direct intimidating input in either or both losses, Sonny didn't fit the public image from the time he first was locked up at Missouri's Jefferson City until he died in Las Vegas, December 30, 1971, an apparent victim of a drug overdose.

In between, apparently trusting only his wife, Geraldine, state penitentiary Father Alois Stevens, and maybe early coaching tutor Monroe (Pops) Harrison, Liston lived a troubled life obviously short by his 39 years or as Bob Burnes suggested, maybe 10 years older.

Benchwarmer Burnes, sports editor of the old *St. Louis Globe-Democrat*, was a hero who answered Father Stevens's plea for the fistic monster in prison. At Jeff City, ham-handed Liston quickly proved his potential to Harrison and then to many others.

From a one-round knockout over Don Smith at St. Louis in 1953 until he stopped Chuck Wepner at Jersey City in 1970, six months before his death, Liston was devastating—50 victories in 54 fights, 39 by knockout.

Sonny's left jab was almost too good, so strong that it pushed his foe out of range, too far from a sluggish right. The right, however, was at its best if you ducked inside, as Patterson did and was clobbered with a mallet chop.

The Arkansas cotton chopper's kid gave out similar mistreatment in robberies after running away from his father and joining his mother in St. Louis when he was 13. Sonny had so many brothers and sisters, he couldn't recall whether there were 12 or 13.

When he couldn't control himself in skirmishes with the law, his time in St. Louis was short. His career shifted to Philadelphia, then Denver, finally Las Vegas and the final bell.

Father Stevens summed up the bitter with better. He remembered Sonny as a semi-literate with only one power, his fists. Said the padre about the passing, "I'm glad I helped give Charles his chance. I was with him when he won the title. . . ."

Super Century

Bob Hayes Ran a Record 100 Here

A highlight of St. Louis's celebration of the city's bicentennial came on the longest day of the year 1963, when Bob Hayes ran the fastest 100-yard dash—here at Public Schools Stadium—in the National AAU track meet.

Getting the AAU to St. Louis was a trick in itself. Turning tired, worn-down Public Schools Stadium acceptable with a rubberized, up-to-snuff running track was a chore and a challenge. But in a forerunner of the pre-Olympics effort 30 years later, we did it.

The Public Schools Stadium, like other stadiums of modest athletic facilities, is gone now, but memories of the '63 AAU meet remain.

Especially, that is, if you were in position to watch Florida A&M's football phenom, Bob Hayes, come at you in an explosion.

Weight on his six-foot body pared down from 192 pounds for football to 186, Hayes came at you with the neck of a bull and the waist of a ballet dancer, pigeon-toed, stepping on himself when he ran. He burst the tape at a record 9.1 seconds.

The cheering crowd included the general manager of Los Angeles' championship-bound Dodgers, Buzzy Bavasi, who exulted, "Look at him, as Jake Gaither says, 'A halfback who runs like a rabbit with his tail on fire.'"

Peter Cottontail, age 20, starred for Gaither, a lovable old guy who, as he put it, liked his players "mo-bile, a-gile, and hos-tile."

Strong, too. Track buff Bavasi remembered Hayes when he ran indoors at L.A. Said Buzzy, "They actually had to open a door to keep him from running right through it."

Before the race, in the lovely June summer solstice, football Cardinal trainer Jack Rockwell had rubbed down Hayes on an outdoor training table. Said Rockwell, "Positively the most relaxed athlete I ever worked on before a big event."

Before the first trial run, amazingly explosive in a quick jump, the wide-shouldered, wasp-waisted, and thick-thighed Hayes actually seemed to ease up at the finish. Afterward, he cheerfully explained his awkward, wobbly style of sprinting. Pointing to his slashed track shoes, he grinned, "I'm so pigeon-toed, I spike myself every time I run."

Hayes pointed to the track, a rubberized running surface provided by Bill Bangert, a champion for the AAU's gift of the bicentennial event. Bangert, a one-man show himself, was a former college football player, amateur boxer, singer, and mayor of nearby Champ, Missouri. Big Bill had failed at his boldest venture, a proposed 100,000-seat domed stadium there, but not in his bid to bring the AAU meet.

The contractor's springy track resurface caught Hayes's praise. "I like to run anywhere, most certainly here," he said, deflecting questions, "but I'd rather do it carrying a football."

Bob Hayes got his wish, an early draft by the Dallas Cowboys, but as a pass-receiver, not as a ball-carrier, and he was spectacular in a pro career that lasted through 1974 with Big "D" and one more at San Francisco.

The 1964 Olympian caught 365 passes for 6,295 yards and 71 touchdowns. He's one to remember, especially here for that gold moment in the '63 National AAU Tournament, when the Peter Cottontail of the pigskin, Bob Hayes, ran the first 9.1 century run.

★

LIKE A SPEEDING BULLET: Superman Bob Hayes, the great college halfback who wanted to play pro, rounded out his record 1963 National Amateur Athletic Union here in grand style. At St. Louis's former Public Schools Stadium in 1963, Bullet Boy pigeon-toed the century in a record 9.1 seconds. At the same event in the Big Apple a year later, Hayes broke the tape for a new mark in the 60-yard dash, 5.9.

1963
Charley Hustle
Chuck McKinley, Tennis's Big Little Man

Considering climatic differences that favor warm-weather kids able to play outdoors all year, it's remarkable that the St. Louis area has produced prominent players such as Jimmy Connors, Butch Buchholz, Ken Flach—and Chuck McKinley.

Charles Robert McKinley, son of a pipefitter from suburban St. Ann, brought a Pete Rose approach to tennis and won the highest accolade in 1963. He was ranked number one internationally.

For a quick, thick kid with a choirboy tenor and a cheerleader's enthusiasm, this was a climax of a career in which Chuck hit his heights in Davis Cup play and at Wimbledon.

McKinley won the U.S. singles in 1962 at Forest Hills, two indoor singles titles, two clay-court crowns, and, with local boyhood rival Buchholz having turned pro, Chuck teamed with Dennis Ralston. They won three doubles honors at Forest Hills and brought back Davis Cup glory to America.

McKinley and Ralston ended a five-year drought for the Davis, named for a native St. Louisan. And that year to solidify his international top rank, McKinley won the singles at Wimbledon.

Why didn't he turn pro then? Because it didn't pay nearly so well as now. So McKinley turned down one-night, pro touring chances with Pancho Gonzales after his glittery amateur days.

The young star turned from the tennis racket to the ticker tape of Wall Street, ultimately moving to a better thing with the market. By then, twice married, he had a 19-year-old daughter and sons 12 and 8 when stricken with a brain tumor. Shortly before his death in August 1986, the prosperous stockbroker was inducted into tennis's Hall of Fame, but he was too far along with illness to take the trek to Newport, Rhode Island. He was only 45.

At Pattonville High, stubby 5'8" Chuck McKinley was fascinated by the baseball Cardinals' Stan Musial and Marty Marion. He thought tennis was only "a rich kid's sport," but a campus coach urged him to try it. So the kid would bus downtown to the old YMCA on Locust Street, where he met Bill Price.

Price, a great table tennis player, had a notion that the game many sneered at as "Ping Pong" helped sharpen a tennis player's quickness. And McKinley was fast, energetic, and acrobatic. He won a tennis scholarship to Trinity University in San Antonio.

Despite his lack of height, Chuck sprung high to retrieve shots and to attain leverage, giving him a surprising and booming serve. He also had a side-armed volley, hitting the ball on the fly to gain points where others would play it safe.

Physically and emotionally, revved up like Pete Rose, a champion because of his blood and guts effort, he would leap and lunge dexterously. Cunningly, to improve his forehand, he cheated to his left and invited shots to his backhand.

"Slashing around," to use his own expression, Chuck McKinley played with a hustling verve that was captivating and successful. One night at Washington University's Francis Field, he darn near ran out the southwest door to retrieve a shot from Dennis Ralston.

When Chuck was given an award here, Jack Buck had the right quip: "Why, the kid's so good, St. Louis already has named a bridge for him—"

★

NUMBER ONE: *Briefly in tennis, the top U.S. amateur, and in the hearts of many who admired his bouncing tenacity. That was Chuck McKinley, the hometown boy reached the top in Wimbledon, at Forest Hills, and in defending Mr. Davis's cup.*

1964
The Dean of College Swimming

Doc Counsilman

The grand salami of splash, the sultan of swimming, is a former St. Louisan whose name originally might have been confused with Jimmy Conzelman, but the famed James (Doc) Counsilman would make his own name.

Doc Counsilman, who spells his surname slightly different from the multi-talented late football coach, was a kid who played around the Forest Park fisheries, finished 113 in a senior class of 116 at Blewett High School in 1938 and, as he puts it, understandably had a "poor self-image."

Though the captain of the Blewett track team, he could have chinned himself on a curbstone until he began hanging around the downtown "Y" on Pine Street. A coach there named Ernie Vornbrock interested him in swimming, and, as Counsilman recalled, "convinced me that I was human and should go to college."

Fast forward a half-century to 1990 when 69-year-old Counsilman retired as the swimming's winningest coach ever. At the University of Indiana, from 1958 to 1990, taking over a humpty-dumpty Hoosier swim team, Doc won 23 Big 10 conference championships, 20 of them in a row, and took 140 consecutive dual meets and 6 NCAA titles.

That's not all. Counsilman's swimmers, some of whom he directed as the 1964 U.S. coach in Tokyo and in '76 at Montreal, claimed 41 Olympic medals. And he helped significantly the careers of Sullivan award winner John Kinsella and swimming's most famous performer, Mark Spitz.

Spitz, by his own analysis, stumbled through the '68 Olympic Games with four victories when he might have won six, and two of the four were relays. Fresh out of high school at age 18 and earmarked for Long Beach State, Mark turned to Counsilman.

Doc—he loved that nickname based on his Ph.D.—thought his chances were as slim as the thin coat of ice that knocked Spitz on his rear end in a visit to Bloomington. (The coast kid, arriving in a blizzard, didn't even have a heavy coat.)

Over the years Counsilman had learned many things. Through a freshman year at Ohio State, he was national AAU breaststroke champion. Called into service, he became a B-24 pilot. Doc flew 32 missions before he was shot down over Yugoslavia in 1944, winning a DFC. He later had captained Buckeye swim teams to NCAA titles in '46 and '47.

So he was a man of confidence and good humor, energy, and vision who compelled Spitz to stay. Of course, Mark four years later bug-eyed the world by winning seven gold medals in the Munich Olympics.

A disciplinarian and a close friend and dining companion of basketball's brash Bobby Knight, Counsilman could be tough, which became increasingly difficult as he developed an unathletic tummy and didn't mind his kids ribbing him about it. A favorite sugar candy always was available for the Hoosiers, too.

Satisfying his own longtime ambition, the bulky Counsilman in September 1979 became the oldest then at 58 to swim the 21-mile English Channel. He was bothered most during the swim by a Russian freighter that nearly did him in and also suffered a nasty jellyfish sting.

When he gave up coaching 10 years later, afflicted with arthritis, he helped Joe Hunsaker of St. Louis create a unique stillwater pool that bears study. And Counsilman wrote a book—"The Science of Swimming"—that is definitive, translated into 20 languages.

St. Louisan James (Doc) Counsilman has come a long way from the kid who didn't know what he was doing when he first took to the water way back in 1938.

★

MR. DOC: *That's really what they should have called native St. Louisan James Counsilman, seated, shown here with Indiana University athletic director Ralph Floyd. Counsilman, college swimming's winningest coach, liked to be called "Doc".*

1964
High Spot for Shin Kickers
CYC Stars Tie Brit Champs Liverpool

Of all the times St. Louis soccer players fancied themselves equal to Europe's or South America's best—and were embarrassed in international matches—the golden moment came on a mid-May night in 1964. Local amateurs labeled as the Catholic Youth Council All-Stars tied Liverpool, England's professional champions.

Of previous embarrassments, the worst for international teams probably came in 1939 when a basic St. Louis team, though with some imported professionals, met Scottish pros here. Our guys, led by white-haired player/coach Alex McNab, had won consecutive National Open championships in the United States. The touring Scots humiliated them 9–0 and taught them the technical importance of a three-back defensive system compared to two. Now, worldwide, it's four back, making goals as tough as they were that magic moment in '64 when CYC All-Stars matched Liverpool 1–1.

Previously, St. Louis's international soccer highlights had been limited. In 1951, then in a run of national amateur and open titles, Kutis upset Germany's touring Eintracht-Frankfurt team 2–1. In '55, against a traveling German team from Nuremberg, Kutis prevailed 3–2.

But, as researched by the *Post-Dispatch*'s Hall of Fame soccer writer, Dent McSkimming, St. Louis never had won or tied against 18 British teams in visits that began in 1905. In Liverpool's three previous visits to the United States and Canada, the British champions had been tied only once in 33 matches. This time they had beaten Boston's best 8–1, and New York's select side, 7–0.

On a warm night—good for the air-conditioning Liverpool had enjoyed mid-day when the local lads worked—5,700 saw the improbable, a game in which St. Louis's captain, center halfback Bob Kehoe, played probably his best match ever. That's the way the analytical McSkimming saw it.

Kehoe's top task was marking Liverpool's brilliant center forward, Ian St. John. Bobby darn near followed St. John into the visiting clubhouse at halftime, setting a fast pace as the vagabond athlete rising to the occasion.

Unrelated to the more prominent Keoughs, who spell their Irish surname differently, the CYC's Kehoe had a romantic career. He'd quit Saint Louis University High School after his sophomore year, 1945, to spend five seasons in minor-league baseball.

Later, he became a cop and then a fireman, and ran a bar when he wasn't visiting one. He coached high school soccer and briefly the St. Louis pros. The lean athlete, who resembled television's master of *The Twilight Zone*, Rod Serling, had a gift of gab when given a broadcasting chance, but he needed most the lifeline of Anheuser-Busch's Denny Long, the brewery's soccer-buff president.

At age 71, when this series of century recollections began, Kehoe just had quit playing in an old-timers' game, proud of having represented the United States in World Cup matches, but happiest that night in '64 with his CYC teammates.

Said Kehoe wistfully, "Liverpool was better, of course, but we didn't know it. They forced the most corner kicks, yet we got the best shots on goal and got great play from our keepers, Mike Lyons and Roger Rupp. And—just think!—they had to score with four minutes left to tie us. Unbelievable!"

★

FRONT AND CENTER: Pat McBride, one of St. Louis's best soccer players, stands ready (center) to handle a rebound in the game that featured Bob Kehoe, the 1–1 tie with England.

1964
Key Cardinal
Ken Boyer, Captain of '64 Cards

CAPTAIN COURAGEOUS: *By the time the Cardinals won the 1964 pennant, their first in 18 years, power-packed Ken Boyer was the inspiration, the captain, an RBI guy who could hit, field and run—yes, and MVP in the NL.*

St. Louis's 18-year wait for a return to the World Series ended in 1964. After 13 frustrating seasons for sportsman Gussie Busch, the Cardinals conquered old rival New York Yankees, and the Series was climaxed by Captain Ken Boyer's long-awaited celebration.

Boyer's game-winning grand slam in game four was the highlight of the Series, even more than Mickey Mantle's monstrous homer that won the day before for the Yanks and Tim McCarver's 10th-inning blast that took the fifth contest for the Cards.

Then Yankees, as usual, had prevailed in the American League even though their old stars were showing telltale signs of age. Johnny Keane's Redbirds had prevailed miraculously to bring St. Louis an unexpected baseball bunting.

A near-miss ball club in Stan Musial's last season, 1963, winning 19 of 20 in September, the Cardinals flattened out in '64 and, unfairly, general manager Bing Devine was fired in August. Angered players, who had limped through the first half of the season one game under .500, responded and were aided by a Philadelphia fold-up. Six-and-a-half games out with 11 to play, the Redbirds won the last day.

Devine's final stroke had been a major factor, the acquisition of Lou Brock from Chicago in a Brink's heist. True Blue Lou's trading-deadline efforts at bat and on the bases were even more significant than first baseman Bill White's second-half surge and the play of the field foreman, third baseman Boyer.

As a 10-year man, Boyer had fulfilled the expectations of Devine back in December 1957, just after Der Bingle was named general manager. Devine turned down what he regarded as a most attractive offer from the Phillies, i.e. return of former Redbird left-hander Harvey Haddix and fleet young outfielder Richie Ashburn.

Said Devine, "I'm banking on Boyer becoming a full-fledged star."

He did. By 1964, achieving National League Most Valuable Player status with a .295 average, 24 homers, and 119 RBIs, the big guy capped a seven-year period of high-level consistency—.303 average, 26 home runs, 101 ribbies, and four straight All-Star game selections.

The '64 Series offered a couple of interesting postscripts. Not only were both managers St. Louis–born, the Yankees' colorful Yogi Berra and former Redbird seminary student Johnny Keane, but the brothers Boyer from Alba, Missouri, were the rival third basemen.

Seven of the marble cutter Vern Boyer's sons of a family of 14 children not only played professional baseball, but three made the majors. First, Cloyd, nicknamed "Junior" by the Cardinals, was a pitcher handicapped by injury. Next was Kenton, also originally a pitcher, and finally Cletis, a gifted third baseman with the Yankees and a better fielder even than obvious family leader Ken.

Clete had known Series success. So, many fans pulled for Ken, but things didn't seem right by the fourth game. After a Series split in St. Louis, where legendary Whitey Ford folded physically, and where the Yanks lucked out the second game over rarely rattled young Bob Gibson, the mighty Mantle broke up the next game at New York.

In the home ninth of a tight duel between the Yanks' Jim Bouton and Cards' veteran southpaw Curt Simmons, Mick hit the knuckleball reliever Barney Schultz's first pitch sky high into the right-field seats. New York was up 2–1 and headed to a rout the next day with a first-inning three-run dismissal of 20-game winner Ray Sadecki.

The only bright play for the Cardinals, other than admirable long relief by Roger Craig and Ron Taylor, came after a double by Mantle. Mickey reacted mirthfully to shortstop Dick Groat's reenactment of Mike Shannon's silly leap the day before, trying to flag down Mantle's far-flung homer. Slyly, Groat picked off the relaxed Mantle at second base.

The dark comedy took a delightful turn in the sixth when the Cardinals filled the bases against lefty Al Downing. In the spotlighted clutch, Ken Boyer reached down and hooked a grand slam into the left-field seats.

When Ken circled the bases, brother Clete impishly stood in the baseline at third. Passing kid brother, Ken playfully slapped him on the family fanny.

That 4–3 win held up. Thanks also to Gibson's pitching and fielding, the Cards won the final game at New York 5–2 on Tim McCarver's three-run homer in the tenth. The Series edge enabled the Cards to withstand an old-fashioned Yankee-slugging 8–3 victory in the return to Sportsman's Park.

In the seventh game, with Brock and Boyer homering, Gibson withstood three late home-run shots as Keane, in his last act and leery of his bullpen, stuck with the starter. As the manager put it, "I'm sticking with the man's heart."

Actually, Keane could have meant Boyer as well as Gibson. The dramatic 7–5 success was summed up the next day in one of the most remarkable *Post-Dispatch* Page One displays ever: "Cardinals Win Championship . . . China Drops Its First H-Bomb . . . Soviets Oust Khrushchev . . . Yankees Fire Berra as Manager . . . Keane Spurns Contract Renewal . . ."

★

1965
Consolation Conquest
Big Red Win Runner-Up Bowl

The football Cardinals' post-season victory in 1965 was worthy for more than being the only playoff win in St. Louis uniforms. It was against a team headed for destiny, Vince Lombardi's Green Bay Packers.

Back there in early January 1965, the Big Red met the Pack in the Playoff Bowl before a record crowd of 56,216 in Miami's Orange Bowl. The Playoff Bowl, more accurately labeled the Runner-Up Bowl, was between the two top second-place teams, a means—as in baseball's period of two All-Star games—to supplement the players' pensions. Until the cleated Cardinals beat Green Bay 24–17, no Western Division team had won. Detroit had won it the past three seasons for the East. And in '64 the Packers had whipped Cleveland 40–23 and were favored over St. Louis by seven points. Offensively, in a game where the Cards' Charley Johnson outperformed the Packers' Bart Starr, the star was the Big Red's number three, second-year wide receiver Billy Gambrell from South Carolina.

The little second-year Gamecock caught six of Johnson's 14 passes for 184 yards and two touchdowns. Billy the Kid was voted Most Valuable Player in a game that, in a time of lower salaries, yielded $800 to each Big Red player.

A highlight, too, was a St. Louis defense that shut down Lombardi's vaunted power sweep and halfback Paul Hornung's option pass. When Jimmy Burson intercepted Hornung's pass in the end zone, he locked up the victory.

The defense was outstanding as the Cardinals held rugged Jim Taylor—with a 1,000-yard season—to just 30 in 12 carries and Hornung to just 15 in five tries.

With a nod to defensive coach Chuck Drulis, head coach Wally Lemm noted that the Big Red had used a special defense that limited the Pack's great running game to 52 yards. Explained Lemm, "We tried to give a little different look on every play, going from a 4–3 to 4–2, and we combined it with a lot of red-dogging."

Ah, memories of old recount the seventh time Starr was dumped on his britches by Joe Robb, Luke Owens, Larry Stallings, Bill Koman, and Don Brumm. Johnson, by contrast with 243 passing yards to just 126 for Green Bay, was sacked just once.

Gambrell, taking over for injured Sonny Randle at mid-season, scored on an eight-yard play and from his 10. His 164 yards were a Playoff Bowl record, breaking one set by Bobby Mitchell of Cleveland against Detroit.

Johnson, the Phi Beta Kappa quarterback, hailed the award to Gambrell and also to the key interceptions by Burson and Jerry Stovall.

Said Dr. Johnson, the Ph.D., "We don't throw deep too often, but Billy is fast enough to go deep when he has to. He has to know me as well as I know him. I was looking for Jackie Smith on the big one, but when he didn't look around, I saw Billy."

They were gifted guys, the Playoff Bowl kings of 1964. When for instance, Bobby Joe Conrad suffered a shoulder injury, Jim Bakken replaced him—and of course, win, lose, or draw Bakken always kicked a field goal.

★

WILDCAT: Larry Wilson, longtime best free safety in pro football, was the football Cardinals' first Hall of Famer, a master of the safety blitz and playing hurt.

1967
Gibby and Company
Bob Gibson Was Great in the '67 Series—and Two Others

Bob Gibson was good enough to win three games in the 1967 World Series, and to pitch on a broken leg, if only briefly.

Gibby the Great, number 45 with a .45-caliber arm as a pitcher, was one of the best—and maybe most competitive—in a career marked by many things, namely a record low 1.12 earned-run average for a 300-inning pitcher, a 17-strikeout World Series performance, and the ability to win seven in a row in the Series spotlight.

Another highlight came in 1967 at the All-Star break when, as the accident occurred, oddsmakers in Las Vegas lowered the league-leading Cardinals' chances. Thanks to the ability of young right-hander Nelson Briles to come out of the bullpen for eight straight victories, the Redbirds didn't miss Gibson in the standings, but Red Schoendienst, a 7-come-11 natural then managing the ball club, couldn't be fooled.

He needed the all-around athlete from Creighton University, and after three tune-up performances Red wanted 13–7 Gibby against Carl Yastrzemski, Jim Lonborg, and the Boston Red Sox.

In a career year, en route to the Hall of Fame, Yaz led the American League in average, hits, homers, and RBIs, turning in a Triple Crown performance and playing remarkably well in the outfield, too.

Lonborg was the top hand in the American League, winning 22 games, and proving essential in the decisive last game of the regular season. So he couldn't start the first game of the World Series, a handicap, but not as severe as Gibson's when Pittsburgh's Roberto Clemente lined that shot off the rangy right-hander's legs. Pole-axed, the competitive fire drove Gibson to his feet for a couple of more deliveries before he collapsed.

Backed by a lineup that lost the National League's two top MVP players, Orlando Cepeda and Tim McCarver, Gibson had to rely on himself and another spirited World Series great who also would be a first-time eligible elected to the Hall of Fame—Lou Brock.

Brock, expanding on a solid regular season of 206 hits and 52 stolen bases, soared to .414 against the Sox with 12 hits and the most Series stolen bases ever—seven.

Thanks only to Gibson's tight first-game pitching—he shut out Boston except for a homer by pitcher Jose Santiago—the Cardinals gained a 2–1 win because wise old Roger Maris bounced twice to the right side of the infield with the second baseman playing back. Gibson, walking one, struck out 10.

Lonborg, delayed a day, used two homers by Yastrzemski and no-hit pitching into the eighth to get a 5–0 victory. The only hit Lonborg allowed was a double by Julian Javier.

Back at St. Louis, blanking Yaz, Briles bulldogged a 5–2 victory, and Gibson, even more effective in an easy 6–0 reprise over Santiago, walked just one and fanned six.

Lonborg again was a giant in a three-hit, 3–1 victory, marred only by a homer by Maris, and then Yaz and Rico Petrocelli punished rookie retread Dick Hughes in the sixth game, 8–4.

So again it was time for the cliché, "There is no tomorrow," and the Boston morning tabloid splashed a short-order headline, "Lonborg and champagne." Jim had only two days' rest and Gibson three, but Gibby was hot under the collar because he had been frozen out of breakfast at a crowded motel.

Rescued by a ham-and-egg sandwich bought to Fenway Park by a sympathetic reporter, Robert (Hoot) Gibson was at his best. He struck out 10 and hit a home run. Lonborg was long gone when three-game Gibby, winning going away 7–1, had his champagne—with his second ham-and-egg sandwich!

★

FALLING INTO FORMATION: *The 1967 Cardinals, led by manager Red Schoendienst (far right), form a pregame lineup for the hometown crowd anticipating a Series victory.*

Birth of the Blues

Love for an Ailing Son Was Sid Salomon's Finest Hour

The birth of the Blues, hockey's Blues, resulted entirely from the love of father for son, of Sidney Salomon, Jr., for young Sid the Third. Only a smart businessman, which the elder Salomon was, would have paid more than he needed for a building—and later paid more for players than he should have.

Sid Salomon III was ill much of his adult life, battling a low-keyed Hodgkin's cancer even when playing golf almost as well as and even more often than Sid, Jr., who came up the hard way. The New York–born kid held down five jobs at one time during the depression, including insurance sales. He began selling at age 19 and made the Million Dollar Round Table routine.

Yet his first job leaving Culver Military Academy as an all-around athlete was writing a weekly golf column for the old St. Louis Times, which bellied up in 1932. When Sid came out of World War II a major, he had his handsome son as an inspiration.

By then, briefly a Cardinal stockholder under Democratic friend Bob Hannegan—Salomon often headed the national Democratic committee—he dabbled with Bill Veeck and the Browns and even moved a Triple-A farm club to Miami, but it was the boy and the sport the kid loved—hockey—that turned around both their lives.

When the National Hockey League planned a six-club expansion for 1967, St. Louis wasn't on the list. The sixth franchise was earmarked for Baltimore, but—wait!—the Chicago Wirz family had a building to unload—the seldom-used St. Louis Arena, a white elephant. If Mr. Salomon would pay an overpriced $4 million for a building once offered for sale at $250,000, the building was his and—yeah—that franchise.

So to please the 20-year-old boy, Sid paid through the nose and then spent even more than he could afford for veteran player stars and to turn the Oakland Avenue pigsty into a palace. Salomon, a spit-and-polish guy, scrubby-Dutched the building. He ran out the rats and cats from an unfinished dirty-level basement, established a private club there, increased the seating capacity, and gave the building what it needed most except for air-conditioning—escalators. Later when Salomon ran out of money, Ralston-Purina added the cold blowers that turned the Arena into a year-round building, one that even won NCAA tournament approval.

Trouble was, trying to placate young Sid's love for his team and desire to give the Blues the best schedule edge, the Salomons didn't invite as much business as they could or should have. Even though at times as "The Thing" in town, filling up with handsomely dressed men and women, the Blues fell short in receipts and profits despite leading the league in attendance. The bottom line turned red.

But except for the other bottom line in the standings—the Stanley Cup—they reached the final three straight years under a different playoff format. They signed up future Hall of Famers, paying veterans like Glenn Hall, Jacques Plante, Doug Harvey, and Dickie Moore more than they ever had seen.

The Blues established Scotty Bowman as a championship coach and Barclay Plager, Al Arbour, and Noel Picard as local legends.

Time was too short for the Salomons with the team and town they loved. Sid, Jr., nursing a bad heart, died where he used to entertain his players—Florida—at 76 in 1986. Young Sid, who had fought the good fight against the big "C," was only 51 two years later when he followed his father the way Pop used to follow him on the golf course.

★

10,000 WORDS: If that's what they said about a meaningful photo, they were right. This one reflects the deep love of father for son. Sidney Salomon, Jr., striding with characteristic cigar at his back, a good golfer clucking like a mother hen over his competitive young son, Sid III. Young Sid's good game was handicapped ultimately by a fatal illness.

A Schocking Result

Ron Schock's Overtime Goal Put the Blues in the Stanley Cup Finals

Before Ron Schock shocked the Minnesota North Stars with a double-overtime goal for a playoff victory on May 3, 1968, catapulting the Blues into the Stanley Cup against perennial champion Montreal, the playoffs had a feature almost as exciting as the finish.

Young coach Scotty Bowman would recount later with a smile how he hoped the Blues' minor-league farm club at Kansas City would lose the night before the seventh game of the first round of the playoffs. The Blues' foe was the regular-season champion of the Campbell Division, Philadelphia, and the Blues had carried Philly into the seventh game there.

Available for the Blues, because Kansas City had lost the night before, was a pink-cheeked veteran with a jelly-bean nose, player-coach Doug Harvey, longtime defensive standout of the Canadiens. What Doug did that game was to slow down the pace with grace and skill. The Hall of Fame geezer was in complete control.

Like a member of a popular holiday ice show—the easy-does-it graybeards, "The Old Smoothies"—Harvey took charge so that in the final minute the Blues held a one-goal lead as Philly lifted its goalie in a face-off at center ice.

How many times did you ever see a player win a face-off at mid-ice and score? Red Berenson did it that night, hitting the bull's eye in a 3–1 upset.

So with Cesare Maniago outplaying St. Louis's great Glenn Hall in the semifinal round of the playoffs against Minnesota, the seventh game went into a tense double overtime. Before the game, 43-year-old Harvey was told his mother was desperately ill back home in Montreal, and team captain Al Arbour returned from the injury list.

Beforehand, general manager Lynn Patrick urged Ron Schock, whom he had signed as a big-bonus baby

at Boston, to shuck his helmet. Patrick had a hunch it would be a big night for Schock, who had started just one game previously in the series.

A record Arena hockey crowd of 15,586 watched the big one scoreless until fewer than four minutes remained when a deflected shot eluded Hall.

The Blues skated onto the ice with time running out. Forty-three seconds later, Dickie Moore tied the game on a screened shot that eluded Cesare Maniago. For one, young Bob Plager knew future Hall of Famer Dickie Moore would score. Said Plager afterward in awe, "I knew Dickie was going to score when he went over the boards. He was holding the stick so tight, the veins were standing out in his arms. And he had that special look in his eyes. When he gets that look, he's going to score."

Yes, and Moore played with a heavy heart because his father-in-law had died in Canada.

Death that season of Minnesota's Bill Masterson had caused Schock and many others to go to a helmet, but as Patrick noted, Ron hadn't played well with the headgear. So, bareheaded, he shocked the Blues into the finals with his bell-ringer two minutes into overtime.

That cliffhanger, as Gus Kyle would put it, sent the weary Blues, many of them over-aged, into a next night's playoff against captain Jean Belliveau's well-rested Canadiens. It really should have been no contest, but Mr. Goalie, Glenn Hall, came up big when the chips went down.

The Blues went down to heavily favored Montreal four straight, but every game was just a one-goal difference, twice in overtime, and capping the climax of that unforgettable first Blues' season, the goalkeeper of the losing team was named Most Valuable in the Stanley Cup playoffs.

★

SHOCKED: Himself and all others when seldom-seen Ron Schock scored probably the most significant goal in the Blues' history, an overtime effort over Minnesota that put St. Louis in the 1968 Stanley Cup against Montreal. The man who benefitted, Scotty Bowman, didn't sip from Lord Stanley's cup here but did numerous times elsewhere as hockey's winningest coach.

1968
Sweet 17

Bob Gibson Records 17 Strikeouts in Series Opener

In many ways, considering the bright blue-skies' weather, the hitting ability of the Detroit Tigers, and significance of the situation, Bob Gibson's 17-strikeout first game of the 1968 World Series just might be the best exhibition ever of fanning the foe.

Strikeouts for a game rarely have reached 20 in the majors, however, the incidence is increasing in part because of the hardball pitching of king-sized pitchers and also full-cut swinging of hitters who unlike a Ted Williams, Joe DiMaggio, or Stan Musial of a generation ago, don't see the stigma in striking out, or, as they probably like to put it, "of lining out to the catcher."

Once upon a time, the strikeout was infrequent, especially in the World Series, played in the daytime until 1973. Surprise starter Howard Ehmke of the Philadelphia A's raised the strikeout record to 13 when he slow-curved the Chicago Cubs out of a blurred Wrigley Field background in 1929. Brooklyn's Carl Erskine used a great overhand curve and change-up to get 14 against the Yankees at Brooklyn in 1953, and master southpaw Sandy Koufax of the whistling fastball and sharp curve made it 15 against the Yanks in the opening game of the Series sweep in '63.

Koufax, who retired at his peak because of painful rheumatic problems with his left arm, called the turn on Gibson's total or, more accurately, Sandy's personal pique when Gibby was at his peak. Then doing baseball nationally on the radio, Sandy explained the day before the 1968 Series began at Busch Stadium that Gibby had not been given his just due.

Koufax noted with admiration that Gibson hung in there with an arthritic condition only slightly less severe than Koufax's own. Yes, said Sandy, and a fabulous 1.2 earned run average and 13 shutouts, overshadowed by glamorous Denny McLain's 31 victories for Detroit.

Said Koufax, "He'll eat him alive for lunch tomorrow," meaning Gibson would chew up McLain. Sandy might have added, "And for dinner, too."

The game was played in bright bluebird weather, the '68 Series that was won by the Tigers largely because of number-two starter Mickey Lolich's three-game string.

In the well-publicized opener between the pitching giants, Gibson struck out the leadoff man and third-spot hitter Al Kaline in the first inning. Round two, Gibson struck out the side—Norm Cash, Willie Horton, and Jim Northrup—and when he threw a called third strike past Bill Freehan in the third, he had fanned five in a row. McLain even obliged by bunting a foul third strike.

The strikeouts mounted, but not so fast. Kaline was called out in the fourth, and Don Wert was caught looking in the fifth. Mickey Stanley, who had two of the Tigers' five hits, struck out in the sixth, Northrup and Freehan in the seventh. When Eddie Mathews, pinch-hitting for Wert in the eighth, dragged his bat back to the bench, it was 14 strikeouts going into the ninth.

The packed house—54,000 plus—was buzzing in the ninth when big number 45 with the wide shoulders and narrow hips strode to the mound. He had walked only one and led 4–0, but he gave up Stanley's second hit.

Now, another future Hall of Famer, Kaline, who would rally to hit .379, whiffed for the third time. With the scoreboard flashing a record-tying 15, catcher Tim McCarver hurried out to pep talk the pitcher. Growling, Gibson told Timmy to get his bucket behind the basket.

Gibby struck out Cash for the third time for the record, and then he made it 17 by breaking off a game-ending slider that froze Horton.

At least, said a jubilant McCarver, "Gibby didn't tell me what he'd told me before—'The only thing you know about pitching is that you can't hit it.'"

★

GIBBY THE GREAT: As Dizzy Dean used to say, "Show me a guy who doesn't follow through, and I'll show you a guy who ain't foggin' the ball." Big No. 45 Bob Gibson, as if he was firing a .45, followed through, fogged the ball, and, as Ol' Diz noted, still got back into fielding position. He was a great fielder, good hitter, a winner, and greatest competitor.

1968
Masterful Finish
Bob Goalby and the Green-Coat Masters

Bob Goalby could have used a break, but he didn't need one that big; Argentine's Roberto de Vicenzo signed the wrong card after the 18th hole at Augusta's fabled Masters. As Belleville's Bob said it with a touch of his competitive fire, "I like to think I could have beat him in a playoff."

But there wasn't the extra round the Monday after the 1968 tournament ended even-Stephen, because Tommy Aaron, scoring for de Vicenzo, recorded a "4" on the 17th hole, where the Argentine birdied with "3." Recklessly, the emotional South American signed his card that toted up one more than Goalby's six-under 66.

So the penalty cost the stroke and gave Goalby his first major victory—the Masters major—after several near-victories. For instance, in the 1961 U.S. Open when he sat in the clubhouse with a lead after a 71 finish, Gene Littler snuck in by a stroke. And a year later in the PGA he closed with a 67, only to have Gary Player finish even better for a one-stroke difference.

So, yeah, Goalby, then age 38, had paid his dues in the game he had begun to play as a caddy over in Belleville; and he was a favorite of the East St. Louis's deep-throated sports editor of the old *Journal*, the late Ellis Veech. To Veech, a prep and college football and basketball referee, the home-area kid was a favorite even though Ellis once had to point a warming finger at the roughneck.

Goalby, you see, was red-faced and ruggedly handsome—good enough to have the University of Illinois football quarterback job in his golf sack—but he loved the humbling game of golf too much to stay in school. Trouble was, his competitive zeal cost him in tiffs with caddies, reporters, and galleries. His own worst enemy for too long was himself.

But Robert George Goalby had the skills, best reflected one sunny spring in the '61 St. Petersburg Open when he birdied a record-straight holes. The result was a brilliant 261 score for the 72 holes, five strokes off the record for St. Pete's 6,296-yard Pasadena course.

As spectator Don McGranaghan put it—McGranaghan, a good-luck New York state police lieutenant fan of the baseball Cardinals—Goalby was only "two blades of grass and a three-putt green" away from tying Sam Snead's PGA record of 59.

Big-winner Snead, veteran Doug Ford, and golfing rival Gene Littler were firm friends who found Goalby so much on his game before the '68 Masters that Snead huffed after losing too many five-dollar Nassaus, "Hey, Goalby, I haven't seen your name in the papers much about winning. What are you trying to do, take it all out on old Sam?"

So Goalby was right-on in the Masters, 11 under at 277 on rounds of 70–70–71–66. It was the first major victory in a pro career that began 11 years earlier, as sweet as defeat was sour for de Vicenzo on the Latin's 45th birthday.

Except for senior golf money-winnings, Goalby never would have quite the kind of career for which he and area fans had hoped. His nephew and pupil, Jay Haas, did pretty well, too, but no one ever could take the title or the prestigious green coat away from Belleville's Bob.

When Goalby arrived back from Atlanta by plane, a crowd of well wishers, including his wife and children, overwhelmed him, impressing all others except one. Arriving on the same plane was Georgia's controversial governor, Lester Maddox. Maddox thought the cheers for him and came down, waving his arms. Sorry, Guv!

MASTERS FOR A DAY: Grinning Bob Goalby of Belleville was front and center in the 1963 version of the famed Masters tournament at Augusta, Georgia, drawing from a happy predecessor, Gay Brewer, the pleasure of putting on Goalby's traditional green championship jacket. (right) Goalby in true form.

★

1968
The Bigger They Are . . .
The Harder They Fall to Dan Devine's Tigers

In Dan Devine's divine decade of the 1960s—Missouri lost only 22 of 102 football games—Ol' Mizzou was at its finest against the prestigious Big 10 and against two of the game's big-name coaches: Michigan's Bo Schembechler and Alabama's Bear Bryant.

Tiger triumphs over Michigan at Ann Arbor and over Alabama in Jacksonville's Gator Bowl highlighted a period when the team twice turned down bowl bids and won four out of five. Overall, Ol' Mizzou was the only major school that did not suffer a season with more than three defeats.

Included in the centerpiece 10 of Devine's 13 seasons as football headmaster at Columbia was his record against the Big 10, arguably the top college conference in any period. Devine's teams went 9–1–1 in that stretch against the storied old Western Conference, losing only to Northwestern in the 1963 opener of a 7–3 season for the Tigers.

Parenthetically, that game preceded one of Devine's—and Missouri's—most significant victories by a week. At Little Rock, Mizzou played Arkansas, coached by Frank Broyles, who had jumped ship after the single 1957 season at Faurot Field. Broyles, like Devine, was headed for the College Football Hall of Fame, but he left Mizzou angry and agitated. Devine, reflecting the attitude, was a sidelined jumping-jack in the 7–6 victory.

Although soft spoken, Dan could be testy. For instance, when he graduated from Minnesota's Duluth State and the superintendent of schools at International Falls, Minnesota, didn't think he had a big enough name. After trundling across country to Michigan with a wife and twin daughters, and a baby crib on the top of a battered car, Devine did so well coaching unbeaten East Jordan high school teams that he earned—and won—a break. Michigan State hired him as junior varsity coach, at less than half his $3,600 salary so he could get a Master's degree. Head coaching success at Arizona State led him to Missouri in 1958—and back to Michigan.

As mentioned in KFNS's century series, a 1959 come-from-behind win over the Wolverines, 20–15, set the tone for the timber and quality of Devine's teams. By '69, mighty Michigan was back with a brilliant new coach, Bo Schembechler, and Ol' Mizzou was pretty hot stuff, too.

Fact is, when they kicked off at Ann Arbor, Devine had perhaps his best ever Missouri team. The Tigers were headed to the Big Eight championship and a trip to the Orange Bowl.

Michigan, using a final-game upset of Ohio State, went to the Rose Bowl. So the match-up was monumental. Michigan led early, muffed another scoring chance, then fell behind, and yet closed to within five points in the fourth quarter. Here, the Tigers' Mike Bennett blocked a kick, setting up a 24-yard field goal by Henry Brown, and then Joe Moore zipped 62 yards on a draw play for a touchdown, leading to a deceptive 40–17 score—the only home game Schembechler lost in his first 10 years as coach of the Maize and Blue.

Bigger, still, was the Gator Bowl game the year before, 1968. Proud 'Bama was a heavy favorite and college's winningest coach, Bear Bryant, the topic of a week-long build up. Devine, who had a habit of making his teams very sorry for themselves on road games—you know, us few against their many—loved the underdog role.

Missouri, throwing only two passes, ran for 402 yards, including 179 for bridegroom tailback Greg Cook. Quarterback Terry McMillan kept 18 times for 76 yards on the option. And the Black and Gold defense left the Crimson Tide black and blue, dumping quarterback Scott Hunter on the seat of his white pants—45 yards lost in a game of only 65 yards total offense.

Beneath that checkered hound's tooth hat, Bear Bryant groaned hoarsely, "They ran up and down the field just as if we were a barber's college."

★

DANIEL IN THE TIGERS DEN: Low-key Dan Devine was a fireball in games where Ol' Mizzou faced the biggest challenge—on the road.

1969

To Cooperstown, Early and Late

Steve Carlton Began His Hall of Fame Trip There

If there's any player who took a short course on the long hill to baseball's Cooperstown, where many try and few make it, the honor would go to a rangy Redbird left-hander named Steve Carlton, who joined the ball club at the Hall of Fame and capped his St. Louis career with a major-league record 19 strikeouts.

It's not that the 19 strikeouts Carlton rung up in Busch Stadium in late 1969 was necessarily his best night, certainly not the best season. The rangy big guy was just filling out physically and financially into a power-pitching bull.

But it was in a game—lost, of all things!—to a New York's Mets' Cinderella season of 1969—that Carlton displayed the strength of ability and determination that would drive him to 329 victories, second most ever for a left-hander. Warren Spahn won 363.

"Lefty" to most—tall, dark, handsome, and a Greta Garbo in knickers—the big guy was incommunicado most of his 24 seasons in the bigs, but he was so impressive a miffed media voted him first-time election into the place where he had begun his career—Cooperstown, New York.

Actually, given a $5,000 bonus as a junior college kid in Miami, Carlton had worked a few assorted innings and games in 1965 before the call-up from top farm club Tulsa in '66. The Cardinals were playing Minnesota in the annual Hall of Fame mid-season inter-league exhibition at Cooperstown.

There, listening to Ted Williams outpoint articulate Casey Stengel as both were tapped for Hall of Fame induction, big Steve might have stayed. Four times he was National League Cy Young award-winner, helped the Cardinals win two pennants, and with third baseman Mike Schmidt, he virtually willed Philadelphia out of longtime mediocrity into excellence.

Dealt away in a dispute with angry Gussie Busch after a 20-game season in 1971, Carlton made it St. Louis's worst deal since the Cards gave away a young right-hander named Three-Finger Brown to the Cubs for fading veteran Jack Taylor in 1904.

Immediately with the Phillies, dealt a half-hour before he recanted his salary demands, Carlton responded with a remarkable 27–10 record for a last-place ball club that won only 52 times. He led in innings pitched, 346, with a 1.97 earned run average.

It was just as incredible as that murky, rainy September night in '69 when, too hot to cool down, the marvelous Mets blurred Carlton's 19-strikeout night with a pair of two-run homers by Ron Swoboda. New York was four up over the league leader they had caught and devoured—the Cubs.

The strain was considerable on the left arm of fantastic faddist Carlton, who had built himself into a 6'4" monster. Lefty endured a 26-minute delay at the outset and a 54-minute interruption because of rain.

He struck out Amos Otis four times, Tom Agee, Ed Charles, Al Weis, Gary Gentry, and even Swoboda twice each. Going down on strikes once each were Donn Clendennon, Jerry Grote, and Tug McGraw.

Redbirds' pitch charter then, Charley Galatti, had nine swinging strikeouts and 10 called, 12 on fastballs, five on sliders, and two on curves, a total of 152 pitches—96 fastballs, 22 curves, and the jagged pitch that got better with the years, Lefty's slider, 34 of them.

Ahead were the glory years past 40—six of 20 games—whether for guts, glory, or extra cash, he pitched too long, until age 44. Those last four years, he won only 12 of his 329 victories and was saddled with 34 of 244 career defeats.

Back there, that tide-turning night in '69, Carlton sat exhausted in the Cardinals' clubhouse past 1 a.m., sipping a beer. Big Steve sighed, "I'm exhausted, stiff, sore, and could sit here all night, beaten by the Amazin' Mets and Super Swat."

Swoboda or, as Casey Stengel called him, "Soboda."

★

THE ONE THAT GOT AWAY: Ouch, Steve Carlton was lost in a trade with Philadelphia when the big boss Gussie Busch resented a holdout in 1972. Too late, big Steve agreed to terms. Already dealt to the Phillies, a 19-strikeout whiz with the Redbirds, the 27-year-old lefty responded remarkably. He gained 27 wins for the last-place team, en route to 329 victories and the Hall of Fame.

Goals to Go—6!

The Night Red Berenson Saw the Record Red Light

Like the Red Baron of old, who menaced the skyways as Germany's one-man aerial show in World War I, hockey's Red Baron—the Blues' Gordon (Red) Berenson—zeroed in one night and on target with a record to remember: Six goals!

The event occurred at Philadelphia's Spectrum, then and now a tough place to win even without the Broad Street Bullies. But that spectacular night— November 5, 1968—even hard-nosed Philly fans cheered as the Red Baron shot out the lights.

Berenson's six goals in an 8–0 game tied a modern NHL record, set by Detroit's Syd Howe in 1944. And when the Blues' 29-year-old star pounded in four goals in the second period, he matched a mark set by Chicago's Busher Jackson back in '34, oddly the one single season St. Louis had a club in the league before expansion in 1967.

Berenson was one of the many good players who benefitted from the NHL's doubled size. Unusual, especially for a Canadian player, he came armed with a college degree from the University of Michigan, where he majored in business and in scoring goals for the Wolverines.

He was a red-haired son of red-haired parents, son of a Regina city fireman of Norwegian descent and a Scotch-Irish mother. The Saskatchewan province city of $100,000 was near enough to fishing and hunting, which appealed to the outdoorsman.

At age 19, Red married Joy Cameron, his attractive high-school sweetheart. At Ann Arbor, Joy worked as a secretary to help supplement his hockey scholarship. Summers, Red worked as a security patrol officer at Chevrolet's Detroit plant.

A $10,000 contract with Montreal wasn't bad by standards, but Red liked it less when traded to New York—the Big Apple had too many folks for him—and he was hunting deer in the Catskills when he got the good news he had been traded to St. Louis.

Berenson and Blues' coach Scotty Bowman hit it off well, the coach appreciating the free-skating, forechecking skill of the 6'1", 193-pound forward. Red appreciated many things, including the night he hit the target like Germany's fabled Manfred von Richtofen.

At 16:42 of the first period, Berenson grabbed a loose puck in the Flyers' zone, powered past defenseman Ed Van Impe, faked out goalie Doug Favell.

The next four goals in the second period came probably in the shortest period ever—four in 9:09. First, Red picked up a pass from Bill McCreary, juked defenseman Joe Watson, and beat Favell with a high corner shot. Next, he drilled Camille Henry's drop pass over Favell. Thirty-two seconds later, he zipped in on a rebound and scored when the puck banked off one goalpost to the other and found the net.

In the third period, Berenson assisted on a goal scored by Henry, and then, with Philadelphia fans leading the cheers, he skated around Van Impe and twanged the cords from 45 feet out.

Here, a chant rose of "Go, Red, go" to standing ovation and applause. Favell saved another with a great shot 58 feet away.

Afterward, gallantly and a team player, Berenson said, "You know, I think I'd rather have had seven assists."

Good man, that blue-eyed redhead—later a coach of the Blues and then of alma mater Michigan's NCAA champions—Red Baron Berenson.

★

RED-HOT REDHEAD: Gordon (Red) Berenson, University of Michigan graduate by way of Canada, later coach of the St. Louis Blues and an NCAA championship team at his alma mater, had his—and one of hockey's—finest hours when he fired in six goals at a most unlikely place, Philadelphia's Sprectrum.

1970
"Turn Out the Lights"
The Party Was Over in St. Louis's Finest Monday Night Win

Monday Night Football, a television institution for a generation and rarely a St. Louis achievement, was almost as rare as the football Cardinals' 38–0 shutout over Dallas that first season of Monday television, 1970.

Charley Winner's '70 team, en route to one of the Big Red's greatest seasons that fizzled at the finish, was on a gambler's roll. Three straight weeks, the cleated Cards shut out NFL opponents—Houston, 41–0; New England, 31–0; and then—socko—Dallas, 38–zip.

The climactic contest down there in the Cotton Bowl marked the first time the Cowboys had been blanked in regular-season play in the franchise's 11-year history. And it came with embarrassing ease, especially to television's new kid on the block in the infant Monday night venture, Don Meredith.

With the unexpected death of former Cardinal and Mizzou quarterback Pitchin' Paul Christman, a colorful commentator, the role went to recently retired Meredith.

Dandy Don would go on to a few colorful seasons teaming with the controversial Howard Cosell. He would venture forth also to a few good films as a good or bad guy in movies, but he was obnoxious most of the night for those not among the 69,333 spectators.

There, the crowd saw Dick Voris's defense put up a great show, which included a shut-down, closed-up, and strung-out night for Meredith's successor, Craig Morton. Only the last minute substitution of a kid with a date with destiny—Roger Staubach—silenced the clamor for the often booed Morton.

Offensively, meanwhile, with Jim Hart passing well, MacArthur Lane running the same, and Johnny Roland running as if at his peak, the cleated Cards buried Tom Landry's highly touted team. The Cowboys dropped two games behind the division-leading 7–2 Big Red.

Roland, benched as first-string running back, came back as the second-string fullback with Cal Edwards hurt and put on a show with 78 yards in 16 carries, plus a couple of additional efforts. The former Mizzou All-American ran back a first-period punt 74 yards for a touchdown, romped in for two more touchdowns from 10 yards and then three. He also caught two passes for 17 yards.

With press box observer Red Miller detecting the weak-side linebacker and defensive end pursuing strong on every play, flanker John Gilliam rushed 48 yards for a touchdown. And a killer came on a 29-yard scoring romp by Ray Shivers in the final minutes.

Meanwhile, assuring the third straight shutout in which St. Louis scored 113 points to none, second-season defensive master Roger Wehrli intercepted an end zone pass.

The brothers Bidwill, still on speaking terms, took it big. Stormy put on a cowboy hat and "ya-hooed" with a Texas accent that seemed Chicagoan. And brother Bill grinned through post-game toasts from Dallas brass.

From this height, 1970 Big Red nose-dived with only a tie, a victory, and three consecutive defeats, giving the New York Giants the division title and costing Charley Winner his job as coach, creating an area of conflict between the Bidwills.

Winner's roller-coaster records of 8–5–1, 6–7–1, 9–4–1, and 4–9–1 before that 8–5–1 cost the coach, whom Billy liked better than Stormy. But none distinguished better than that November Monday night when Don Meredith was forced to concede: "Turn out the lights. The party's over!"

★

JOHNNY OH OR OH JOHNNY: A college Hall of Famer at Missouri, veteran Johnny Roland (23) came off the bench to star in the Big Red's rout of the Cowboys. Jim Hart (inset)

1972

The Granddaddy Upset

Al Onofrio's Over Notre Dame

Said the senior Mizzou fullback from Webster Groves, Don Johnson, who scored two touchdowns that drab October day in rainy 1972 at South Bend, Indiana, "It felt as if the whole state of Missouri was running with us. It was emotional, like playing a big bowl game. Playing a great team like Notre Dame was a great honor. I guess you'd say we were "up'!"

Yes indeed, Don, "up" as in as high-as-an-elephant's-eye for perhaps the greatest college football upset ever. The final score, flashed on the wire service score sheets—MISSOURI 30, NOTRE DAME 26—prompted more than one newspaper editor and radio and television producer to ask for a double check.

This was, you see, just the week after Bob Devaney's Cornhuskers bid for a third straight national championship was sealed by a 62–0 rout over Missouri.

For Al Onofrio, the Tigers' second-year head coach, the debacle at Lincoln came after a devastating last-play defeat at Oklahoma State and, counting the prevous season, left him with only a 3–13 record. Hardly good for the successor to his old friend and longtime boss, Dan Devine.

Here, Onofrio reached a dangerous decision as a head coach. He saw the Nebraska game film privately and then stored it away. There would be no customary game review or finger pointing.

Al kept up his spirits, simplified his offense, and eased up on the team. He felt relaxed as the Missouri team flew to South Bend, greeeted by the steady drizzle that would keep the that packed house of 59,075 as miserable as the game for the obvious home field fans of the Fighting Irish.

For probably the finest hours in Ol' Mizzou's football history, then 84 years, the 1972 Tigers handled themselves with professional poise, their footing as sure as if they had web feet and the ball as if it were wet only on one side. Notre Dame's unbeaten Irish were a four-to-five-touchdown favorite.

Missouri did not fumble, had no interceptions, and not until late, when they were killing the clock at the finish, did they suffer a penalty. Only Knute Rockne, the Irish's perfectionist, could have appreciated the precision that went into the ball control off the Wishbone and the "I," but Ara Parseghian tried.

The brilliant Notre Dame coach, saluting the manner the Tigers controlled the ball, said, "There are only so many minutes in a game." Mizzou rushed 72 times to Notre Dame's 46 and totaled 79 plays to 63. The Irish gained 27 yards more, but they turned over the ball four times, twice each on fumbles and interceptions.

In-and-out quarterback John Cherry lived up to his surname—Cherry on the cake—with a pinpoint passing performance. Junior college transfer Tommy Reamon from Newport News, Virginia, brought good news with 76 yards on 16 tries outside, setting up inside traps for fullback Don Johnson, who rumbled 28 times for 87 yards and, as mentioned, two touchdowns.

With coach Onofrio's Columbia neighbor Greg Hill kicking three field goals, motivated Missouri scored on the first five possessions and built a 16-point lead into the fourth quarter.

Afterward, Onofrio walked around in a warm, golden haze with a silly grin of disbelief. Back home, he got a letter from Nebraska's Devaney, the coach who had annihilated him and had seen Notre Dame beat Michigan State. Said Devaney, to make a long letter short, "I honestly believe that your preparation—mentally, physically, and technically—was the best done by any coach in the history of football. . . ."

★

GIANT KILLER: Al Onofrio, who had a roller-coaster career in seven exciting seasons as head coach at Ol' Mizzou, is carried off after the most glamorous of his upsets over Alabama, Ohio State, Southern California, and three times Nebraska. It was at South Bend in 1972 over unbeaten Notre Dame, 30–26, a week after a 62–0 loss to Nebraska.

Wunderbar at Wimbledon

Arthur Ashe With Teacher Hudlin as His Guest

If there was drama enough in an African American for the first time winning tennis's most famous byline—Wimbledon—it was another to have one St. Louisan watching another win or, more accurately, the man who helped Arthur Ashe over the cold spots in a hot, meteoric career.

Seated at Wimbledon that early July 1975, was a veteran longtime teacher at St. Louis's Sumner High School, Richard Hudlin, the first black captain of a Big 10 team and the man Ashe's father in Richmond, Virginia, entrusted to see to it that Arthur got a fairer square, a better deal in tennis and life.

That's an extraordinary task considering that St. Louis then and now still has enough racial misunderstanding to make many uncomfortable, but presumably there was another difference for the Ashes to feel that their young man would have a better chance up north in Missouri than down south in Richmond, Virginia.

Hudlin, with whom Ashe stayed, had a raspy-voiced tone like Hollywood's comedic master of sarcasm, Groucho Marx, and the old 1927 University of Chicago tennis captain, could be salty about missed opportunities and other things that weren't right. But, overall, he was a patient teacher and proud of his prized pupil.

So from Dick, Arthur received the kind of concentrated, hard-play tennis that enabled St. Louis to become a home for champions over all-weather winners, such as kids from Florida, California, and Texas. If from age 15 you learned to play on the slick varnished basketball floor of the old St. Louis Armory, you had an edge most certainly on clay and even on grass.

And if you were as distinguished and noble as Ashe, who would die much too soon of AIDS, you could do impossible things—for instance, beat Belleville's Jimmy Connors, a whopping 3-to-20 favorite as defending champion. No final had been so top-heavy for the winner since Australia's Rod Laver ruled the English courts a decade earlier.

With Hudlin there as his guest, Ashe worked on the world's top-ranked star like a surgeon. He won 6–1, 6–1, 5–7 and 6–4. The Wimbledon win came just after the World Championship of Tennis crown for the young man.

Ashe, seeded sixth at Wimbledon, sounded like Gene Tunney of boxing in Hudlin's heyday explaining how he beat Jack Dempsey. Said Arthur, "I didn't play my usual game. What I played was the kind of game that would beat Jimmy Connors. Somehow, I don't know why, I've always felt that this would be my year, and I was not surprised when I won."

Previously, Ashe had played and lost to Connors three times, always on clay or cement. This, their first meeting on grass, was the first all-America men's final at Wimbledon in 28 years, since Jack Kramer defeated Tom Brown in 1947.

From the outset, Ashe served wide to Connors' forehand to eliminate the blistering returns by the big banger from Belleville. The first set took just 19 minutes and the match two hours and four minutes.

Connors, subdued and gracious, noted that Ashe had played as well as Jimmy ever had seen. Said Connors, a product of his tennis mother's zeal, his grandmother's, and his own, "It was tough for me to get into the match. He didn't give me much to hit at."

Jack Dempsey would have said the same about Gene Tunney in 1926 and '27. To Ashe, it was the second-greatest victory of his career.

Said Arthur, "First was winning the Davis Cup for my country and at Forest Hills."

As for Richard Hudlin, characteristically unsmiling, he left for a plane back to the States without seeing his young champion. As he said, softly, "It wasn't at all necessary."

★

KING OF THE COURT: Finally, but only briefly, the late, great Arthur Ashe, prepped here by Sumner's colorful Richard Hudlin, died much too soon a victim of AIDS.

USA
DAVIS CU

1974
Jimbo the Giant Killer
Mama's Boy Jimmy Connors Was No. 1

Aptly described as the blue-collar player in a white-shirted game, James Scott Connors went into the International Tennis Hall of Fame at Newport, Rhode Island, in 1998—no longer pugnacious and lion-hearted, but still momma's boy.

Jimmy Connors's mother, Gloria Connors, the former Gloria Thompson, was one of the St. Louis area's best a couple of generations back, and she had the same intensity, desire, and fire that turned her boy into one of international tennis's best ever.

She called him "Jimbo." He called her "Mom," of course, but it could have been "teacher." In those youthful years Mrs. Connors would have him out on the court with drill-sergeant authority, but the guy with Gas House Gang spirit remembers it more tenderly.

"My mom gave me this game," he said, the day he was tapped for tennis's Hall of Fame. "Mom gave me this game, Mom and her mom. They rolled balls to me when I could hardly hold a racket. For all these years, Mom has been three things: mom, coach and friend. And it's still that way."

With a Wimbledon highlight back in 1974 when he killed popular Aussie Ken Rosewall's comeback hopes in straight sets, Connors was the best and often least-liked—fierce and argumentative, a chunky left-hander with the equivalent of a 100-mile-per-hour fastball for sizzling strikes.

As a result, his box score at a semi-retired age 46 was a record 109 pro singles titles, eight of them major.

He was the most highly decorated U.S. tennis male since red-haired Don Budge earned six majors in 1938.

Jimbo never grand-slammed, but he regarded his highlight in 1991. As he put it, "Eleven days, including U.S. Open. Even though wrist surgery saved my career, I was supposed to be washed up. Heck, I was rated number 939 coming in, the wildest wild card, but I reached the semifinals. It was crazy. Pandemonium. It's the way I wanted tennis to be."

Indeed, he was always exciting, whether vulgarly grabbing his crotch or speaking his mind, often provoking fines and suspensions. He was not a choirboy, that Catholic kid from Belleville, Illinois.

Then, as he confessed, he liked it, as a tough kid who once saw a man killed in a saloon when accompanied by his grandfather, but he mellowed with age. He's happy that his teenage son and daughter grew up well and credited his ex-wife, sorrowing that he was a "loner" who didn't fit marriage well. Early, you'll recall, he and young woman Chris Evert had a romance.

Still able to win in occasional excursions away from his gambling-boat interests, James Scott Connors left a legacy of having been ranked number one in the world for 268 weeks, second only to Ivan Lendl's 270.

Semi-retired at age 46, careful not to be carried away by competitive instincts and invitations, Jimbo has his own focus. "I'm on top," he said, "I'll always be on top."

And he'll always be momma's boy, too.

JUMPING JIMBO: *From the time he was a freshman at Assumption High School, Jimmy Connors (far left, first row) reflected his efforts and his mother's teaching. He led the school to a 14–1 record in 1968. Mother Gloria Thomson Connors called him "Jimbo." Everyone else, internationally, called him champion.*

1974
Savior at Sunrise

Only Bake McBride's Great Speed Ended the 25-Inning Marathon

On May Day 1920, the Brooklyn Dodgers played a 26-inning tie at Boston, and everybody said it wouldn't happen again, but it almost did in 1974, except that the Cardinals' lean, lanky Bake McBride scored all the way from first base on a pick-off throw.

That incredible first-to-home early morning September 12, 1974, capped a 25-inning 4–3 game that drew 13,460 to New York's Shea Stadium. Most fans were long gone—except for Commissioner Bowie Kuhn and wife Louisa. The game ended at 3:12 a.m.

Baseball's second-longest marathon lasted into virtually a doubleheader behind the regulation game, first because Redbird third baseman Kenny Reitz hit a two-run homer off Mets' left-hander Jerry Koosman with two out in the ninth inning.

Back in 1920, the Dodgers and Braves had wanted to go one more to make it 27 innings, the equivalent of three full games, but darkness prevented the added inning.

In the St. Louis/New York marathon 34 years later, only the motor acceleration of McBride ended a game that seemed to have no end.

With the hidden heroes veteran Redbird left-hander Claude Osteen and rookie Mets' right-hander Jerry Cram—Osteen worked nine scoreless innings in relief, Cram eight—the showdown came with young Hank Webb opposing the Cardinals' seventh pitcher, Sonny Siebert.

McBride opened round number 25 with an infield single. Webb, trying to pick him off, balked, so actually the Baker had second unmolested; the rest was a risk on his own. Late, dead tired like many, McBride said by the time he hit second, he was going all the way. Yeah, right through third base coach Vern Benson's stop sign.

With none out and both Joe Torre and Reggie Smith previously thrown out at the plate, Benson wouldn't send McBride, but, as manager Red Schoendienst said in defense of the runner, "Bake was moving so fast, he couldn't see the sign. When you've got McBride's speed, you make the other side nervous."

Indeed, catcher Ron Hodges dropped the hurried throw from first baseman John Milner and, unromantically, was charged with an error. But McBride, who lay on the ground sputtering dirt from his eyes and mouth, insisted the catcher couldn't have tagged him. Said Bake, "Hodges was way up from the plate and I was sliding behind him."

The happiest man was plate umpire Ed Sudol, on his feet for the seven hours and four minutes. The wisecracks came as fast as McBride's merciful flashing feet. With his post-game guest, homer-hitter Reitz, Jack Buck intoned, "Tonight's Star of the Game is Ken Reitz—good night, Ken!"

A hot club closing in momentarily on league-leading Pittsburgh, the Cardinals followed their 25-inning victory with one in nine over the Mets, then went to Philadelphia for a 17-inning game. And after two more there in nine, they moved to Pittsburgh and won in 13.

Back in 1920, Sunday ball was banned in Boston. The Dodgers left behind their pitcher Leon Cadore who had gone the full 26 against Joe Oeschger. Brooklyn went back to Ebbets Field for a Sunday game, lost to Philadelphia, then returned to Braves Field for games that went 13 and 19 innings.

The prize for Wilbert Robertson's team in '20 was one that eluded Schoendienst's Redbirds in '74. Nicknamed the "Robins" for their manager Uncle Robby, Brooklyn won the pennant for their overtime prize.

★

MOTOR MAN: *Only the blazing speed of Bake McBride, like early day Helen Stephens the Fulton Flash, kept the famed 25-inning marathon ball game in 1974 from lasting forever. The lanky weary outfielder sped from first to home on a missed pickoff throw.*

1974
Hail to Hale

Irwin Became Open Champ, Then Senior Golf's Best

If there's anyone who has good reason—with proper pride—to drive a car with a special Missouri license plate, it's golf's Hale Irwin.

The celebrity plate has two words: "US-OPEN."

Great! The man who is behind the wheel of that slick silver Mercedes drives that caliber of car because he won the National Open three times.

Only three others have won the 105-year Open once more than the 54-year-old Irwin. They're heavyweights of the game, too—Willie Anderson, Bobby Jones, and Ben Hogan.

And Irwin did it the oldest—age 45—in June 1990, at Chicago's Medinah course. Back there in 1974 at New York, Mamaroneck's Winged Foot, he was the first to win the Open wearing glasses. And, yes, the first big-time football star to be champion.

Not only good at football, Irwin had enough guts to dash up from the secondary at the goal-line for a game-saving tackle against Oklahoma, and his fellow Colorado Buffaloes showed similar fortitude when they faced fourth-and-goal at the one with only 10 men on the field! The academic All-American plugged the leak.

Technically, Hale Irwin is a Missourian. His family, living across the border in Oklahoma, wanted a Joplin hospital for his birth in 1945. He grew up to age 14 at Baxter Springs, Kansas, then moved to Boulder. The happy coincidence permitted him to meet his wife.

Sally was from Kirkwood, so their move to Frontenac gave St. Louis the pleasure of the budding golf champion's companionship and his dedicated service to a children's hospital with contributions—also, a daughter and son.

At age 26, Irwin won his first tournament as a pro. Three years later at Wing Foot, 1974, he shot a 287 for his first Open. Five years later at Toledo's Inverness, after a strong next-to-last round, he had a toss-and-turn night, chattering with dear Sally. Barely able to keep down a cantaloupe, he ran on half-tank and wasn't happy about his final-round 75, except his even-par 284 was two-up as money in the bank.

By 1990, Irwin's exemption as a former champion had run out, but the golf association gave him a courtesy invitation. Two weeks before, he dreamed that he would win and told Sally so as a family secret.

At Medinah, a capricious course and a record 7,185-yard distance for an Open, the weather behaved himself into the last day. So did Irwin before a remarkable run, gaining five strokes on the last eight holes. The back-breaker was at 18, where he gained a playoff with a wonderful 60-foot putt.

Now, Hale Irwin is a reserved professional, but at Medinah he looked like Mark McGwire after hitting his record home run. He played patty-cake with patrons on both sides of the gallery.

Tricky, gusty winds made Medinah a dangerous flirt in sudden-death overtime. Opponent Mike Donald had done well all week at the first hole, but Irwin won it there with a 10-foot putt, then had a family celebration.

He also picked up his largest purse, $220,000, but, shucks, turning to the senior tour even just part-time, he made over-50 his private preserve, winning six events and $2.5 million in 1998.

Heck, the man with the silver Mercedes and "US-OPEN" plate could drive a solid gold Cadillac.

★

GRIDIRON TO GOLF: *A former defensive back for the Colorado Buffaloes, Irwin is a three-time U.S. Open champion and a dominant player on the senior tour.*

1974

Happy Anniversary to Lou-Lou

One After Another for Speedy Lou Brock

Before the '00 that apparently even had the computers scared, 1999 had to have marked more happy anniversaries for Lou Brock than for any other.

1999 marked 35 years since baseball's biggest Brinks heist, the Cardinals acquiring Lou Brock; 25 years since the 1974 season in which Brock broke Maury Wills's single-season stolen base record with 118; and 20 years on the nose since Brock ended his career by reaching and exceeding the magic 3,000-hit goal.

Oh yes, and how did this get in there? It was 22 years since he caught, collared, and passed Ty Cobb's career stolen base record, 892, with two late in the '77 season at San Diego.

So just as Lewis and Clark discovered the Pacific Northwest as America's frontier explorers, Louis Clark Brock set lasting records, some of which Rickey Henderson broke.

As a result of True-Blue Lou's brilliance at bat and on the base paths, Cardinals' promotion whiz Marty Hendin figures to have Brock on the field more than the Busch Stadium groundskeepers, and deservedly.

Few did any more, and none more cheerfully, than the grinning Hall of Famer who was virtually a career .300 hitter. He topped the figure eight times in 19 seasons and turned into a terror at bat and on the bases in the limelight of the World Series.

1999 isn't an exact anniversary of 1968, but it was in the '68 Series that Brock was at his best. Uh-huh, even though he didn't slide once as many thought he should have.

Truth is, if Lou hadn't been banging out base hits for quantity and quality—13 in seven games good for 25 bases—the Cardinals wouldn't have carried the Detroit donut king, Mickey Lolich, and the Tigers into the seventh game. There, in game 7, Lolich broke the Redbird tradition of triumphing in seven-game Series as they had done six times.

About Brock's failure to slide in the fifth inning of the fifth game, in which the Cardinals were leading 3–2 and finally lost 5–3, his explanation made sense. With Willie Horton making an uncommonly strong and accurate throw from left field, Brock found catcher Bill Freehan up the third-base line a bit, his foot ready to turn left or right to deflect a sliding runner off one side of the plate or the other.

"Actually," said Brock, "Freehan hadn't had time to extend himself to take the throw, so really when we collided, we were on the plate. So, S-A-F-E!"

So, gee whiz, the .464 average and .844 slugging percentage weren't good enough! It's amazing, though, how in the pressure and excitement of World Series play, Brock could be pumped up enough to hit for average and power. Thirty-four hits for 62 bases. Even though when he came over from the Cubs in mid-season of 1964, manager Johnny Keane had convinced him to forego power for base reaching and base stealing.

That's really what Lou did the rest of that spectacular season, hitting .348 and stealing 43 bases, his lowest of any for the next 13 seasons. But he wanted to be remembered as a hitter as well as a runner. That's why 3,000-plus hits meant more than 900-plus stolen bases.

That's why, to use one of the articulate athlete's favorite words, he "orchestrated" his retirement, good and graceful, one of the best ever, .304.

★

THIEF OF BAGS: True-Blue Lou Brock, acquired from the Cubs in a 1964 mid-season heist, set a career National League record for stolen bases with 118 in 1974. Shown above in 1971, famed No. 20 stole his fifth base in the third inning of a game against the Phillies.

1974
Over the Rainbow

Happy Days, the Big Red Win One

For a horrible half, the nightmare stalked Busch Stadium again. The football Cardinals, who couldn't win for losing, once again looked in late 1974 as they had in similar circumstances four years earlier. They were blowing their first division championship against the New York Giants.

Not that New York was ready to take the NFL's Eastern Division title in '74, as they had back in 1970 when they upset the Big Red in the next-to-last game of the regular season. The '74 Giants were an also-ran, but you couldn't tell it by the halftime scoreboard, 14–0 Giants. Happiness this final game day soon would be realized by finger-licking George Allen and his Washington Redskins.

In the 1970 game, ultimately an 8–5–1 farewell for coach Charley Winner, the stumbling Cards slumped after three straight shutout wins, but they still could have prevailed at home against the Giants.

Instead, they lost to the Giants in a rout, 37–14. Afterward, coaching New York, Alex (Red) Morrison said, sympathetically, "They were so tight, they squeaked!"

And there was a squeaky oh-no-don't-let-it-happen-again feeling in '74 when Don Coryell's Cardiac Cards were down by two touches at the half, scoreless at 14–0. Elusive running back Terry Metcalf had dropped four passes. Why, big lumbering quarterback Jim Hart led in rushing with eight yards. The crowd of 47,414 booed.

What happened at halftime? "Nobody threw a blackboard," snapped Dan Dierdorf. His steak-shop colleague, Hart, was assured he was throwing well. And coach Coryell of a short fuse and sputtering lisp was composed.

So the Big Red, who hadn't won anything since a division title 27 years ago, simply came out and blew the Giants away. First, linebacker Mark Arneson met New York ball carrier Joe Dawkins head on in a third-and-two play. Dawkins, who had romped in the first half, was stopped.

Next, Roger (The Dodger) Wehrli, one of the best yet not in the Hall of Fame, set up the offense with a 32-yard punt return. Hart capped a 40-yard drive with a four-yard touchdown pass to fullback Ken Willard.

Fifty seconds later, cornerback Norm Thompson deflected a pass by Craig Morton. Jim Tolbert intercepted, and Hart found Jackie Smith with a 28-yard scoring pass, tying the game and providing a springboard to two more TDs.

Meanwhile, Metcalf, the team's most valuable player with 2,058 combined yards, found the offensive linemen his best friends. Instead of pulling guards and other things fancy, they stayed with the basics. Terry could romp and receive with the skill that broke him big yardage on running plays, flat-zone flips, and kick returns.

So the 26–14 final made it pennant raising time at the old ballpark because, though Washington also finished with a 10–4 record, the Big Red had skinned the Skins twice.

The 1974 season would end in a disappointing climax, a 30–14 playoff loss at Minnesota, and even after a better 1975 of only three defeats in 14 league games, the season ended in a 35–23 playoff loss to the Rams in Los Angeles.

Still, it was a far cry from three successive 4–9–1 seasons, '71 through '73, and those late-season losses that kept the Big Red at home empty-handed, when pro football began its second season.

★

AS GOOD AS HE SOUNDS: Dan Dierdorf emerged from pro football articulate, with a wit and wisdom of analysis, an aftermath of an All-American career at Michigan, and Hall of Fame stature as a tackle with the Cardinals of the '70s. Inset, '74 co-MVPs, Terry Metcalf (left) and Jim Hart (17).

REMARKABLE: Not only did the brothers finish first in the Olympics, but also they each briefly held boxing's highest crown, the heavyweight title.

1976
Brothers Valiant
The Fistic Spinkses Win Olympic Gold

The 1976 Olympic Games at Montreal were not Uncle Sam's best, except in the boxing ring where five Americans prevailed and, amazingly and happily, two from St. Louis—the brothers Spinks, Leon and Michael.

With their dear mother a spectator, thanks to the thoughtfulness of St. Louis attorney John King, Leon won the gold medal in the light-heavyweight division and Michael the gold as king of the middleweights.

The other Olympic fist fighters to win, wearing the red, white, and blue to beat out favored rival Cuba, were flyweight Leo Randolph of Tacoma, Washington, lightweight Howard Davis of Glen Cove, New York, and a light welterweight named Ray Leonard of Palmer Park, Maryland.

For the Spinkses, Leon, 24, had to finish up the one year of a Marine Corps enlistment. Michael, 21, would say only that he would look for a fine job, but that, meanwhile, "Right now, I just want to put my hands behind my head and rest."

In the finals, Michael hammered Russian Rufat Riskiew with a third-round knockout. Leon floored Cuba's Sixto Sorta in the second round and stopped him in the third.

For the United States, seven overall boxing medals were the most since the 1904 Olympics in St. Louis, but then all entries were American. The five golds matched the American total in 1952 at Helsinki, led there by Floyd Patterson.

For the Spinkses, the once-upon-a-time fairy tale began in St. Louis's Pruitt-Igoe complex, imploded as a disaster in 1975. The brothers seemed to have little chance, too, raised by an attractive Bible-quoting mother who kept the kids and the faith, hers and theirs.

At Montreal, Mrs. Spinks bubbled with joy. "It was a wonderful thing to see them win. I'm just glowing over. It was something else when the flag rose. It seemed like a tribute to the whole country. When we walked outside, it was raining—and I thought the rain was even beautiful."

Had the boys seen her before the title bouts for which she was a late arrival? Yes, they had. And what, fellas, did you say to your mother?

"All I said to her was . . . 'Hello, Momma.'"

★

1978
Leon Spinks v. Muhammad Ali

Even Muhammad Ali, boxing's and maybe sport's number one celebrity of the twentieth century, could be over-confident; not for long, but long enough for a St. Louis kid named Leon Spinks to wrest away Ali's heavyweight boxing championship.

First as Cassius Clay, a colorful popoff kid from Louisville, as fast with his poetic quips as with his fists, the boxer gained fame. Next, taking a Muslim name, he became legendary with his skills and with conscientious objection to military service. From then on, Muhammad Ali had international stature.

As champion, except for Pier Six brawls with Joe Frazier, Ali was invincible, though as the years would show, he took more punishment than imagined. Part of that punishment came from that 24-year-old Olympic champion from St. Louis, Leon Spinks, who had only seven professional fights served as a tune-up in February 1978 for a later box office bout.

About over-confidence, an insidious thing seen often, it was explained best by Swedish champion Ingmar Johannson, knocked out by Floyd Patterson in a return bout. In his cracked-ice English, Ingo said, "If I'd known I was over-confident, I like to think I'd have done something about it."

Bingo! Ali was not prepared for ex-Marine Spinks, whose trainer, Sam Solomon, 62, had shown the wisdom of his biblical namesake. Sam told the kid to fire out with a strong first round and to follow the trainer's orders—attack the body, the kidneys, and work on the left shoulder so that Ali's great jab would lose effectiveness.

In late rounds, Ali's jab was more of a flick than a darting weapon. By Round 6, Solomon thought the kid could win, but he warned him to fight cautiously the next few rounds, to coast so that he could finish strong against the champ, by then battered and perspiring.

The three judges couldn't agree—with one giving Ali the nod by one point, the other two Spinks by one point and two—but all three awarded rounds 13, 14, and 15 to the grinning, gap-toothed contender. In Solomon's wise words, Spinks's ability to take punishment in the tenth round surprised—and discouraged—Ali. Yet the trainer insisted Spinks had to win number 15.

The decision brought roars of surprise and approval from the Hilton Palace Crowd in Las Vegas. The great ex-champion sat in a suite, and said, soft-spoken, "I underestimated him. He's a tough kid, but I am not through."

Ali's trainer, highly respected Angelo Dundee, said he didn't think the champion had lost, but that it was too close for comfort. "There's no cop-out," said Dundee. "People make a mistake when they talk down Spinks. All I could think of all week was, 'I hope lightning doesn't strike again like it did for Ali against Liston.'"

But it did, of course, but, as always, cream rose to the top. Six months later in a return bout at New Orleans, Ali regained the championship, capping a career as a legend who obviously took more punishment than it seemed. He retreated into a status of virtual mild-mannered mute before the millennium.

Spinks? Ah, with his nose flattened against the candy store like an underprivileged kid, Leon couldn't cope with fame and fortune. Knocked out a year later in one round by a stumblebum, he burned life's candle at both ends—and even faster than he had that famous February night in '78.

★

GAPING GRIN: A vast underdog, Leon Spinks achieved the impossible dream, briefly taking Muhammad Ali's title. Yeah, the hometown kid missed his two front teeth—and then some.

BELIEVE IT OR NOT: Bull-like Glenn Brummer, third-string catcher, stole home with the winning run in the 12th inning of a 1982 game against San Francisco. No wonder Whitey Herzog won the pennant— Brummer surprised everybody, including the manager. Shown: The disputed play, a home-plate hug with Tommy Herr, and the engraved, autographed home plate.

1982
One for the Book

Heavy-Hoofed Glenn Brummer Stole Home

If a third string catcher built like a fullback can steal home with two out and two strikes on a hitter, why couldn't a ball club win a pennant? Thanks to bold Glenn Brummer's memorable swipe on really what might have been an inning-ending third strike, the Cardinals did take the flag in 1982!

What the run-sheep-run Redbirds of go-go guy Whitey Herzog did in '82 was to win the pennant, the Cardinals' first in 14 years, and add their most recent world championship, too.

And the Cards did it with the unexpected, incredible help of Brummer, a blocky seldom-seen backstop, who surprised manager Herzog, third-base coach Chuck Hiller, a stunned Sunday crowd of 46,877 at Busch Stadium, and—yeah, quite probably—the umpire, Dave Pallone.

Pallone's non-call at best—non-call on the pitch, not the slide—was the difference in a 12-inning victory over Frank Robinson's San Francisco Giants, 5–4.

Brummer, entering the game midway and catching only the 19th of 21 games he would play, singled and moved up on the fourth hit by Willie McGee, hitting hero with Ken Oberkfell. Third baseman Obie's two-out double in the ninth had tied the score.

Brummer, facing lefty Gary Lavelle with one out, got a hit. So did McGee. Ozzie Smith's grounder moved up both men.

Edging away, pitch after pitch on the next hitter, Dave Green, Brummer whispered to coach Hiller that he could go. Chuck didn't answer, so the bull-in-the-china-shop went.

Happily, Green didn't swing or he might have parted the scalp of the guy from Olney, Illinois. As Glenn slid in, umpire Pallone instinctively stepped to the left and made the "safe" call. But what about the pitch! A third strike would take precedence!

In self-defense, Pallone said he had called it a "ball," but manager Robinson argued profanely. Replays indicated the Giants' skipper was right, but, sorry Charley . . . er, Frank!

★

1982
Wonderful Willie
McGee's Greatest Day Ever

As Whitey Herzog, the White Rat who became the cat's meow as manager of the Cardinals, put it, if Willie McGee's performance in the third game of the 1982 World Series had been in New York—especially if Willie still wore the Yankee stripes earmarked for him—McGee's performance might be regarded as the best ever.

In a Series won by St. Louis in the late innings of the last game at Busch Stadium, the one-man show by the shy center fielder was extremely precious. The scared-rabbit switch-hitter went on to become a box-office legend past age 40 with the Cardinals and a quiet philosopher.

Actually, McGee, the most famous Willie since Mays, came aboard only because fourth outfielder Dave Green, acquired from Milwaukee in Herzog's remarkable shake-well changes to the roster, was hurt in early May.

Herzog beckoned to Louisville for McGee, who had been obtained from the Yankees' Nashville farm club for a seldom-remembered pitcher, Bob Sykes.

McGee, moving into center field, was a standout for Herzog, whose dealings were so good that both the Cardinals and their primary shopping partner, Milwaukee, won pennants. Harvey Kuenn's Wallbangers, power hitters, were favored in the Series and showed why in a 10–0 rout at St. Louis behind lefty Mike Caldwell's three-hit pitching. Both players en route to 3,000 hits and the Hall of Fame, Robin Yount got four hits and Paul Molitor a Series record five.

After the Cardinals staggered to a 5–4 win, the shift to County Stadium brought forth from McGee the great performance. Willie warmed up with a leaping catch of Molitor's home run bid in the first inning. And in the fifth inning of a scoreless duel between Joaquin Andujar and Pete Vuckovich, McGee drilled a three-run homer. Still not done, he homered again in the eighth and then capped the 6–2 contest, a deceptive score, by depriving Gorman Thomas of a homer by leaping higher than the fence.

Buoyed by their money-in-the-bank acquisition, the Redbirds raced to a 5–1 lead the next day. Highlighted was McGee's base hit and stolen base and a walk to Ozzie Smith. The run-sheep-run Redbirds were never better than when both moved up on a wild pitch and then both scored—Smith from second—on an outfield fly!

When chubby St. Louis southpaw Dave LaPoint dropped a one-out throw in the Brewers' seventh—"he musta thought it was a cheeseburger," Herzog grumped—the floodgates opened for six runs and a 7–5 Milwaukee victory.

So, the Americans went one up in a 6–4 fifth game behind Caldwell when Yount became the first player to get four hits twice in a World Series.

Rain came to spoil the visiting Brewers' parade in the sixth game at St. Louis when the Redbirds backed rookie John Stuper with 13 runs, including a three-hit game for designated hitter Dane Iorg, a .529 hitter even hotter than Yount and Molitor.

So it went to the seventh game, familiar in the Cardinals' tradition, and Vuckovich out-battled Andujar into the home sixth, 3–1.

With one out, the unrelated Smiths delivered, Ozzie and Lonnie. The Wizard singled and Skates doubled him to third, bringing in lefty Bob McClure. Gene Tenace, pinch-hitting for Ken Oberkfell, walked to fill the bases.

Here, in a long duel at the plate, Keith Hernandez of the Cards won with a two-run tying single to right center. Immediately, Silent George Hendricks, an old pro, poked an outside pitch to right for the leading run.

Bruce Sutter came in and finished with a flourish, and battery mate Darrell Porter, the Series MVP, chortled, "H-o-o-i-e, I been to two county fairs and a goat roast—and I ain't never seen nuthin' like this."

Or like Willie McGee in Game 3.

★

WONDERFUL WILLIE: In the rookie season of what would become a legendary career, one which ended in 1999, Willie McGee emerged as a legend and starting center fielder on the St. Louis baseball writers' half-century All-Star team. An early factor was one of the most remarkable World Series performances ever. In game three of a 1982 World Series won by the Cardinals, McGee hit two home runs and made two great catches at Milwaukee, one shown here.

1983

Depression Gimmick to Titletown

St. Louis's Hoc-Soc Led to Indoor Soccer Honors

Indoor soccer, kissing cousin to a game concocted by two enterprising St. Louis men in the depths of the depression, has had some of its biggest successes in Soccer Titletown, U.S.A., but not too many championships.

Born as Hoc-Soc, invented by Walter Giesler and Charley McBride for kids who couldn't get jobs in the tough times of the 1930s, indoor soccer came full blast years after World War II. The bow still could go to the deceased innovators, Giesler, a sporting goods operator and longtime U.S. soccer delegate, and McBride. Charley fathered the first young American to win spurs with European players, Pat McBride.

Single-named foreigners starred when indoor soccer was at its commercial peak. One, a Yugoslav named Steve Zungul (as in jungle), was devastating in New York and good box office here, too. Zungul, almost as good as he thought he was, hammed it up with infuriating pratfalls that euchred officials into too many bad calls.

By 1981, the St. Louis Steamers, originally owned by a New Jersey dentist who had loose regard for book-balancing, had been acquired by former basketball Hawks' owner Ben Kerner and others, like Stan Musial and Joe Garagiola, who felt that if promotion-minded Kerner would help, they wanted in.

Kerner, an older father with young sons who hadn't seen his Hawks, fell back on razzle dazzle. The Steamers surged onto the Arena surface under steamy clouds. They threw roses to the fans and kicked soccer balls into the stands as substantial gifts.

The Steamers won, too, but not quite enough. On a Sunday afternoon showdown in March 1981, Zungul and the New York Arrows prevailed. The Arrows were managed by a Yugoslav with St. Louis connections, Don Popovic. With Zungul scoring five goals, the last one trickled past popular hometown goalie Slobo Illijevski—"Slobo" was name enough. Zungul's winner came with 30 seconds left, 6–5. A record sellout 18,000 were disappointed.

Why St. Louis didn't continue to prosper at least at the gate, especially when often in the title hunt, was perplexing and a disappointment, certainly most to the modern sportsman owner, Dr. Abe Hawatmeh, a ranking urologist. Abe had played the game in his native Jordan and was well connected with royalty there.

When Kerner and company bowed out to new ownership—Ben insisted on no profit in sale—the franchise was in slow Titanic descent. Well-meaning owners couldn't bear the losses as the local teams, with rosters usually loaded with hometown talent, tried and failed.

As the Stars in the old North American Soccer League, then the Steamers and Storm in the Major Indoor Soccer League, St. Louis was better on the artificial pitch than at the gate. Enter Doc Hawatmeh with money and enthusiasm, but not too much patience.

Still, his team, in the new National Professional Soccer League, prevailed in their third season, 1994–95.

Pridefully, they made much of it. St. Louis had known national amateur and open success and, of course, college, but this was not only the old Shin-kicker Capital's first overall professional soccer title, but also, mind you, the city's first championship team since the 1982 World Series Cardinals.

Acquired by Dr. Hawatmeh from Tulsa in 1992, the Ambush struggled to 19–21 the first year, 25–15 as division champs the next, and then, following a robust 30–10 regular-season record, they prevailed over the Harrisburg Heat in a five-game finale.

Despite low ticket prices in the new Kiel Center, it was difficult to maintain the overall 200,000 crowd of that championship season. Led then by hometown goalie Jamie Swanner, high-scoring Mark Moser, and defensive genius Darryl Doran, the team couldn't sustain success on the floor or at the turnstiles. The game invented by Giesler and McBride—a soccer ball kicked at the old Neighborhood House gym with rubber shoes and ten-pin goal posts—had come a long way. Uh-huh, in salary too, and Hoc-Soc's kissing cousin was in jeopardy as the new century began with new faces on the Ambush. Still, that magic old name—Steamers—has resurrected for a new league in a new building, St. Charles Family Arena.

★

AT FULL STEAM: Local striker Don Ebert (bottom left), goalminer Slobo Illijevski (top left), and local Darryl Doran (above) were Steamer mainstays. Doran player-coached the Ambush to the championship in 1994–95.

Yes, We Have No Hits

A Redbird Record Two for Bob Forsch

From George Washington Bradley's first National League no-hitter in that league's first season, 1876, until Jose Jiminez's in 1999, the last season of the century, only nine ever pitched a no-hitter. So Bob Forsch is special—he did it twice!

For length of service and reliability as a Redbird, Robert Herbert Forsch was a latter-day Jesse Joseph Haines, the senior citizen of Cardinal pitchers. Like good Ol' Pop, himself a no-hit pitcher, Bob was good, but not great, a quiet, gutsy guy who well might hit a batter in the seat of the pants—and, ah, consistent!

That's why it's an oddity of the Grand Old Game that Forsch's two greatest games came in only two of the four super seasons he had with the Cardinals in 15 years.

A 20-game winner just once and 15 twice, the big 6'4", 200-pound Californian, a transplanted infielder, was struggling at 11–17 in 1977, a fifth-place year for the ball club. But he reached the heights on a June Sunday at Busch Stadium, where he zeroed the Phillies before 11,495, 5–0. In the one-hour 56-minute game, he walked two and one reached base on a controversial error.

In the eighth inning when any silly official scorer would make sure the first hit was a clean one, third baseman Ken Reitz missed a ground ball hit by outfielder Garry Maddox.

The second no-hitter in late September 1983, the year the champion Cardinals sagged to fourth, came as manager Whitey Herzog had suggested the veteran might drop down to the Winter Instructional League to work on a knuckler.

Forsch, 10–12 for the defending world champions, walked out there on the chilly night, warming in the clubhouse between innings. He was never better. Second baseman Ken Oberkfell reached down and felt nothing on a second-inning grounder by Chris Speier—an obvious error—and no other Expos reached first base.

With 12,457 standing and cheering, wasn't Forsch superstitious or excited? "Naw," he said, "the World Series was more exciting. Besides, I was born on Friday the Thirteenth."

Admiringly, Herzog responded, "He's one of the gamest guys I ever met. Just when you count him out, the so-and-so comes back. He's something."

Which is just about the way Red Schoendiest, then manager, put it years earlier when young Forsch pitched a private intra-squad game in St. Petersburg, Florida. Said Red, "He's not overpowering, but he's a battler. You'll see. . . ."

Indeed. The parallel with Pop Haines, the 18-season veteran, is considerable. Haines, the better pitcher with marginal Hall of Fame credentials, was with better teams and the only Redbird player to share in five World Series. Pop had character and, as mentioned, the same willingness to spin the caps of hitters who crowded the plate. Ditto Forsch.

Bob, 186–138 overall, finished his career at Houston, then doubled back to St. Louis. His elder brother Ken, 114–113, also pitched a no-hitter for the Astros.

To single out Forsch in chapter tribute was in deference to that double no-hit acheivement rather than not to say more about Grin Bradley's first no-hitter against Hartford back in '76—1876!—or Haines's Tuberculosis Day no-hitter in 1924, Paul Dean's in the '34 pennant race, Lon Warneke's stretch-drive contribution in '44, and the magic moments in '99 when Jose Jiminez outpitched the great Randy Johnson twice in a week, first with a no-hitter, second with a two-hitter.

About the past, there's an amusing postscript. In Haines's no-hit game against the Boston Braves in '24, colorful Casey Stengel would chortle that he had made the last out. Ten years later when Stengel was managing Brooklyn, Paul Dean pitched a no-hitter after brother Dizzy hurled a three-hitter.

"And," moaned Stengel, coaching third base, "I never saw a friendly face all day. . . ."

★

ELDER STATESMAN: Not only did he write Redbird history with two no-hitters, but Bob Forsch was an old reliable of the pitching staff, like an early day Jesse (Pop) Haines.

1984
Bittersweet Success

Al Joyner, an Olympic Champion Lost His Love

Upstaged athletically in life by his famous sister Jackie Joyner-Kersee—and his attractive wife, Florence—Al Joyner looked to the new century and millennium as an Olympic victor returning with a purpose—his own and his dear daughter's.

Shortly after wife Flo-Jo died unexpectedly in early fall 1998, Alfrederick Joyner found himself father and mother to eight-year-old daughter Mary Rose.

The job would not be easy, and Al would best forget about the sport in which he had been a surprise triple jump winner in the 1984 Olympics, but, suddenly, his precious little missy asked a penetrating question after bedtime prayers: "Are you training, Daddy? I know Mommy never would want to stop training. Neither would I."

So, at 39, Al began training for the 2000 Olympics in Australia, aware that 1984 was the first—and only—time he upstaged his fabulous sister, Jackie Joyner-Kersee, six times an Olympic medalist, and his wife, who won and placed four times in the glamorous international quadrennial.

For Al Joyner, a family junior, he learned early—as did sister Jackie, two years younger—that life was no rose garden. They grew up in an East St. Louis neighborhood on Piggott Avenue, a four-bedroom, one-bathroom house cramped with two grandparents, their own parents, and two kids, an athletic pair.

Al was born in 1960, Jackie in 1962, to a boy 16 and a girl 14. They could remember a time when there wasn't food. They could remember, too, sadly, when their young mother died when they were college-age kids, fortunately athletically gifted. Al's daughter—his and dearly departed Flo-Jo's—is named for the Joyners' mom, Mary Rose.

Mom certainly would have liked it back in 1984 when Al and Jackie came back to the East Side in triumph, given a new house for the family and twin Mustang cars. Ah, sweet success, but, ah, what hard work, too.

Their own polite teacher and coach, then husband and brother-in-law, was Bob Kersee, who had coached Florence Griffith Joyner in junior college, then moved with her to UCLA, where he would meet superstar Jackie, his wife-to-be.

For Al Joyner, street-smart and dedicated, love with Flo-Jo could be excused if it came at first sight. To her family and close friends, she was "Dee Dee," but not ever to the young man who worshipped her. She was formally Florence.

Florence was eager to write and to do many accomplished things before she died. Al persuaded her to write a book called *Running for Dummies*, a delightful how-to for couch potatoes. And pitchman Al quickly promoted his wife's fitness gospel.

If this piece is short on Al Joyner's athletic activities, hopefully it's long on sentimentality and romance. At Flo-Jo's casket in late September 1998, Al lamented the loss, tearfully noting, "Not everybody saw she gave unconditional love. She was my dream. I stayed focused on her for seven years until she looked my way."

Before little Mary Rose fell asleep in Auntie Jackie's arms, she sang one of her mother's favorites—*When Wind Blew on Me*.

Al Joyner really doesn't enjoy running, but he does in tribute to, as he put it, "to my coach and best friend."

So if he doesn't make it with the triple jump in the 2000 Olympics, he'll take a breather and then in 2000, Al Joyner will start to train for what Florence was doing at her death—the marathon. He said softly and simply, "I'll run the five she wanted to run."

★

FLO JO'S FELLA: Al Joyner's triple-jump success led to marriage to lovely Miss Griffith, who died much too soon for husband and daughter.

WIZARD AT WORK: Ozzie Smith, acrobatic shortstop of the
Cardinals, hits his most dramatic homer—and first ever left-handed—to
beat Los Angeles, 3–2, in a League Championship Series won by the
Cardinals in 1985.

1985

A Date With Don Denkinger

Ump's Faulty Call Killed Storybook Season

Fifteen years later into the round-figured new century, 2000, St. Louis's Public Enemy Number One still is an American League umpire named Don Denkinger, the man who spoiled the "I-70 World Series" with Kansas City.

Actually, reflection really is too tough on Denkinger—except that his "safe" call in a glaring "out" situation was quite poor in execution—because Kansas City's pitching muzzled the Cardinals' hitting. And in the critical sixth-game moment, the Redbirds all played as if the starting nine had been "captured" by the Busch Stadium tarpaulin.

The loss of Vince Coleman, leadoff man and catalyst in "Whitey Ball," the run-sheep-run offense of manager Whitey Herzog, was devastating. A creeping tarp had caught Coleman's leg in an earlier pre-game rain delay.

Still, when pinch-hitter Brian Harper bounced a run-scoring single up the middle in the eight inning of the sixth game at K.C., it looked honestly as if St. Louis had won a seventh World Series with the worst offense. The run-shy Redbirds scored just 13 runs in six games and would bat a woeful .188 overall.

Pitching in relief with that 1–0 lead was just about the hottest bullpen man ever. In a rousing six-game upset over Los Angeles in the National League Championship Series (NLCS) and World Series, left-hander Ken Dayley appeared in nine games and conceded only three hits and four walks, struck out eight, and allowed none of what the Royals needed most—runs.

But in a questionable move in the ninth, Herzog brought in his other game-saver, right-hander Todd Worrell. Pinch-hitting, Jorge Orta began the inning with a soft grounder to Jack Clark at first base. Clark lobbed to Worrell, covering, and—as instant replay would make his mistake even more obvious and infamous—Denkinger belatedly put palms down—safe!

To digress years later, a fretful Herzog, unable to argue Denkinger into changing his decision, said he wished he had walked over to commissioner Pete Ueberroth and demanded a look at replay. If the commissioner refused, Whitey said he should have pulled his team off the field, obviously outrageously in a forfeit loss.

Smiling, he cracked, "I'd have been right, but I'd have been fired!"

The Cardinals came apart after Denkinger's decision. Forced to hold Orta on base, Clark had to chase a foul near the dugout at an odd angle. The ball fell untouched and, of all people, a strikeout batter, Steve Balboni, then singled.

A bunting force-out at third helped, but only long enough for catcher Darrell Porter to commit a damaging passed ball. Pinch-hitter Hal McRae drew the obvious call, a bases-loaded intentional pass. Former Redbird Dane Iorg, also pinch-hitting, lofted a single to right, and when Porter was timid covering the plate on Andy Van Slyke's strong throw, the winning run followed the tying tally. The final was 2–1.

The Cardinals unravelled in the seventh game when big-game lefty John Tudor faltered early and tore up his hand punching a mechanical clubhouse fan. With Denkinger unfortunately working the plate, both Herzog and hot-tempered Joaquin Andujar were ejected. The 11–0 rout was the low point in Cardinal Series history and a sad conclusion of a sensational 101-game season in which both Andujar and Tudor were 20-game winners, the southpaw crafting an incredible 10 shutouts and another in the Series.

With bullpen ace Bruce Sutter having leaped to an astonishing contract at Atlanta, Herzog crafted a championship "bullpen by committee," basically Worrell, Dayley, and unsung middle-man Jeff Lahti.

Against L.A. in the NLCS, the improbable, if not impossible, occurred to help the Cardinals take the lead in the fifth game, the last at Busch Stadium. Ozzie Smith hit his first left-handed home run in nine major league seasons, beating stunned Tom Niedenfuer, 3–2, with a blow that bounced off a right-field upright, prompting Jack Buck's famous call, "Go crazy, folks, go crazy."

And two days later at Dodger Stadium, after mighty mite Wizard of Oz stung Niedenfuer with a triple in the eighth inning, Clark came up in the ninth, one short and two on. A hitting sensation crippled the second half of the season, Jack the Ripper ripped out Tommy Lasorda's heart. His three-run shot put the Cardinals into the Series and a date with Don Denkinger.

★

1986
Wick's Big One
Doug Wickenheiser's Great Playoff Goal

For the finest hour in Blues hockey history, earned by overall merit rather than automatic promotion into the Stanley Cup finals, the greatest come-from-behind achievement was capped by a young man destined for an early death—Doug Wickenheiser.

Over their generation in the gold-tinged note of the Blues, St. Louis has had shattering experiences of man's mortality—the motorcycle casualty of Bob Gassoff, the gutty cancer demise of admirable player and coach, Barclay Plager, and then the big "C" that finally felled Wickenheiser in 1998 after a long battle.

So it's a rich opportunity to salute the popular player by recalling his two-goal contribution to the remarkable rally that knocked off Calgary in the sixth game of the conference championship series in 1986.

Doug's overtime goal at 7:30—his second of the unforgettable game—brought a 6–5 victory before a screaming Arena crowd of 17,801 that probably couldn't believe what it had seen. That is, three tying goals in the last 12 minutes of regulation, the last of which were highlighted by Greg Paslawski, second only to Wick as a standout.

With barely four minutes to play, Paslawski scored twice; the second twanged the net with only a minute and eight seconds to play.

By then the SRO crowd was ready to throw a fit, aside from throwing things at referee Kerry Fraser. The striped shirt was caught in roughhouse play caused as much by the Blues as the Flames. In the midst of 20 first-period penalties, assistant captain Rob Ramage, irate at Fraser, threw a paper cup at the referee and drew a crippling 10-minute misconduct.

After two periods, Calgary's 4–1 lead seemed safe, but coach Jacques Demers's team, reacting as if club owner Harry Ornest were a big spender rather than a pinch-penny, already had shown a desire and ability to come from behind. The Blues had rallied to beat Minnesota in the first round of the playoffs and then Toronto in the division finals.

Now, facing his weary blades in the dressing room, Demers was quiet. Said Jacques, "I didn't say much, 'Just keep your head up. No matter what happens, we walk out of here with our heads up.'"

Tactfully the coach suggested, "I think we can get about 20 or more shots and, if so, there'll be a seventh game. We don't know how to lose."

Early in the third period, Wickenheiser got his first goal, unassisted, but then former Blue Joey Mullen, a fly in Ornest's soup, extended the lead to three goals again.

Then the Blues began to celebrate scoring star Bernie Federko's 30th birthday early. In the third-place season of 37–34–8, Federko had scored 107 points, many more than Mark Hunter, Ron Flockhart, Doug Gilmour, Dave Barr, and Brian Sutter.

A minute after Mullen's goal made it 5–2, Sutter batted in a rebound of a shot by Paslawski. Next, assisted by Sutter, Paslawski scored and, as mentioned, Greg took charge.

Stealing the puck from defenseman Jamie Macoun, Paslawski wheeled and scored. And in overtime, celebrating his birthday, Federko set up the score with a pass to Hunter, whose shot rebounded to Wickenheiser.

Doug broke it up, 6–5, the greatest-ever playoff goal, but they had gone about as far as they could go—the Blues, that is, and Wick, too. They lost the seventh game at Calgary, 2–1, and Wickenheiser later would face a more serious foe.

★

IN THE 'WICK' OF TIME: Doug Wickenheiser's finest hour—maybe the Blues', too—in a career cut short by death was the overtime goal that gave St. Louis a remarkable come-from-behind victory over Calgary, 6–5, in 1968. Wick scored another that sixth-game playoff series that sent the series to a seventh game. Unfortunately, like Wickenheiser in a short life, the Blues lost that one.

For the Love of Mike

The Younger Spinks Achieved the Rarity for a Light-Heavy—the Big One

As the old saying goes, a good little man can't beat a good big man, especially when the difference is the size and poundage between light-heavyweight and heavyweight boxing champions. Unless, that is, if you're a Bob Fitzsimmons of old or a much more modern Michael Spinks.

The younger of the brothers Spinks—Michael—succeeded in the mid-1980s where so many 175-pound champions had failed, that is, since freckled Cornishman Bob Fitzsimmons—Ruby Robert—succeeded early in the twentieth century.

Fitz, slender-legged with a blacksmith's upper body, knocked out James J. Corbett for the heavyweight title in 1897 and then, kayoed by James J. Jeffries, led the light-heavies from 1903 to 1905. So it's really the reverse of the task Spinks accomplished and so many other failed.

In boxing, traditionally, the heavyweight championship purses are considerably larger than for any other division, including just one flight-down. Good 175-pound champions who failed at the jump included Georges Carpentier, John Henry Lewis, Billy Conn, Archie Moore, and Bob Foster, among others—especially Foster.

Arizona sheriff Foster was devastating with many quick knockouts in his division for years, but when he tried for the big belt and the big money, he was knocked out by Joe Frazier in two rounds in 1970 and by Muhammad Ali in eight four years later.

Even the gifted Sugar Ray Robinson, perhaps pound-for-pound the best, couldn't make it when he tried to go up from the welterweight division to middleweight and then light-heavyweight. In a steamy night in New York in 1952, he couldn't get past safety-first Joey Maxim.

So for Michael Spinks's St. Louis fans, it was sobering, when former U.S. Olympic middleweight champion sought, from 1981 to 1985 the top prize after holding the light-heavyweight belt.

For one, eminent trainer Angelo Dundee had fingered Michael Spinks over brother Leon when the Olympic kings came home for a professional card in 1977 at Kiel Auditorium. Leon scored a third-round knockout, and Michael took a six-round decision, but Dundee observed, "I like the little one," meaning, of course, the younger and lighter brother.

For the abortive leap from light-heavy to heavy, Michael put himself in the hands of a remarkable fitness man, Mackie Shillstone, who also helped Ozzie Smith fill out for baseball. That's exactly what Shillstone did for Spinks, building him up a bit and yet not sacrificing the special need for speed.

So, in September 1985, facing Larry Holmes in Las Vegas, Spinks's extra 25 pounds helped him to a unanimous decision over a 220-pound champion. Six months later, this time at 205, Michael again outpointed a heavier Holmes.

If there was one disappointment in Michael's career, it was his quick, one-round fade-out against wild-swinging menace Mike Tyson, who overwhelmed the 212-pound champion.

Chances were, Michael was too smart to linger long in the rugged game where guys often wind up on Queer Street. Also, the mother of his dear young daughter had been killed in an accident. He had a child to raise.

Perhaps with a view of the descent of brother Leon—there but for the grace of God go I!—Michael Spinks retired, moved to Wilmington in tax-friendly Delaware, and lived happily, a former light-heavyweight boxing champion who was good enough, if briefly, to be king of the heavies.

★

THAT'S HOW: As Michael Spinks seems to indicate after doing what comes most unnaturally. That is, a light-heavy champion overcoming the heavyweight title holder, which had been done only once before in the nineteenth century. Obviously, Mike doesn't mean it as an easy-does-it gesture, but it's fascinating that he upset heavyweight champion Larry Holmes in 1985 at Las Vegas, his weight bulked up without loss of speed, and then beat Holmes again six months later.

Farewell to Flo-Jo

Lovely Mrs. Joyner Won Races and National Acclaim

If you will, she was Diana, the queenly goddess of love—or was that mythical Greek figure merely the goddess of the hunt?—but Florence Griffith Joyner, or Flo-Jo, the Olympic track star, was cut from the same regal cloth.

If it's easier to write glowingly about the dead, especially those deceased at only 37, it's because the athlete, wife, and mother brought to women's track and field an appealing change. She was a curvaceous cutie with talon-style fingernails and flashy one-legged running suits—and she could run like the wind.

At the 1988 Olympics in Seoul, she burst into the international scene with four medals, including still-enduring world-record performances in the 100- and 200-meter dashes.

At the Olympic trials, she not only ran the three fastest 100 meters ever—at 10.49 seconds—but she did it in a purple body suit adorned with a turquoise brief bikini and absolutely nothing on her left leg.

Said Olympic gold medalist Evelyn Ashford, "What Florence brought to track was a flash and a flair, good for the sport and the rest of the women athletes. Her charisma and personality reflected kindly on the rest of us women."

Despite her success, there were whispers about steroids and drugs, which infuriated her and her husband, Al Joyner, sister of female track's greatest performer, Jackie Joyner-Kersee. Al was a gold medalist himself in the 1984 triple jump.

Understandably, Al's bitterness spilled over at the funeral, where sister Jackie held Flo-Jo's eight-year-old daughter, Mary Rose, in an hour-long ceremony in Los Angeles.

Al and Jackie had known tough times in East St. Louis, but so did Florence Griffith, who grew up hungry in South Central L.A., the seventh of 11 children and mocked as a kid for wearing mismatched socks, riding a unicycle, and walking on her hands.

After Flo-Jo graduated from high school, hoping to be a beautician, designer, artist, poet, and "everything," she went to Cal State at Northridge, then followed coach Bob Kersee to UCLA. Kersee, of course, is so important in the Joyners' lives.

At UCLA, Griffith graduated with a degree in psychology and continued her interest in track, which led to NCAA championships in the 200- and 400-meter dashes. As a bank teller who had finished second in the 1984 Olympics, she almost quit running track, but by '86 she was working out full time, 15 pounds heavier and stronger.

With a sudden surge—Flo-Jo dropped to her knees and asked God's help—she turned track upside down and brought sexy success to Seoul.

There, in the capital of South Korea, she won worldwide attention with three gold medals and a silver, and then she turned to things she loved, as model, actress, writer, beautician, poet, children's advocate, clothes designer, wife, and—what she loved most—mother.

She really never slowed down, as indicated in her amusing book for couch potatoes, a guide called, *Running for Dummies*.

In 1996, she suffered a heart seizure on a flight from Los Angeles to St. Louis, but she still was a woman in motion, training for a marathon, when, sleeping with dear Mary Rose at her side, Flo-Jo died peacefully of a brain malformation that had existed from birth. The time was late 1998, too young to die.

★

FLOWING GRACE: *Flo-Jo, everybody's nickname for delightful Florence Griffith Joyner, raises the national banner high after another victory and flows toward husband Al Joyner at the left.*

Nick of Time

Rich Grawer Ended Billiken Basketball Descent

With end-of-the-century honors deservedly Charlie Spoonhour's for having taken Saint Louis University a rung higher in basketball, it's nice to pay tribute to Rich Grawer for having put Billiken basketball back on the ladder of success.

A kid who made good in the hometown, Grawer came to the college campus in 1982 at age 39 after 12 years as a conqueror at DeSmet High School. There, he had a handsome 296–85 record, including three state championships and, oh yes, a genial giant, Steve Stipanovich, who made it big at Missouri and into the pro ranks.

The cynical might suggest that Grawer's payment for having helped Stipo stay close to home was the coach's own ticket to Norm Stewart's staff at Ol' Mizzou. Chances are, though, the wily Grawer knew he needed the exposure for the job he had dreamed about, Saint Louis U.

Many others had floundered out there on Grand Avenue. Fact is, good Jesuit fathers, who take an oath of poverty but not their work-a-day financial problems, were thinking about dropping the sport or scaling down into Division II. That lower label stigma would have been even more costly in a community that believes in the best, even if old St. Lou doesn't always get it.

Still, Billiken blue and white had been black and blue after a decade of losing two out of every three games when Grawer came along with a reverse ratio in his high school record.

After three sad seasons of what the Billikens had become accustomed to—defeat—the little coach climbed a big mountain. He persuaded local talent to stay home, well enough for him to obtain Monroe Douglas and a high-school teammate Roland Gray, a diamond in the rough. Similarly, he corralled the gifted athlete, Anthony Bonner, who would become St. Louis's all-time leader with 1,972 points.

This is the center cut for which Grawer deserves to be remembered in a career of 10 seasons, only one short of Eddie Hickey's 11-year record. Hickey left for greener pastures and greener money at Marquette, whereas Grawer was ushered out with a season left on his contract after a 5–23 pratfall.

In a remarkable rebuilding of the campus as a Midtown oasis, the university president, Lawrence J. Biondi, S.J., had included sports in his higher standards. The aggressive, progressive padre had established a top-25 ranking as the standard for round ball.

It was unthinkable then—almost the cause of a muffled laugh—but not now, because of Spoonhour and the other guy, Grawer, who became athletic director at Clayton High School.

At Saint Louis U., Rich stopped the bleeding with an 18–12 season in '85, then he brought back the Bills to tournament heights the next year with a 25–10 record. They beat St. Peter's at home, then lost to ultimate champion Southern Mississippi.

They were so close in those days, not quite lofty enough for the NCAA tournament, but twice they reached the NIT finals. In 1989 after a 27–10 season, the Bills capped the year with tournament wins over SIU–Carbondale, at Wisconsin, and over New Mexico and Michigan State before losing in the finals to the dimpled darling of Madison Square Garden, St. John's.

Saint Louis reached the finals again in '90 after a 21–12 year, after beating Kent State, Wisconsin–Green Bay, DePaul, and New Mexico before a two-point final loss to Vanderbilt.

So ultimately, athletic director Debbie Yow, asked by Father Biondi to get a coach to take the Bills a bit farther, came up with Charlie Spoonhour, a bell-ringer. Rich Grawer, the other guy in the round-ball revival at the place he always wanted to coach, wound up the century watching son Brian play, wearing Missouri's black and gold.

★

BENCH BOSS: *Rich Grawer, pointing to what has to be done, raised Saint Louis University's basketball standards after a successful high school coaching career at DeSmet.*

1990
Show-Me Showcase

Norm Stewart, a Legend at Ol' Mizzou

It's simply not true that the first Kansas coach Norm Stewart opposed was Doc Naismith. It just seems that way because Stormin' Norman became a legend at Columbia, as established as the campus columns.

Like the six columns of an old university administration building that burned—not five columns as Chancellor Richard Wallace misspoke—Stewart was an Ol' Mizzou mainstay until that shocking April day 1999, when he announced he would step down as basketball coach at his alma mater.

After all, in 32 of the 96 seasons played by the Tigers since 1906, Stewart won more games at the university—634—than the 11 coaches combined that preceded him at Columbia. Their total was 630 and, mind you, for the last three-quarters of the century, Missouri had only three coaches previous to Stewart.

A big country kid from Shelbyville, Missouri, Norm was a good athlete, All-America in basketball, and a pitcher on Missouri's 1954 College World Series champions. And he came back after a pro basketball demitasse with the St. Louis Hawks and a brief baseball encounter with the Baltimore Orioles' minor leagues.

With a look-see as an assistant to his old coach, Sparky Stalcup, and a six-season successful run as head coach at Northern Iowa, he was right-on ready when athletic director Dan Devine beckoned in 1967.

Under Columbia native Bob (Van) Vanatta, who could win anywhere except where he wanted to win most, Stewart chipped out of life's rough. First year, he was 10–16 with a team that had won only three games each of the previous two seasons.

From 15–11 his second season, 1969–70, and for the next 30, he had only two losing years. In 13 seasons he won 20 or more games, plus eight conference championships, and led the team to 16 NCAA tournament appearances and five NITs. Stewart coached 28 first-team all-conference players, eight first-team All-Americans, and 29 drafted by the NBA.

Only Kansas's Phog Allen, a successor to the man who invented the game, Dr. James Naismith, and Oklahoma State's Henry Iba coached longer in the same conference. Fact is, Stewart saw 36 head coaches come and go in the conference since his first Tigers won their '67 opener at Arkansas, 74–58.

Six-time Coach of the Year by respectable groups, including the AP and UPI, Stormin' Norm never earned honors more significant than in successive seasons, 1994 and '95. First, the '94 team went 28–4 and on to the NCAA's Elite Eight after going through the entire Big Eight season unbeaten.

In '95, with eight seniors gone and Freshman of the Year Kelly Thames out for the season, a 20-win surprise led to a crushing letdown and a near upset of ultimate NCAA champion UCLA. Swift little Bruins' Tyus Edney, put in the game with 4.8 seconds left, streaked the length of the floor at Boise, Idaho, for a two-point basket and one-point win.

A most certain highlight for Stewart as coach in the Big Eight for all of its 20 years was in 1983 when his peach of a pair, Steve Stipanovich and John Sundvold, produced a 26–8 record for a fourth straight conference title.

Norm Stewart, eating food as hot as he could become, collapsed in 1989 with colon cancer and other wounded intestines. He could have bowed out then, but he waited a decade later until heeding the friendly sideline foes at Kansas who chanted, "Sit down, Norm, sit down."

The way it's told, Stewart informed new athletic director Mike Alden of his decision when Alden was discussing Tiger basketball's future with the 64-year-old coaching indestructible.

Many held their breath, fearful of an ugly ending. But bless his soul, Stormin' Norman was a sentimental pussycat at the end in a graceful denouncement. He drifted into retirement with a golden million-dollar parachute.

★

STORMIN' NORM: A legend as a great basketball player and good championship baseball pitcher, Norman Stewart came back to his alma mater Ol' Mizzou as a basketball coach who showed the Show-Me State—and everyone else. He wound up one of the winningest coaches ever, raising the barrier of expectancy for basketball's Bengals.

1992
The Mostest Gal

JJK Rose from Poverty to Scholarship, Athletic Excellence

If the cow had jumped over the moon, before man spoiled a good fable by doing it himself, chances are the dear bovine would have been accompanied by a fair lady who just might have been the best woman athlete ever—Jackie Joyner-Kersee.

If Jackie wasn't the best, maybe it then had to be a Texas tomboy, Mildred (Babe) Didrikson, champion of tough times in the depression before she married burly wrestler George Zaharias and became the top woman pro golfer.

Fatal illness cut down the Babe, but, though handicapped by hamstrings, Jackie Joyner-Kersee still was regal in her last tournament bow-out at Southern Illinois University–Edwardsville, close by East St. Louis, the struggling community of her youth.

Joyner-Kersee, who survived a youth at times without any meals or heat, used a rundown old East Side recreation center as an oasis. And there, in the brown-suede high heels of a woman accomplished, she spaded out the first shovel of ground in gratitude as a driving force for the new Jackie Joyner-Kersee Youth Center. For all her great achievements, it's charming that at her track and field farewell, she already had taken her biggest athletic leap into the future!

A *Post-Dispatch* Scholar-Athlete, skilled enough to lead Lincoln High School to three Illinois state track titles and three girls' basketball championships, she won a scholarship to UCLA, a college of various championships. From UCLA Blue, the sky was the limit.

Twice All-American in track and field, twice All-American in basketball, she began in 1983 six successive years as heptathlon champion.

A year later with brother Al Joyner, Jackie competed in the summer Olympic Games at Los Angeles. Al won the gold medal in the triple jump, Jackie the silver in the heptathlon.

In 1985, coached by Bob Kersee, who would become her husband, she won the Broderick Cup as the nation's top woman collegiate athlete and—this summarizes the complete dear lady—she graduated in the top 10 percent of her class with a degree in history.

In the heptathlon, she set a record of 7,148 points in the 1986 Goodwill Games at Moscow, then topped it with 7,158 at the U.S. Olympic Festival and won the prestigious Sullivan award as the nation's top amateur athlete in 1987.

At the 1988 Olympic Games at Seoul, Jackie won gold both in the heptathlon and long jump. Her 7,291 points in the heptathlon was a world's record.

By the time she won the gold medal in her specialty and the bronze in the long jump at the 1992 Olympics, Bruce Jenner of 1976 Olympic decathlon fame dubbed her "the greatest multi-event athlete ever, man or woman."

By the time she took a brief fling in the American Basketball League in 1996—one heck of a volleyball player, too—Jackie Joyner-Kersee really had driven her 5'10", 153-pound body far enough, especially when she had higher sights set in her efforts to help humanity. She more than fulfilled the mild admonishment given years earlier to athletes by Monsignor Louis F. Meyer. Said the monsignor, "Put something back into the pot."

The clergyman was talking to the athletic jocks, but none ever followed with the warmth of a girl the legendary six-time Olympian first coach Nini Feenoy remembered as "all legs, pigtails, and teeth—smiling teeth"—a happy hero.

★

HIGH HOPES, HIGH HURDLES: *Jackie Joyner-Kersee had both, as an underprivileged East Side girl who became a topflight student, athlete, and leader of youth.*

PURE GOLD: Brett Hull, one of the Blues' greatest and certainly most
controversial players, twangs the nets with a goal. Golden Brett,
outspoken with raspy comments, soon would be getting his checks from
Dallas, to the regret of many and the delight of a few.

The Golden Goal Guy

Brett Hull Scored Often in Hockey's Eye and Spectators' Hearts

From Hall to Hull, from Picard to Pronger, from one Plager to the other, from the on-the-ice Brendan Shanahan to same-named Mike in the front office, the hockey Blues have had favorites, but probably none so fetching as Hull, the Golden Brett.

Among his faithful, who far outnumbered those who thought he wasn't quite a team player, the famous son of a famous father, Chicago Blackhawks' Bobby, Hull was a box office draw as well as a goal-getter.

So management had to have fortitude to decide that the Blues would win without Brett, a decision aired to Hull by manager Larry Pleau in July 1998. The 10-year talent moved down to Dallas and helped the Stars to new heights.

The front office's consolation in the millennium season, one with a league-tying record for consecutive victories on the road, was that the Blues made their boldest bid for a sip from Lord Stanley's battered old, tiered wedding-cake trophy.

There is, after all, nothing that beats team success, as the Cardinals' Sam Breadon learned 75 years ago after having boldly let personal feelings deal away his franchise player, championship manager, and star slugger Rogers Hornsby. When Frank Frisch rose to the occasion, Breadon never again was afraid to trade players, though he divested too many.

The Blues, with none of the Redbirds' success, had little reason to risk offering another multi-year contract after Hull had shown a volatile temperament. Like many, broken-beaked Brett couldn't get along with a difficult foreman, Mike Keenan, whom management obviously had granted too much authority.

Keenan spoke his mind too often and too strongly from beneath an oddly unemotional blank stare. Raspy-voiced Brett would respond gravely, further rocking the boat and actually turning away many who had regarded highly his professional support as much as they did his efforts for charity and good causes.

Make no mistake about it, coming to town in March 1988, acquired from Calgary for Rob Ramage and Rick Wamsley, Hull loved the town. Immediate applause pleased him and also impressed Mike Shanahan, then the club's goodwill man upstairs.

Reflecting his easy-going approach, inherited with strong wrists and forearms from dear Dad, young Hull joined the senior with 500-plus goals. The Golden Boy scored 72, 86, and 70 goals in successive seasons, achieving one record worthy of famed old Maurice Richard—50 in 50.

Brett won a couple of the major awards, the Hart trophy as the National Hockey League's MVP and its Lady Byng as gentlemanly player.

When Hull came aboard back in '88, he was 23 with a famous name, a big shot, and only one NHL season, as the Post-Dispatch's Dave Luecking noted in Brett's farewell, and junior was grateful for the fact that excitable Ron (Professor) Caron dealt for him.

The kid thought he didn't have much, but he had that quick-trigger power shot, speed and power, and the ability to turn on the red light and big celebratory boat horn. By '90 he had negotiated his first $1 million contract.

But Keenan came in with the trade-itching technique of baseball's Frantic Frank Lane. He traded away Curtis Joseph, Kelly Chase, and fan favorite Brendan Shanahan. By the time he also got rid of Hull's close friend and line-mate Adam Oates, Keenan brought out the worst in Hull and, as Luecking wrote, "vice-versa."

Public exchange of insults didn't help, nor did Keenan's taking away the team captaincy, insisting it wasn't "personal." Brett suggested that you could bet your bippy it was deliberate.

With the coach insisting he hadn't inherited "his kind of team," a patient front office finally cashiered him with cash after two-and-a-half years. That really wasn't enough for Hull's happiness, despite his becoming the fourth fastest player ever to reach 500 goals.

Management saluted him then and, of course, the faithful Hull fans came as they always did. But new, low-keyed general manager, Pleau, couldn't reach agreement on Brett's value and future. Al MacInnis received top dollar and leadership, along with a big young defenseman named Chris Pronger.

So Golden Brett Hull, originally a free-swinging bachelor, left with a wife, three kids born here, and, to paraphrase Luecking earlier, a love affair with St. Louis that was "vice-versa."

★

1992

Bellerive

A Magic Home to Gary Player, Nick Price, and the Area's Tourney Hopes

Bellerive, as tough as Queen Victoria's finest troops when Britain ruled the waves, proved twice that for her former majesty's golfing best.

Two natives of South Africa, Gary Player in 1965 and Nick Price in 1992, won the last two majors played in St. Louis, both at Bellerive. Player, a champion in class, won the U.S. Open in 1965 and named his new South African ranch "Bellerive."

Finally finding a Price that was right, Nick scored his first major at the same course in 1992, winning the

Professional Golfers Association. Buoyed by the success, Price won a second PGA title two years later at Tulsa's Southern Hills Country Club.

Here, in weather mild for June until a playoff round with Australia's Kel Nagle, Player prevailed.

In the St. Louis major a quarter-century later—you know the old crack about keeping dogs from going wild in August is by shooting 'em in July—Price found August as nice as his golf. The 35-year-old former Rhodesian soldier fired a final-round 70, one under par, three up at the finish. Nick's four-day score was 278, six under.

Winning $280,000 and fellow pros' plaudits for more than one previous near-miss, Price overcame past mishaps in majors, and Bellerive's awesome 7,148 yards and pin placements. And he finished with a flourish, a par putt for the check and Wannamaker Trophy.

THE PRICE TO PLAY(ER): Nick Price was always on the approach before he conquered Bellerive in the 1992 PGA. Gary Player raises the U.S. Open trophy at Bellerive in '65.

In '65, Player, matching Gene Sarazen, Ben Hogan, and Jack Nicklaus as one of four to win golf's four pro majors, played cautiously against Nagle, head to head, aware Kel was upset after having hit two women spectators with shots, bloodying one. The dear lady felled at the fifth hole was back at the finish, greeting the Aussie cheerfully with six scalp stitches. She accepted three golf balls and his apologies.

Player, a wily little man in black, brown-armed like a blacksmith, had traveled Kel's troublesome path. His 71 to the shaken Nagle's 74 was deceptive, because Gary bogeyed the last two holes.

For the little man with long fingers and brawny biceps, the U.S. Open was one more to chalk up for courage and conviction. When recovering from a broken neck at age 15, he got his first golf clubs as a gift from his father, a Johannesburg paint salesman. Within three years, without having won an amateur tournament, Gary turned pro. First off, using his own clubs, the Black Knight parred the first three golf holes he ever played.

A physical fitness faddist, exercising regularly, eating raisins and nuts for instant energy, he had instant success—even when he switched to bananas and honey, the first to line his stomach, the second for a quicker lift.

Much like the grand champion with whom he was compared, Ben Hogan, Player was nerveless and cool on the course, but gregarious off it. Those thick fingers pushing back his hair, he hit with home-run oomph off the tee.

His intensity as a three-time Masters' champion was manifest when he gave 1999 winner Jose Maria Olazabal a pep talk about confidence. The Spanish golfer increased his practice and won Augusta's green coat.

For the 5'7", 150-pound Player, St. Louis was only a stepping stone. By century's end, at age 64, Player had 19 Senior PGA victories, 21 regular PGA titles, and nine majors.

With $9 million, minus the $36,000 he gave away here in gratitude in '65, the Black Knight had traveled 10 million miles and collected nine grandchildren. He began the millennium seeking to become the first golfer ever to win an official PGA-sanctioned tournament in six different decades.

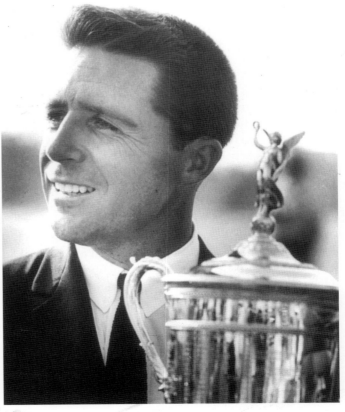

Gary Player could do it. Before the National Open playoff against Nagle in '65, he borrowed a coin from tournament director Joe Dey of the PGA. He'd gone without a farthing and needed a coin to mark the ball. Afterward, with a grin, Player gave the penny back to Dey—and a check for $25,000 for junior golf.

★

1993
The Old Barn's Last Barn-Burner
Missouri Over Illinois in Triple Overtime

When they closed down the old barn that was the Arena on Oakland Avenue, the last basketball attraction there was a barn-burner. Missouri beat Illinois in triple overtime in their annual Braggin' Rights battle.

In a mixed metaphor of sports, "barn-burner" was the favorite radio expression of a hockey man, former coach and Blues broadcaster, Gus Kyle, but it's an apt way to describe the last basketball attraction before the move to the building put up by hockey ownership—Kiel Center.

Over the years of a 7-come-11 natural rivalry—oddly the series score was 7 to 11 in '99, in favor of Illinois—the Illini showed a basic advantage over Missouri in players and procurement. But the remarkable triple-overtime shootout in '93 figured to be a favorite even if not the last game at the Arena.

For Norm Stewart's Tigers, reeling from a 120–68 walloping by Arkansas at Fayetteville and a shaky one-point win over Coppin State at Mizzou's tough home court, Hearnes Center, the dramatic tug o' war triumph over Illinois was a springboard to a great season, 28–4. Included was a perfect 14–0 Big Eight record, unbeaten home and away.

For Lou Henson's Illini, the second loss in eight games took its toll in a 17–11 season in which they finished 10–8 in the conference. In the game, spunky freshman Kiwane Garris missed two free throws on the clock at the end of the second overtime. Either would have won the contest for the Orange and Blue.

For the Tigers, senior Jevon Crudup was the spark before he fouled out, scoring 22 points. With a look that could have killed the referee when he waved him off the court, Crudup later captured the game properly. "This one," he said, "will go down in Missouri history."

Indeed. And at the finish, having had five players foul out, Stewart used a patchwork lineup of Kelly Thames, Jason Sutherland, Derek Grimm, Lamont Frazier, and Reggie Smith, who hobbled on one knee.

Said a happy Stewart afterward, "We had the sick and wounded playing. Next up were women and children."

Actually, Smith had missed the last four games with an injury and was scheduled to be out three more weeks, but he played the final overtime. And Chris Heller, who had sprained an ankle a couple of days earlier, was in there.

Missouri, ahead four points at the half, 42–38, extended the lead to 16, 61–42, but Illinois silenced Mizzou rooters in the mixed-interest crowd of 18,273. The Illini went on a 26–4 run to take apparent command with a nine-point lead and just over a minute to play, 74–65.

Reflecting later, coach Henson commented, "When you've got a chance to close a door, you have to do it."

Actually, they did, as one writer cracked, but the Illini slammed the door on their own thumb. With Illinois missing in a typical parade to the free throw line, Missouri hit with four three-pointers. The last was rung up by captain Frazier with 10 seconds to go, 79–79.

Fatigue obviously was a factor in the overtime, as were Garris's two free-throw clunkers with nobody on the floor in the second extra period.

In the third overtime, aggressive Sutherland, who hadn't scored previously, hit two of four field goals in the clutch, including a three-pointer to open the third overtime. Overall, though, Crudup was the hero. He stood defiantly next to the Tiger bench. Rival coach Henson saluted Crudup, calling him "devastating." Devastating in a devastating game.

★

WIN WITH WINFIELD: Arm-raised Julian Winfield (center) joins in after Missouri's amazing triple-overtime win over Illinois in the final Braggin' Rights battle at the Arena.

1994

Spoon Fed

Charlie Spoonhour Brought Talent and Humor to Saint Louis U.

A country kid from Arkansas, with a smile on his face and a quick wit on his lips, Charlie Spoonhour finished what predecessor Rich Grawer had started. He took Saint Louis University basketball back into national prominence, then decided at only age 59 that he had gone as far as he could go.

When the Will Rogers of round ball stepped aside gracefully a year in advance of the new century—at his request and to others' sorrow—he proved he could do just about anything with Doc Naismith's basketball except get the good big man who could put him and the Billikens over the top.

By the time the turtle-necked, close-cropped graying blond left for a seat in the baseball Cardinals' dugout and occasionally behind a wheel of chance at his adopted second home, Las Vegas, the hay was in the barn and the fans in the stands. Even without a true center, the Blue and White Bills were one of the nation's attendance best.

Spoonhour himself was partly the reason, a pink-cheeked man on the sidelines who wanted his teams to play as neat as he looked. When his seventh Saint Louis U. team couldn't win enough to satisfy the coach—they were one game under .500 in the 1998–99 season—Charlie asked out.

Few could have bowed out so gracefully, partly because he had raised the basketball bar for the Bills, and partly because as coach and commentator he was colorful, capable, and entertaining. He left pleasant successor Lorenzo Romar with a difficult standard—sound and coach as well as you look.

Spoonhour—"Spoon" more than "Charlie"—earned his reputation the hard way. From that coaching beginning at Rocky Comfort, Missouri, high school, through stepping-stone seasons coaching junior college and a couple assisting the Oklahoma and Nebraska universities, he built a sound background as a wit and a winner.

When, at 53, he left Southwest Missouri State after nine seasons as head coach, he not only won hands-down election to the Missouri Sports Hall of Fame, located there in Springfield, but set up the situation by which he would win national Coach of the Year honors from the U.S. basketball writers. That would be his

second season at Saint Louis U., 1994, a year the Bills reached the NCAA tournament for the first time in 37 years.

That 23–6 year, which climaxed in an NCAA bid, included 14 straight season-opening victories and hot perimeter shooting from Scott Highmark, Erwin Claggett, and H. Waldman.

With a crowd of 17,000 for a game with Southern Illinois University–Carbondale at the Arena, shortly before Kiel Center opened new doors downtown, SLU accommodated 20,000-plus and eventually ranked among the top six college teams in attendance.

A 16–12 record in a rough-cob conference and an NIT trip preceded a sub-par 11–19 and then Spoon's greatest acquisition, hometown freshman Larry Hughes, a national McDonalds High School All-American.

Hughes was good, but hard-pressed for financial help for his mother and ailing brother, he decided to opt for professional basketball after his first year in college. The 22–11 record and first-round NCAA victory over prestigious Massachusetts accomplished with Hughes were high-water marks.

For Charlie Spoonhour, winning even more friends than ball games, results without Hughes were not good enough. So Spoon said a cheerful, smiling good-bye.

★

SPOON AND FRIEND: *A dear friend, the highly gifted Larry Hughes who gave Charley Spoonhour and St. Louis U. just one sensational season before turning pro for personal financial reasons. That could have been enough to tell the amusing, talented head coach it was time to retire.*

1996
Gateway to the Stars
Rusty Wallace

If at century's end you figured pro football was the game of the future—and, hey, that Super Bowl miracle didn't hurt a bit—you'd better slow down like an auto racer facing a caution flag.

Over the twentieth century, the old Mississippi riverboat town progressed too much like a poky old barge, plodding ahead, and, as baseball's Branch Rickey would put it, with too much addition by subtraction.

When the Arena went up in 1929 and Kiel Auditorium in '34, the Coliseum came down. Playing fields with proper seating disappeared, including the old Federal League park, Handlan Field, Saint Louis University's Walsh Stadium, and Public Schools Stadium.

Even when ingenuity, tax relief, and corporate funds helped handsomely in 1966 with Busch Stadium, a downtown savior, Sportsman's Park was too old to be necessary as a "second" stadium.

Ultimately, because pro football's charm had caught national fancy, St. Louis—city, county, and state, too—could join in with a fascinated citizenry to build a domed stadium concurrent with a new convention center. Yes, and finance pro football with cash-in-advance payments for the team that came to the giant TransWorld Dome.

But was the Believe-It-Or-Not Ripley arrival of the Los Angeles Rams any more remarkable than the occurrence just across the river: the site—uh huh, sight and v-r-o-o-m, vroom sounds of a big-league auto-racing track and crowds to fill them?

A geezer who for too long regarded racing basically as an appeal to the red-necked, white-socked, brown-shoed crowd, was most wrong in his career with this estimation. The geezer? Me!

Working with guts, gusto, and the knowledge that enthusiasm for speed racing wasn't just a southern-

fried tradition, individuals from Wayne Meinert in 1967 to Chris Pook in '64, aided by the Illinois government in '66, worked to turn Gateway into an international raceway and a cash cow for much of the East Side community.

Also, it provided a hometown showcase for St. Louis–born Rusty Wallace, nearing 50, a former Winston Cup champion and constant national contender who considers retirement only another excuse to fly his private plane. Wallace, rookie of the year in 1979 and by '89 first in the Winston Cup, went into the new century with close to $20 million in winnings.

Following Rusty and the rest, showing auto-racing fans' attitude, aptitude, and income that made football even more formidable than baseball, Gateway's full-house crowds showed this box score personality: Average age, 36, seven under the national average; sex, 25 percent women; income, nearly $50,000, $12,000 above national; education, 37 percent high school and 30 percent college; habit, 83 percent reading a daily paper, 76 percent a weekly news magazine; 68 percent exercising regularly.

Back in April 1967, the *Post-Dispatch* reported that a new "multi-million-dollar auto-racing facility would open in the Metro East area." Wayne Meinert had left Pacific Raceway and became president of Gateway, then called St. Louis International Raceway.

By 1970, the American Hot Rod Association had brought its Spring Nationals to the original eighth-mile drag strip—seating capacity 6,000.

In '71, Meinert acquired more land and expanded the strip to a quarter-mile, paving the way for the first "Gateway Nationals." A year later, the national hot rod group's Grand American Series, 10 races, included St. Louis.

By '74, still promoter and owner, Meinert expected 75,000 fans for a three-day meet in July and, sounding like baseball's Bill Veeck, he decided he'd sell beer for 10 cents, unintentionally cracking a funny when he observed, "We thought we needed to add a little fuel to the fire."

A bit of financial flat-tire was ahead. In '82, after a squabble over who owed what to whom, the concessionaire brothers Trover, Phil and Jody, took charge. In '84, Jody became number one, aided by new general manager Ted Haines, but when proposed funding for a road course fell through, Kevin Eichner of St. Louis Financial Collaborative stepped in. He formed a corporation with Trover and made $2 million plans to upgrade the facility, a sleeping giant.

A new 2.2-mile road course in 1985 brought four professional road races, but under Fenton's Rodney Bryan, a driving hobbyist and former stock driver Bob Geaschel, a scale-back continued, as it would under Geaschel's replacement as general manager, Robin Weinrich.

The track, now called Gateway International, attracted the eye of a California man, Chris Pook, who has operated successfully since 1973 with an annual race on a temporary street course in Long Beach.

With St. Louis as one of the largest markets without a major auto race, Pook beat Bruton Smith to the starting gun. Smith owned Charlotte and Atlanta motor speedways.

When Pook announced plans for a motor-sports park—suitable for drag strips, an Indy-style oval for big and stock cars, and also a road course suitable for sports-car racing—he sold his idea to the Southwestern Illinois Development Authority.

They bought. So did the man in Springfield. April 10, 1996, when the Illinois governor put his Jim Edgar on "moral obligation" to back $21.5 million in bonds for the Disneyland on wheels, Madison and Collinsville were richer—and good ol' St. Louis, too.

★

TAKING THE TITLE: Rusty Wallace (27) battles seven-time Winston Cup champion Dale Earnhardt (3). Wallace's finish was good enough for his first Winston Cup Championship, 1989.

1997

Lady Fair

Washington U.'s Colorful Volleyball Coach, Teri Clemens

Washington University, a heavyweight of intellectual pursuit, education, and research, has a heart, too. The Hilltop campus that straddles the city's western limits gave its prized 1999 Citizen Award to a beloved sportswoman, recently retired championship volleyball coach Teri Clemens.

Behind the awarding of the William Greenleaf Elliot Society designation for campus community service was the dramatic story of a warm, inspirational person who had the charm and compassion to attract players to a non-scholarship program, enrich them with dedicated teaching, rear six adopted children, and fight off tenacious asthma that became life-threatening.

So threatening that at age 45, still sought by big-name athletic universities, she already had resolved herself—for loyalty's sake—to continue to wear Washington's colors, but to call it quits ultimately for health's sake.

Even before Juniata College of Huntington, Pennsylvania, soured the swan song for the coach, Clemens finally heeded concerned medical advice. She left behind seven national Division Three champions, college volleyball's winningest record—87 percent— and five NCAA Division III Coach of the Year awards.

She accomplished more in her glittering 529–77 record that included a 59-game winning streak, nine straight trips to the Final Four, and 11 years without a conference loss.

She came aboard Washington's Myrtle and Maroon or, if you prefer, the Red and Green in 1985 after having coached Incarnate Word High School girls for three years. As a lovely lass at Parkway West in 1974, she had missed her turn as the *Post-Dispatch*'s Scholar Athlete only because of the policy of an every-other-year turn. That season a boy took the honor.

But in 1997, coach Clemens, motivator and winner, was the first woman as principal speaker at the *Post-Dispatch* dinner and relished the role. And she relaxed the event for some 150 people present, beginning her remarks by calling out a kid she knew in the first row and throwing her dinner roll to him in an accurate pass.

Her remarks, as always, were as good as her team played. Smiling, she wouldn't repeat a funny story about the peewee baseball prospects of one of her own small fry.

The adoption of a half-dozen kids by Teri and husband Tom Clemens, a financial advisor, deserves applause.

With her kids as well as her summer camp youngsters and those who played for her at Francis Field, she gave her honest best as mother, teacher, coach, consultant and friend.

Her own children, to illustrate, got old-fashioned discipline, limited use of the one-in-a-house television set and follow-the-leader reader rather than video games' diversion.

As for herself, she suffered years of attacks from asthma, which became longer, more painful, and threatening, limiting her inhales after troubled exhales. It soon became time to follow the doctor's advice. . . .

"I've been great at faking how I'm doing, but I spent many days in the hospital." To repeat the way she put it before the Juniata game, her last win denied—"my lungs feel fine, it's my heart that's broken. Still, I don't feel for myself."

As Teri Clemens would have it, don't cry for me, Argentina!

★

NOW HEAR THIS: *Coach Teri Clemens knew all the right words to help inspire Washington's Lady Bears to repeated Championship Heights.*

1998
Century's Mount Everest
When SuperMark McGwire Climbed the Highest Mountain

The most significant playing-field moments in the long, colorful career of the Cardinals came in what amounted to a two-layered wedding cake. That would be the day Mark McGwire said "I do" to continued action wearing the Bat and Birds—and a magnificent honeymoon celebration barely a year later.

That celebration would take place September 8, 1998, when the red-haired Redbird scaled baseball's highest mountain, breaking the single-season home-run record with 62, en route to an incredible 70.

The previous September 17, McGwire, who could have become the richest free agent ever, put personal greed second to satisfaction and decided to stay in St. Louis, capping a brief love affair with our town's fans.

With a bow to the new ownership's efforts, the acquisition of McGwire just before the August 1 roster deadline had been regarded here and elsewhere as merely a rent-a-player acquisition, one for which the Cards gave up a few promising young prospects to inherit for a couple of months the contract of a player too rich for Oakland.

Patronizingly, American League president Gene Budig, confident that SuperMark would be back as a big AL box office draw, complimented Redbird CEO Bill DeWitt, Jr., hailing the athlete as a player and a person. The next time they met, after the "wedding," Budig repeated his praise but told DeWitt wryly, "There will be no American League Christmas Card for McGwire."

If this is a long way to tell a short story—not nearly as long as one of the super slugger's home runs—it's intended for proper perspective. The only moment more significant to McGwire's feat occurred off the field, when Branch Rickey began the Cardinals' farm system in 1920. That one led to nine pennants and six world championships over a 21-year period, the springboard to a century total of 15 flags, nine titles, and one division honor.

Back too many years ago, the Cardinals sold players rather than bought them, passing up additional success for purposes of economy. This time the attraction of a hefty three-year contract, $28.5 million, along with the early enthusiasm of St. Louis fans helped win McGwire's approval. Just before the end of the century, Big Mac accepted a fourth-year option at $11 million through 2001—again no haggling.

So, health willing for a player handicapped often and early by back troubles, Cardinal Country faced the happy outlook of a real-life Casey at the Bat. When the millennium season began, Mark McGwire had averaged 61 home runs over a four-season period—52 at Oakland in 1996, 58 there and with St. Louis in 1997, the unbelievable 70 in 1998, and 65 in the century's farewell season.

A menacing man and physical-fitness faddist, McGwire had huffed up into a handsome hulk, 6'4" and 250 pounds, with forearms of a mighty village smithy. Uh-huh, and heart inherited from his dentist father. John McGwire suffered through boyhood polio and limped through life, though still able to box and play golf well. Son Mark was handicapped early by vision fortunately correctable.

From a rookie who walked away from a record 50 homers—his wife and child, Matt, came first— McGwire experienced enough problems that he considered quitting, but he persevered and produced a short, powerful swing. Slightly crouched in his right-handed stance, a devastating low-ball hitter, he wiggle-waggles his bat like a golfer teeing off. And in that compact swing, he accomplishes something photographer-publisher Jim Mense said he'd never seen, a batter's eyes open even at the point of impact.

McGwire endeared himself early with his commitment, emotionally expressed at his "I do" ceremony, to provide a million dollars to help abused children. Dramatically that night, with a crowd on its feet in appreciation of his staying, Big Mac homered his first time up.

By then, as it was in Babe Ruth's day, his fence-busting in batting practice drew crowds early to the park. A ho-hum ball club, the Cardinals achieved rare championship attendance heights—three million plus—as the man possessed toppled records.

McGwire hewed four records in '98: first, Hack Wilson's 1930 NL record of 56 homers; then the high for a right-handed hitter, 58 by Jimmy Foxx in 1932 and by Hank Greenberg in 1938; then the two—the Babe's 60 in 1927 and Roger Maris's 61 in '61.

Ultimately, McGwire displayed what Branch Rickey would have called "inner conceit." Prodded by Chicago's Sammy Sosa, who passed him with 66 in the third to last game of the 1998 season, Mac ripped off a tying homer in 45 minutes, then buried Sammy with two each the last two days.

SuperMark ripped off five for a total of 70, nine more than Maris and 10 more than the Babe, even five more than ten-year-old son Matthew had wished for!

On father John McGwire's 61st birthday, big Mac tied Maris's record, with Matthew at home plate to bear hug and kiss, and the Maris family in the stands as Cardinal guests. A night later, with the shortest homer and longest remembered, McGwire went into the stands to greet Redbird Rog's kids, a climax to the remarkable occurrence of the number 62, a line shot that came at 8:18 P.M., September 8, 1998.

Whether or not you saw the joyous occasion and Mark's grand-circle route of the bases—an 11-minute game delay that will live forever—the base-path handshakes, high fives and high joy, the fireworks, huzzahs and encores, and, oh yes, the superstar's patented Pillsbury punch to the belly at home plate, chances are you'll know what you were doing when big number 25, redhead in Redbird red, wrote an unforgettable chapter in baseball history.

★

SUPERMARK: *The fabulous impact of Mark McGwire was that he was not only, by far, the most prodigious long-ball hitter in St. Louis history, but also the single-season major-league champ with 70 in 1998. Over a four-year period, Big Mac averaged 61 homers a season with 52, 58, 70, and 65 respectively—a grand baseball finale to the century.*

Super Season
The Rams Incredible 2000

Professional football in St. Louis reminds me of Otis, not battering fullback Jim, but the man for whom the elevator was named. Good ol' St. Lou had more ups and downs than Mr. Otis's elevator until . . .

From a city lucky enough to have a franchise much of the century, let alone a team good enough to earn a home playoff date, the minor sports miracle of the millennium in 2000 was the best—Super Bowl champions.

Back in the early 1920s, led by local football hero Ollie Kraehe, the Gateway City had a brief, losing venture in the National Football League with the St. Louis All-Stars.

Better remembered were the Gunners, a strong independent team led by a bareheaded fullback named Chester (Swede) Johnston, 1931–34. The Swede, who outlived 'em all without a helmet, lived to celebrate the final success of the team for which he really had played.

Better on the field than at the depression box office, the Gunners folded in 1935, after having inherited bankrupt Cincinnati's NFL franchise late in '34. As Johnston and others scattered—Swede joined Green Bay's 1936 champs—the league revived the franchise in '37 and moved it to Cleveland. Nickname? Rams!

Eight years later, a heartless visionary, owner Dan Reeves, unrelated to the current coach, moved to Los Angeles, establishing the first major sports team on the coast. For years at the L.A. Coliseum, the Rams flourished.

Meanwhile, St. Louis football came back in 1960 after a 15-year wait, as the city was awarded the Chicago Cardinals when the Big Red couldn't keep up with the Bears. Here, in 28 frustrating seasons of only three division winners, none good enough for home-field advantage at Sportsman's Park or Busch Stadium, unhappy Bill Bidwill moved his Gridbirds.

At Phoenix, rebuffed with the kind of stadium he couldn't get here either, poor Billy became a senior citizen awaiting the success he hasn't known since he was a ball boy for his father's 1947 Chicago champions.

St. Louis, also starved for victory and a franchise, got the one with the other in 1995. With a giant domed stadium downtown, built with public and private funds, the region reeled when, with haughtiness, the NFL refused to permit former St. Louisan Georgia Frontiere to move her team. Obvious as the nose on Commissioner Paul Tagliabue's face, the league was most concerned about preserving television's second-largest market.

With neither the guts nor the ability to keep maverick Al Davis from running his own franchise shuttle from Oakland to L.A. and back again, the league chose Charlotte, North Carolina, and Jacksonville, Florida, over the distinguished old riverboat town.

With chutzpah even greater than St. Louis's asking interested fans to pay for the privilege to buy seats, the NFL imposed harsh financial penalties on Frontiere and minority owner Stan Kroenke. They gulped but didn't flinch, and this once frugal Germanic community prevailed— bless 'em—by guaranteeing more than 70,000 seats. Even cheerleading former Senator Thomas F. Eagleton was astonished.

So now, St. Louis had the place (TransWorld Dome) and the team (the Rams), but things looked painfully too much the same.

Oh, the Rams got off and running under a new coach, Rich Brooks. Rookie Isaac Bruce was virtually a one-man show in the 1995 opener at Green Bay, where the Pack would suffer its only home loss in two years.

But the team and town soon learned the significance of the quarterback, which would be driven home soon again, when one concussion too many cost the services of Chris Miller, author of five victories in the Rams' first six tries.

A sub-par season followed, and another cost Brooks his job. The Rams brought in dynamic Dick Vermeil, a dusted-off relic of college and pro success. But, alas, Vermeil couldn't win for losing, defeated in 23 of his first 32 games.

GUNNERS: *Colorfully dressed, briefly in the NFL, the powerful independents had top talent. One seated on the cannon was the bareheaded fullback still alive in 2000—Chester (Swede) Johnston.*

Now, changing his coaching mood and many players, jettisoning young Tony Banks, in whom he had the most confidence, the coach and ingenious front office acquired native St. Louisan Trent Green, coming off a great season at Washington. The 1999 high-salaried savior and the team's high hopes apparently went up in severe injury after a most encouraging pre-season.

Kurt Who?

Kurt Warner was a seldom-seen backup, a small-college quarterback, a hero of the miniature gimmick game, Arena League, and a star with Amsterdam of the faraway summer European league. In a grocery-stocker cliché the noble-spirited young man finally resented, Warner could have wound up with his own supermarket. After all, they even named a cereal for him.

In a too-good-to-be-true Cinderella season, Kurt passed for 4,353 yards and 41 touchdowns. He and shake-a-leg runner and receiver Marshall Faulk, obtained from Indianapolis, set a remarkable 1-2 punch for offensive coach Mike Martz's imaginative attack.

Faulk's total yards, 2,429, breaking Barry Sanders's record, earned him the NFL Offensive Player of the Year and the Rams' own Most Valuable Player award, and Warner was the league's MVP choice.

With a bow to much I read as well as saw and heard, notably my younger *Post-Dispatch* colleagues, I'd like to wind up this one—and the book—with a snatch from my own *P-D* farewell to the unforgettable:

THE THROW: The many in the clutch by Kurt Warner, including the big ones in the final two weeks, to Ricky Proehl and Isaac Bruce.

THE CATCH: By Proehl, who was fighting off pass interference that probably wouldn't have been called when he cradled the ball at shoulder height and finally controlled it for the TD that overtook Tampa Bay in the NFC championship game.

THE PLAY: A week later, by Bruce, hero of the Rams' first victory as a St. Louis team five seasons ago at Green Bay. When Warner couldn't quite get enough on his follow-through, after being hit hard, the Reverend Ike did the rest.

THE B-R-U-C-E chant as the receiver finished the play, resembling the same cry when the other Bruce

(Sutter) blew a World Series–ending pitch past Milwaukee's Gorman Thomas in 1982. But the Super Bowl finally belonged to St. Louis because of . . .

THE TACKLE: An unsung hero all year as a goodwill man, a good-to-the-community guy and players' conduit to the head coach, linebacker Mike Jones made the final tackle on a play near the goal-line. It will be remembered as long as . . .

THE COACH: Vermeil, who sold me in his first emotional, salty pep talk the day he took the job. If you're a hit in Philadelphia, where they even boo Santa Claus, you must be something special. This emotional man is.

★

(*above*) TROPHY TIME: *The Lombardi Trophy and the Conference Championship Trophy.*

(*above left*) NUMBER ONE: *Dick Vermeil was probably too audacious to be so bold in estimation of his Rams, but as the head coach inferentially held up the hackneyed finger that symbolizes "No. 1," his Cinderella team played that way into an exciting Super Bowl season.*

(*below left*) BRUCE: *Isaac Bruce drew the same musical salute that Cardinals' reliever Bruce Sutter did back in the early '80s, and the Reverend Ike was just as effective with his speed and deception as Sutter was with his split-fingered fastball.*

Top 50 moments

FansSports 590 AM/100.7 FM All-Sports KFNS Radio

1. Mark McGwire breaks the single-season home run record in 1998.

2. Bob Gibson strikes out 17 in the first game of the 1968 World Series.

3. Ozzie Smith and Jack Clark hit game-winning home runs against L.A. in the 1985 National League Championship Series.

4. Stan Musial plays his final game in 1963.

5. Enos Slaughter scores from first base off a hit from Harry Walker in the 1946 World Series.

6. Cardinals win their first World Series Championship in 1926.

7. Bob Pettit scores 50 points in game seven of the 1958 NBA Finals, giving the St. Louis Hawks the NBA Championship.

8. Lou Brock breaks Maury Wills's stolen-base record with 105 in 1974.

9. Ken Boyer hits a grand slam in the 1964 World Series at Yankee Stadium.

10. St. Louis hosts the "Streetcar Series" in 1944 between the Cards and the Browns.

★

11. The St. Louis Blues appear in the Stanley Cup Finals from 1967 to 1970.

12. Jackie Joyner-Kersee wins gold medals in both the heptathlon and long jump at the 1988 Olympics at Seoul.

13. Saint Louis University wins the NIT basketball championship in 1948.

14. The Football Cardinals win the Division Championship in 1975.

15. Cardinals win game seven of the 1982 World Series.

16. St. Louis Blues Ron Shock scores the game-winning goal to beat Minnesota and qualify for the Stanley Cup Finals in 1968.

17. Stan Musial joins the 3,000-hit club.

18. Joe Medwick is removed from the field during game seven of the 1934 World Series at Detroit.

19. The St. Louis Blues play their first game in 1966.

20. The Football Cardinals play their first game on October 2, 1960, versus the New York Giants, and the Rams play their first game at Busch Stadium in 1995.

21. The St. Louis Hawks play their first game on November 5, 1955, versus the Minnesota Lakers.

22. Cardinals win game seven of the 1967 World Series.

23. The Spinks brothers win gold medals in boxing in the 1976 Olympics.

24. Don Denkinger makes the call at first base in game six of the 1985 World Series. Kansas City beats St. Louis in seven games.

25. Cardinals win the pennant in 1987.

26. Lou Brock joins the 3,000-hit club.

27. Bill Walton scores a record 44 points for UCLA in the NCAA Finals versus Memphis State in 1973. In '78, Goose Givens leads Kentucky to the NCAA Championship.

28. The 1904 Olympics are held as part of the World's Fair in St. Louis. The Olympics featured a marathon won by Thomas J. Hicks.

29. Mel Gray makes a phantom catch for the Cardinals in a 1975 game against the Redskins.

30. In a 1970 game in Philadelphia, the Blues' Red Berenson scores an amazing six goals, four of them in under 10 minutes in the second period.

31. Stan Musial hits five home runs in a doubleheader in May 1954.

32. Larry Wilson plays a game with two broken hands.

33. Hale Irwin wins the U.S. Open in 1974.

34. The Blues defeat Calgary in the 1986 playoffs, a victory dubbed the Monday night miracle.

35. Mark McGwire hits his 500th home run of his career.

36. In the 1981 Conference Semifinals, a goal by the Blues' Mike Crombeen leads to a double-overtime victory over Pittsburgh.

37. Missouri defeats Illinois in triple overtime during the 1994 basketball season.

38. Mark Whitten hits four home runs in one game.

39. In a 1999 game in Los Angeles, Fernando Tatis hits two grand slams in one inning.

40. John McEnroe and Mats Wilander battle for the Davis Cup for six hours in a match held at the Arena.

41. Brett Hull scores the 500th goal of his career in the National Hockey League in 1996.

42. The Billikens, under the leadership of Charlie Spoonhour, earn their first NCAA bid in 1994.

43. In 1965, Gary Player wins the U.S. Open at Bellerive C.C., also the site of Nick Price's PGA Championship victory in 1992.

44. The 1958, 1962, and 1965 NBA All-Star Games are played in St. Louis.

45. Glenn Brummer, a third-string catcher, gives the Cardinals a key victory in 1982 by stealing home in the 12th inning.

46. St. Louis Ambush win the NPSL Championship.

47. Brock avoids sliding during a play in the 1968 World Series.

48. The Cardinals' Ray Washburn and San Francisco's Gaylord Perry pitch back-to-back no-hitters in 1968. Bob Gibson also pitches a no-hitter, and Bob Forsch becomes the only Cardinal pitcher ever to record two no-hitters.

49. A line drive by Roberto Clemente breaks pitcher Bob Gibson's leg, but he continues to play despite this injury.

50. SLU, under Rick Grawer, qualifies for an NIT bid with a record 26 wins.

★ St. Louis Rams win Super Bowl XXXIV

KFNS Radio's top 50 sports moments of the twentieth century was compiled by the staff of the radio station, with input from Bob Broeg and Bob Costas. The list was compiled at the start of the 1999–2000 football season. Certainly, the Rams' Super Bowl XXXIV victory would now make the top 10.

★

Photo Credits

The photography for this project came from a variety of sources. Every reasonable effort to properly credit the illustrations has been made. The following organizations and individuals were of inestimable help in compiling this unique collection of photographs. The page numbers in which their contributions appear follow their names.

All Sport Photos, p. 174

Allied Photocolor, p. 18, 32, 51, 68, 88, 126, 131

Arizona Cardinals, p. 128–29, 146–47, 160

AP/Wide World Photo, p. 116, 162, 176, 183, 192

Mike Barnstead, p. 170

Belleville Archdiocese, p. 152–53

Tim Boggan, p. 59

Frank Borghi, p. 91

Bob Broeg, p. 2, 28, 37, 47, 49, 75, 85, 137

Shelley Brummer, p. 166–67

Bob Carson, p. 60, 97, 117

Catholic Youth Council of St. Louis, p. 125

Corbis Photos, p. 169

Elite International, p. 189

Bob Goalby, p. 139

Mathis-Jones Communications, p. 20, 105, 138, 145, 156, 161, 171, 198, 206

Mercantile Library Association, p. 175

Missouri Historical Society, cover, endpapers, p. 7, 9, 57, 71, 92, 95, 99, 107, 159, 207

National Baseball Hall of Fame, p. 14–15, 44

NBA Hall of Fame, p. 103

Steve Prange, p. 199

Val Pelizzaro, p. 100–1

St. Louis Blues, p. 135, 179

St. Louis Cardinals, p. 74, 173, 202

St. Louis Country Club, p. 22

St. Louis Post-Dispatch, p. 42, 53, 79, 120, 166, 181, 190

Saint Louis University archives, p. 10–11

Saint Louis University sports information, p. 80, 87, 112, 185, 197

U.S. Golf Association, p. 21, 23, 193

U.S. Olympic Committee Archives, p. 119

U.S. Tennis Hall of Fame, p. 151

University of Illinois–Urbana-Champaign, p. 83

University of Indiana–Bloomington, p. 123

University of Missouri–Columbia, p. 38–39, 64, 110–11, 114, 149, 195

Jerry Vickery, p. 4–5, 13, 17, 25–26, 29, 31, 34, 38, 40–41, 50, 55, 60, 63, 67, 72, 77, 108, 114, 132, 140, 142, 154, 158, 165, 186, 204–5

Washington University, p. 201

About the Author

Right: *Bob Broeg (left), bow-tied as usual for more than a half-century, finds favorite manager Whitey Herzog decked out similarly for a recent dinner of the Knights of Cauliflower Ear. Broeg thinks the late Eddie Stanky was the best teacher, Whitey the best field foreman overall.*

Below: *Bob Broeg (left) and football favorite Dan Devine late Sunday nights on KSDK–TV when Devine's Missouri teams were annually among the finest. The regime called for the sportswriter-television partner to bring along a five-layer Miss Hullings cake for the sweet-toothed coach.*

Below Right: *The sports editor-columnist, bow tie typically opened at work, sits between heavyweight boxing champion Sonny Liston and veteran Post-Dispatch fight writer Bill McGoogan. The location was the glaring photographic studio at the P-D. Grumped Sonny, who would have known, "Let's get out of here—reminds me too much of a lineup!"*